IMAGES
of America

VERNONIA

I0799429

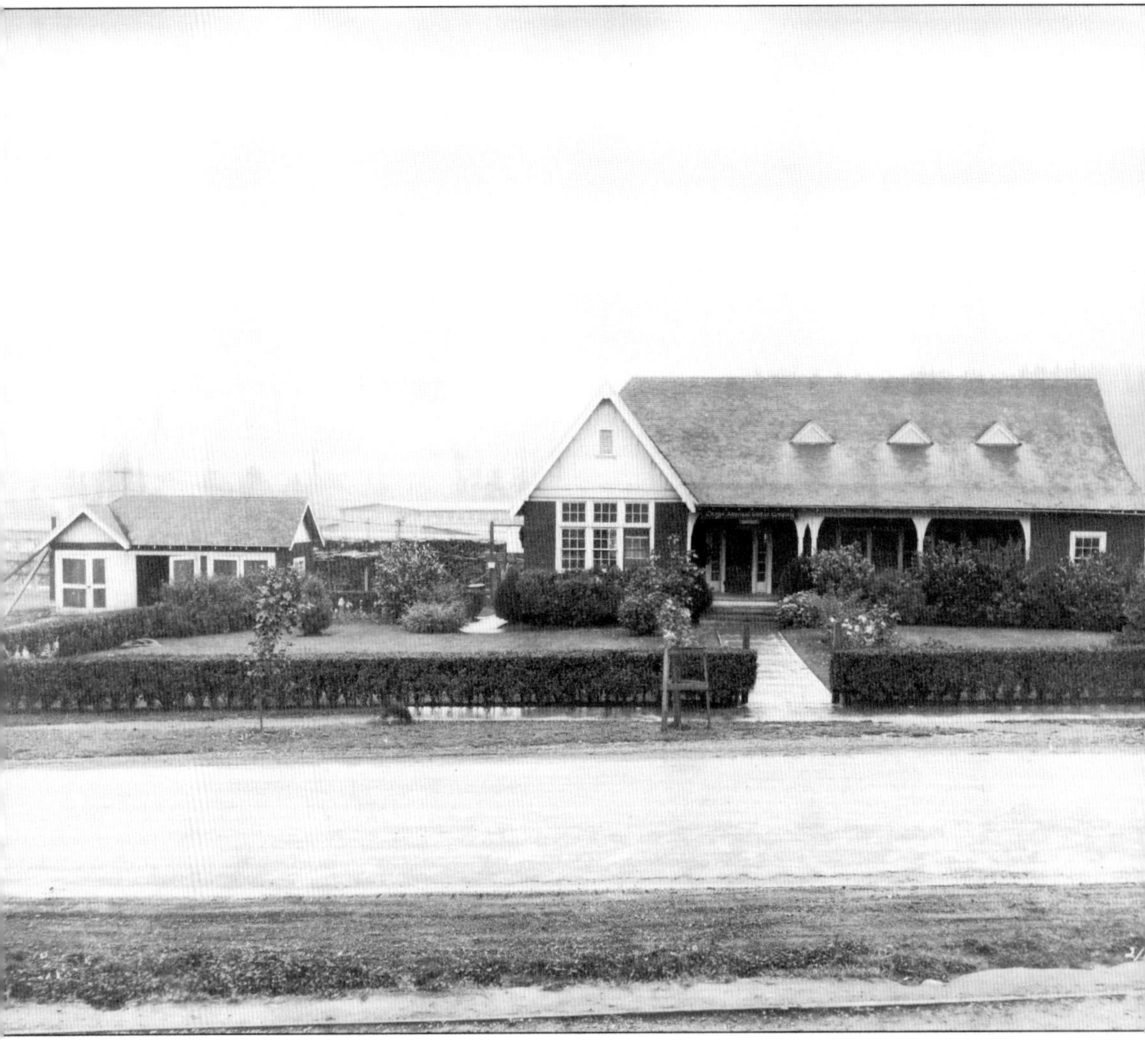

The Oregon-American (O-A) Lumber Company was the economic heart of Vernonia from 1922 to 1957. The O-A office was built in 1924. When the mill closed in 1957, the building was given to the City of Vernonia. Since 1963, the city has leased the building to Columbia County for use as a museum. Added to the National Register of Historic Places in 2002, the Vernonia Pioneer Museum Association volunteers keep the museum open for visitors on weekends and by special arrangements. (Vernonia Pioneer Museum Association [VPMA].)

On the Cover: Bob Spencer, the youngest child of early pioneers Israel and Sarah Spencer, was born in 1890 and lived his 102 years in Vernonia. He is standing next to one of the horses he used for logging in the 1920s. The picture of this Koster Camp crew was taken by noted photographer Clark Kinsey. (VPMA, with permission of the University of Washington Libraries, Special Collections.)

IMAGES
of America

VERNONIA

Vernonia Pioneer Museum Association

ARCADIA
PUBLISHING

Copyright © 2010 by Vernonia Pioneer Museum Association
ISBN 978-0-7385-8041-8

Published by Arcadia Publishing
Charleston, South Carolina

Printed in the United States of America

Library of Congress Control Number: 2009937664

For all general information contact Arcadia Publishing at:
Telephone 843-853-2070
Fax 843-853-0044
E-mail sales@arcadiapublishing.com
For customer service and orders:
Toll-Free 1-888-313-2665

Visit us on the Internet at www.arcadiapublishing.com

To the former curators, past and current members,
volunteers, donors, and visitors
to the Vernonia Pioneer Museum
for their part in preserving Vernonia's history

Contents

Acknowledgments

We gratefully thank the people who shared their memories, treasured family pictures, and historic photographs with us. We are especially grateful to Bill Weed (the Weed family) and Jodi Robertson Queen (Robertson, VanBlaricom, and Christensen families) not only for sharing pictures, but also the narratives sent with the pictures. We thank Frederick "Fritz" von Tagen for his permission to use the Brubaker and Delano aerial photographs. We deeply thank Bob New for his regular e-mails that shared his memories and photographs with the museum.

At the Vernonia Pioneer Museum Board, we are grateful to board secretary Barbara Larsen for accepting the challenge of being the project leader for this book. Her leadership kept us focused and on task, and her long hours of photograph collecting, scanning, organizing, and collaborating were key to getting the job done. We thank treasurer Lilja "Tobie" Finzel for the many hours she spent doing research, writing the text, and working with Barbara to edit and assemble the manuscript. Our president, Carol Cline Davis, and vice president Ralph Keasey contributed photographs and family histories, and also helped with the research and review of the historical content. We thank longtime museum volunteer Donna Webb, former curator Robb Wilson, Noni Andersen, Clark and Rebecca McGaugh of the *Independent*, Jim Blain, Ed Kamholz, Joe Corsiglia, Alexander "Bill" Sword, Ben Soejima, and Shirlee Vike Daughtry for their help in picture gathering, storytelling, and fact-checking.

The photographs used in this book are courtesy of the following: Jodi Robertson Queen (Queen), Barbara Keasey Memovich (Keasey), Mark Greathouse (Malmsten), Bill Weed and Sue Garner-Warsinske (Weed), Janelle Thomas Cedergreen (Thomas), Chris King Redmond (King), Gordon and Mary Ann Cline (Cline), Owen and Claudine East (East), Kathy Minger Eckland (Minger), Kathleen and Richard Gwin (Gwin), Marvin and Ellen Meyer (Meyer), Linda Clark Gisel (Condit), Pat Thompson Wilson (Thompson), Archie and Jeanette Dass (Dass), Ken Anderson (Anderson), Bill Pringle (Pringle), Bill Sword (Sword), and the Vernonia Pioneer Museum Association (VPMA.)

We thank Sarah Higginbotham, our editor, for her guidance and encouragement throughout the project.

INTRODUCTION

Vernonia, Oregon, is located in the foothills of the Oregon Coast Range, northwest of Portland in the Upper Nehalem River Valley. Surrounded by forested hills, the town is more than 25 miles in any direction from larger cities and so has maintained an independent, self-reliant spirit since its founding.

In 1873, thirty years after the Oregon Trail brought settlers to the Willamette Valley and 14 years after Oregon became a state, Clark Parker followed game and Native American trails over hills and through dense old-growth forests from Portland to the Upper Nehalem River Valley to trap beavers. A year later, returning with his wife, Melissa, and their children, Parker staked out a homestead just east of present-day Vernonia. That same year, John VanBlaricom and his extended family established their homesteads near the confluence of Rock Creek and the Nehalem River.

Native Americans appear to have been only periodic visitors to the Upper Nehalem River Valley, possibly due to the dense timber and rugged terrain, as they followed the elk herds along the Nehalem River and caught salmon and steelhead during seasonal runs. By the time the Parkers and VanBlaricoms arrived, the native inhabitants who survived the white men's diseases had been forcibly removed to reservations.

The town was first called Auburn for one settler's hometown. It received its permanent name in 1877 from schoolteacher and settler Ozias Cherrington, a widower, who wanted to honor his daughter Vernona, whom he had left with relatives in Ohio. Whether it was the U.S. Post Office or someone else who added the "*I*" to Vernona's name in the application for a post office is still a matter of debate. Vernona never visited her namesake town and was said to have been unhappy about the spelling change. The first post office was on the Frank Baker homestead on the east side of Rock Creek; Baker became the town's first postmaster. Mail service was weekly due to the lack of roads to outside towns. There were no county roads until 1900; prior to that, road building was done by the settlers who needed access to outside markets.

Most of the original homesteads were established under the Homestead Act of 1862; Civil War veterans, under an 1870 act, were given priority in homesteading railroad land grant areas, typically 160 acres. Rumors of a railroad through Vernonia resulted in a land boom in the late 1880s that brought more settlers and businessmen to the area. The Panic of 1893 and resulting economic depression ended the growth for several years. The population had tripled to 150 by 1893 but declined to less than 50 shortly thereafter.

The late 1890s and early 1900s brought a new wave of national prosperity. The logging industry went from small, family-run operations to large operations with big crews and heavy equipment. Timber speculators bought up large tracts of land from settlers who left the area, and the U.S. Congress voted in 1916 to take the remaining railroad lands under federal ownership. Vernonia went from a small farming community to a timber-based economy. Soon there was a telephone company, a second town school, improved roads, and more small businesses. To keep its tie to farming, however, the Oregon State Grange asked Clark Parker's son, Albert, to organize a Vernonia Grange in 1901. There were 48 charter members. In 1907, they built a grange hall on the corner of North and Washington Streets, where it still stands.

By the early 1920s, the demand for timber, which began before World War I, continued. The Central Coal and Coke Company (CC&CC) bought large forested tracts west of Keasey and made plans to build a mill in Vernonia, which would become the Oregon-American Lumber Company (O-A). CC&CC made a deal with railroad tycoon James Hill to supply the long-awaited and much-needed rail line to the town. The first passenger train arrived in September 1922.

Following the building of Camp McGregor, a logging camp that would house nearly 200 workers, construction began on the modern, electric-powered lumber mill located on a 200-acre site just east of Vernonia. When it was completed in 1923, it was said—incorrectly—to be the largest electric lumber mill in the world. It was unique in its steel and concrete construction. New businesses were established, all eager to serve the rapidly growing population of this now "big payroll" town.

At its peak, the O-A mill employed more than 500 workers on two shifts. The Great Depression closed the mill from 1933 to 1936, although a few men were employed to maintain security on the site. By 1936, the mill was back in operation. World War II changed the employment as the younger men left to join the armed services. Some women performed jobs that had been "men's work," and some left to work in the shipyards along the Willamette River in Portland.

The building boom following the war brought the lumber business back. The late 1940s and early 1950s were prosperous years for Vernonia. That all changed, however, when the last of the big trees on O-A land were gone. The mill closed, and hundreds of people were left without a regular paycheck. Many went to work in other timber industry jobs, some found work at local businesses, and others left town permanently. The O-A houses were sold for as little as $700 each, and the mill site and headquarters were given to the City of Vernonia. Many businesses closed, and Vernonia became a quiet, economically depressed little town. Over time, its proximity to the Portland metropolitan area meant work for those willing to commute. Vernonia became a bedroom community with affordable housing.

Vernonia's fortunes have risen and fallen with both local and wider economic fluctuations, but it continues to be home to resilient and independent souls. Although there are still some residents who are descendants of the first settlers, many others now living in Vernonia made a choice to move there, drawn by its isolation and the natural beauty of the area. In 2006, the first new state park in 30 years opened 11 miles south of town, bringing new visitors. The former railroad line from Banks to Vernonia became a state linear trail. It would be extended to the town of Scappoose on former logging roads to create a 70-mile arc spanning small towns, farms, and forests. The millpond is now a small lake circled by a walking path and stocked with fish. Portions of the former mill site have been designated public parks, and large second-growth trees cover O-A Hill and the mill lands below.

Due to the geography of the Upper Nehalem Valley, periodic floods have been documented since the first settlers arrived. Although the Flood of 1996 was thought to be a 100-year event, the Flood of 2007 reinforced the need to rethink the placement of homes, schools, key community services, and businesses. Floodplain maps have been redrawn, and a new school complex on higher ground has been planned. There is a collective commitment to keeping Vernonia vital and making life in this lovely corner of Oregon sustainable for future generations.

One

Into the Ancient Forest

The earliest settlers found the old-growth trees an obstacle to overcome when establishing farms. They built rough barns and small cabins from some of the timber they felled. Other trees were burned to clear the land. They learned that the elevation, wet springs, and cool summer nights posed a challenge to some types of farming. Root crops, tubers, apples, plums, and hardy grains were some of the crops that thrived. The abundant salmon, elk, deer, and wild berries supplemented the diets of the settlers.

Other settlers soon followed the Parkers and the VanBlaricoms to establish homestead claims. Among these were Judson Weed, Ozias Cherrington, Thomas Lavender, Thomas L. Adams, Israel Spencer, Riley Adams, Thomas Tucker, Edgar E. Brand, Charles Plowman, William Wood, John Kern, and John Pringle.

In 1876, two years after the Parker family arrived in the area, the first log schoolhouse was built on their homestead. The school was also used for community functions in those first years because classes were in session for only two to three months per year due to the expense of hiring a teacher and the need for the children's labor on family farms. Ozias Cherrington taught the first term at the school, and his cousin Judson Weed taught the second term. As the number of homesteads in the area increased, additional one-room, log schoolhouses were built at 2-to-5-mile intervals.

Because it was a three-day round-trip to obtain supplies from Cornelius or Forest Grove, settlers made only a few "going out" trips per year. They relied on themselves and their few neighbors to survive.

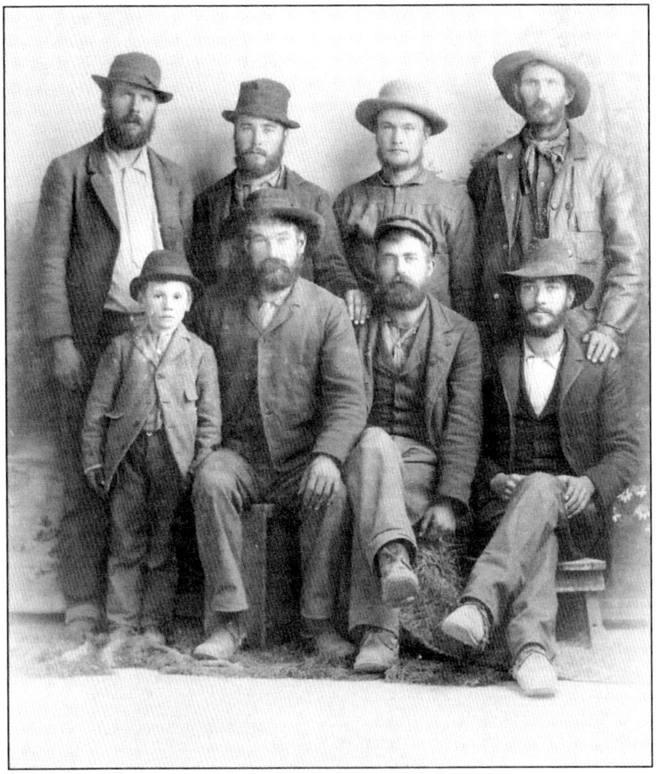

Newt Parker was one of Clark and Melissa Parker's six sons. When Newt's wife died while staying with relatives in Baker City, this group traveled from Vernonia to bring his son, Walter, back home. The group had this photograph taken in Baker City in the mid-1890s. From left to right are (first row) Walter Parker, Newt Parker, Lon Emmons, and Lloyd Detrick; (second row) Charles Kenkle, Albert Parker, John Baker, and an unidentified man. (Keasey.)

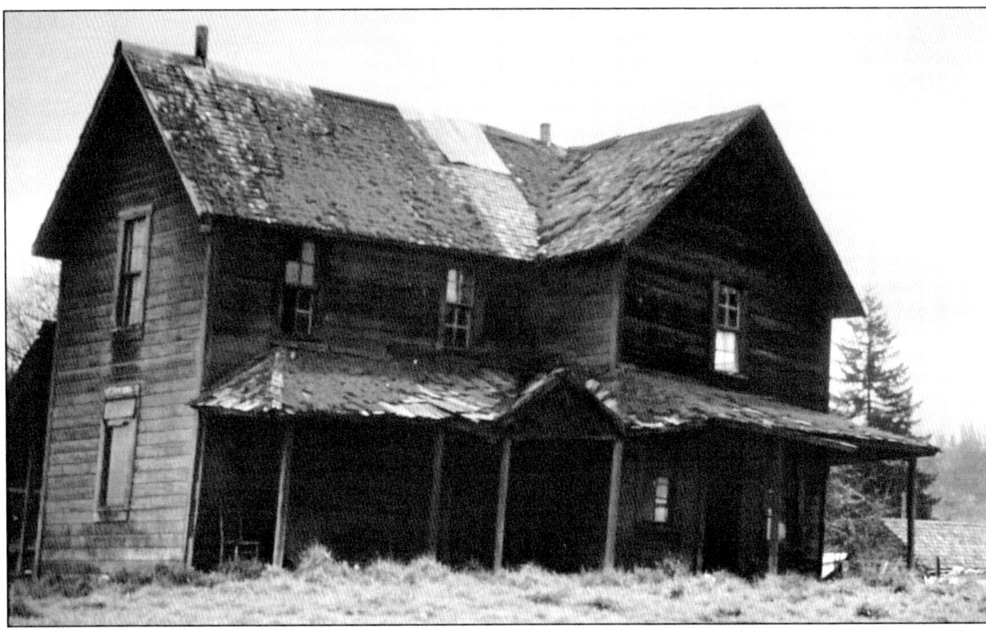

In 1874, Clark and Melissa Parker, along with the first six of their nine children, homesteaded on the east side of the Nehalem River just outside present-day Vernonia. This was the third Parker home; it replaced the log cabin that was built the year after the original split-board cedar cabin. The photograph was taken in the early 1990s before it was demolished for the Heather Park development. (VPMA.)

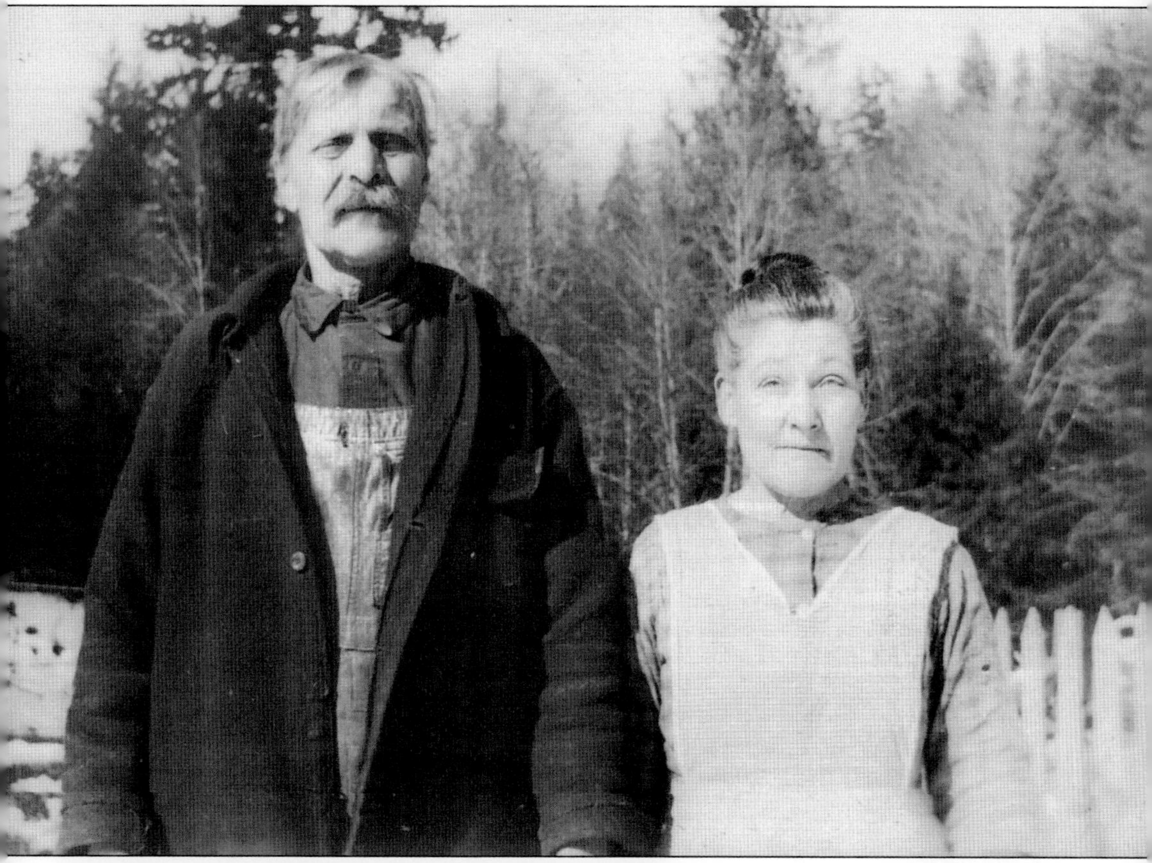

Hans Christensen was born in Denmark in 1865. Anna was the daughter of John and Nancy VanBlaricom's son Phillip and his wife, Hannah. Hans and Anna, shown above in a later photograph, were married in 1885 and had seven children: Harve, Martin, Fred, Vester, Emma, Robert, and Sadie. John VanBlaricom and his extended family were the second group to settle in Vernonia in 1874. His wife, Nancy, died before the family moved to Oregon. John's son Henry and his wife, Catherine, were the first of the VanBlaricoms to establish a homestead. It was located just below the Parkers' homestead. John and his sons John Jr., Joseph, and Hiram homesteaded much of the land within today's Vernonia city limits, as did his sister Drusilla and her husband, David "Frank" Baker. John's daughter Sara and her husband, Saul Sheeley, homesteaded a few miles west on what is now known as Timber Route, as did John's son Phillip. Phillip was killed by a bear in 1879 while clearing land, and his widow, Hannah, married E. E. Brand, who owned the adjoining Timber Route homestead in 1880. (VPMA.)

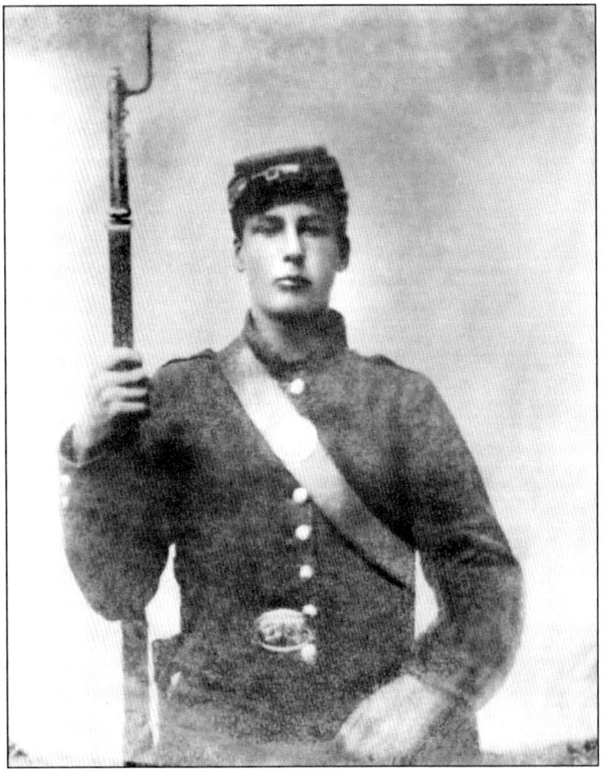

Israel Spencer was a member of the New York Infantry that fought at Gettysburg and in other major Civil War battles. He came west, met Clark Parker and Thomas Adams at the land office in Oregon City, and followed them back to the Upper Nehalem Valley. Spencer purchased his land and a split-board cedar cabin from Henry Beecher for $20. Beecher, not liking the area, had decided to move to eastern Oregon. Spencer is pictured below with other Vernonians who were members of the Grand Army of the Republic Civil War and World War I organizations for veterans. From left to right are (first row) Dr. James Ray; a Mr. Schaffer; Oscar Weed, son of Judson Weed; and Israel Spencer. A Mr. Allen holds the flag and stands next to a Mr. Early in the second row. (Both, VPMA.)

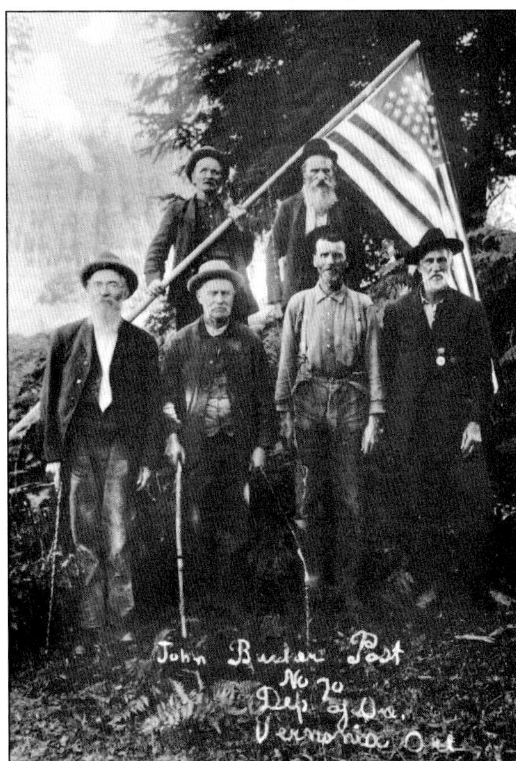

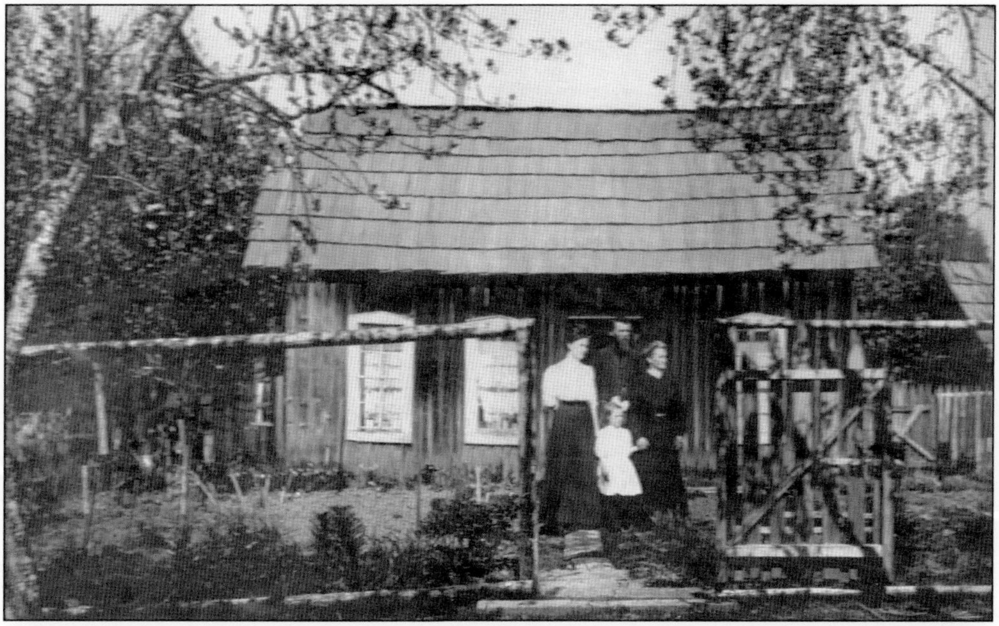

Civil War veterans Judson Weed and his cousin Ozias Cherrington came to the Upper Nehalem Valley in 1876 from Ohio. They shared their first cabin, which was built on the property line between their two homesteads so they could "prove up" their claims together. In 1879, Judson married Emmaline "Emma" VanBlaricom, who came with her family to the valley in 1874. Judson stands in front of his second cabin with his wife, Emma, daughter Ethel (on the left), and youngest child, Lesta. The photograph below of the Weeds was taken in 1938 on the family farm. Seated in the first row are Nancy Weed; Shirley Ann Kaufman; Emma Weed; Emma's mother, Catherine VanBlaricom; Bobby Weed; and Chester Weed. Standing in the second row are Ethel Weed Kaufman, Alma Weed, Elza Weed, Mildred Weed, Ruth Weed, Alice Weed, Melvin Weed, Bessie Weed, and Oscar Weed. (Both, Weed.)

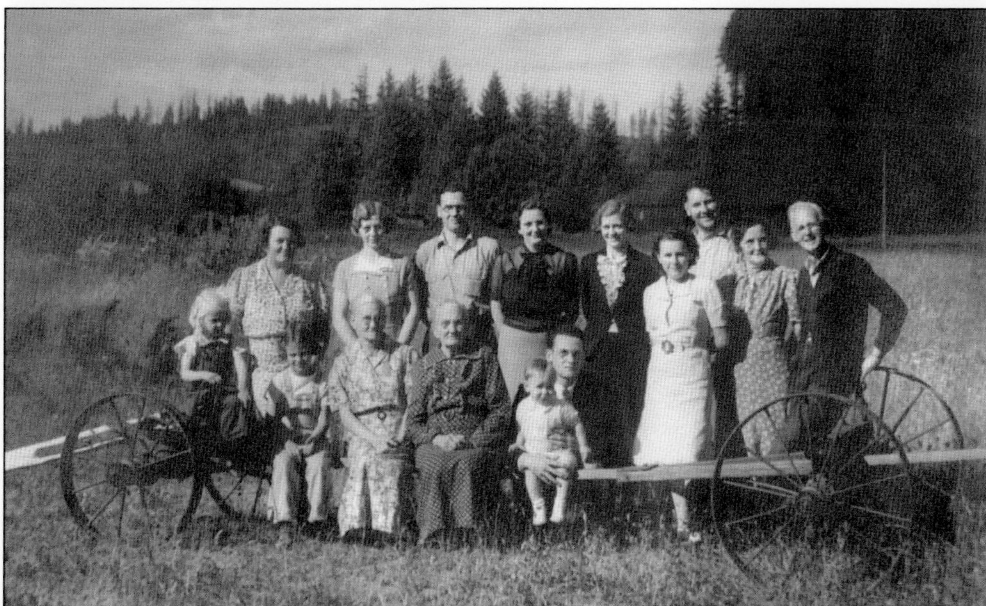

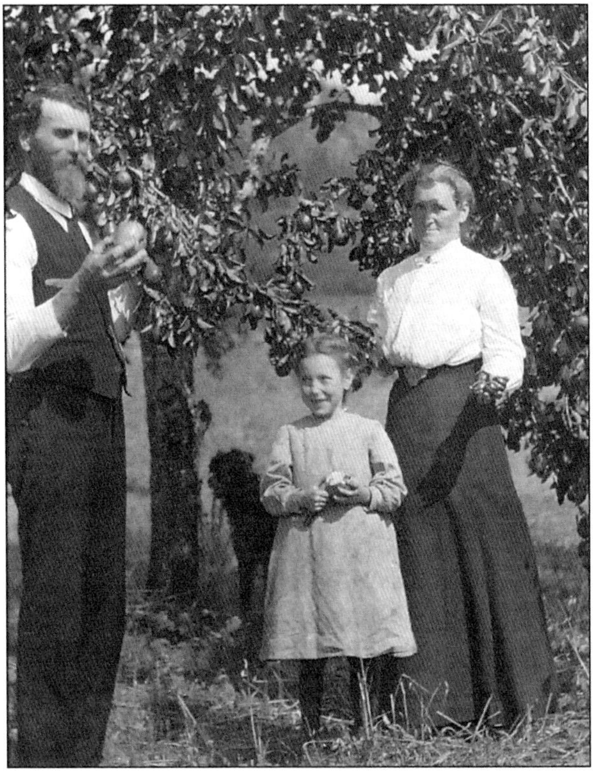

Judson Weed, his wife, Emma, and their youngest daughter, Lesta, pick apples and plums on their Timber Route homestead. Emma's mother, Catherine Gehring VanBlaricom, came to Vernonia with her husband, Henry, and four children in 1874 along with the rest of the extended VanBlaricom family. Like the Parkers, they had to walk in over the Pebble Creek trail. She told of having to cross the creek 13 times on the way in. With no cabin ready, they camped under a huge cedar tree. They split cedar boards to make a wall around the tree, where they lived for several months until a log cabin was built. The photograph below was taken of Catherine by her daughter Emma's husband, Riley Kaufman, in 1939. Pipe smoking was common with both sexes in the early years, and some even grew their own tobacco. (Both, Weed.)

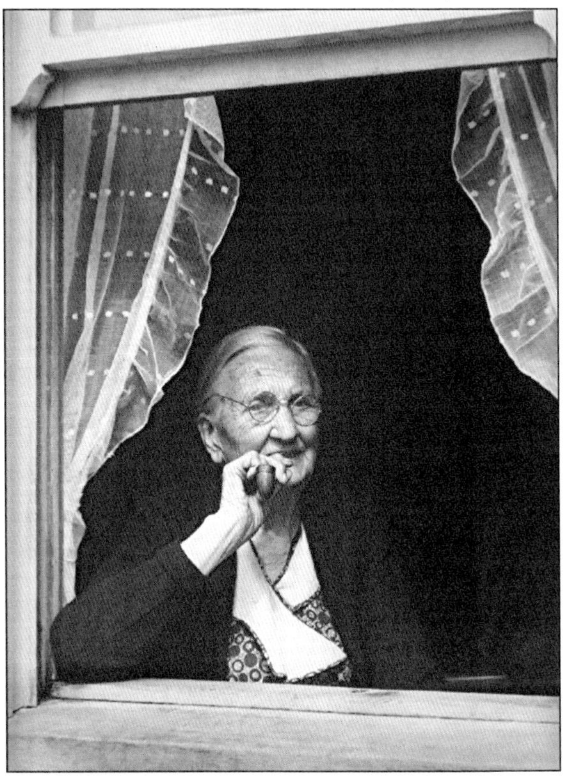

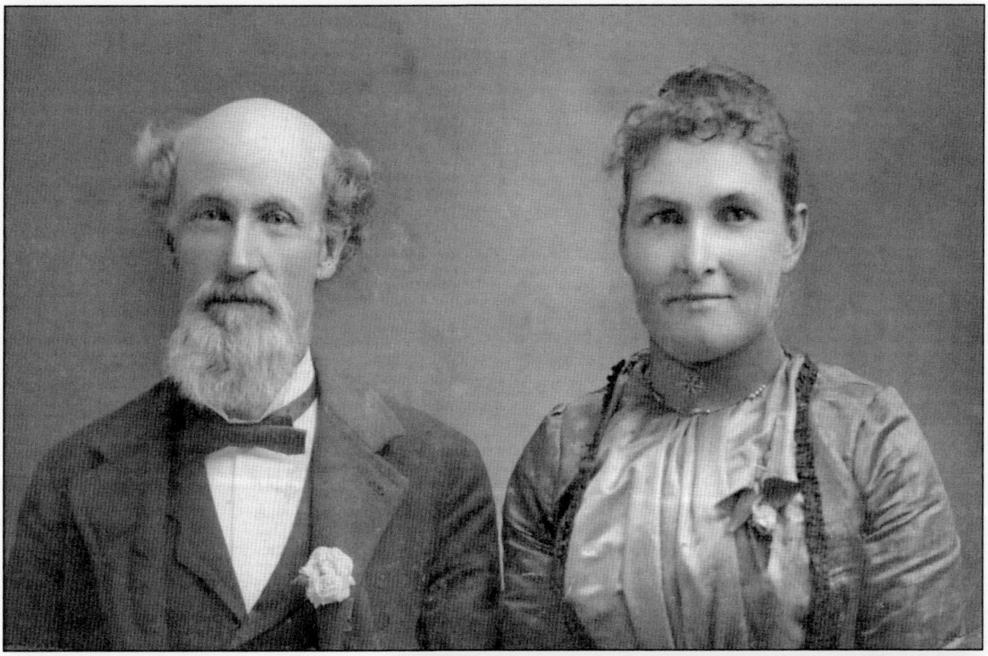

John W. VanBlaricom Jr. and Julia Etta Parker, daughter of Clark and Melissa Parker, were wed on April 7, 1878. They were the first couple to be married in Vernonia. This marriage joined the first two families to settle the area. Born on October 1, 1875, Albert Parker—one of Julia Etta's younger brothers—was the first baby to be born in Vernonia. The photograph was taken in their later years. (VPMA.)

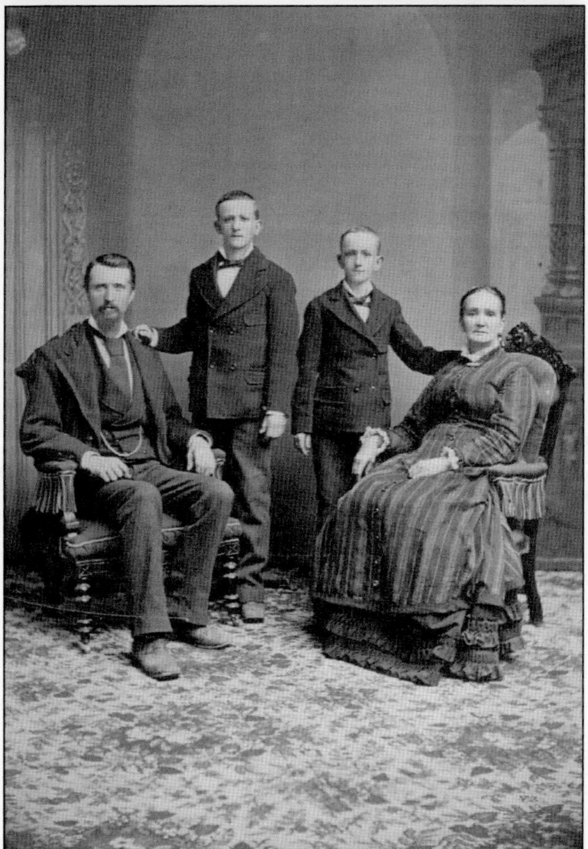

Early settlers John Pringle, his wife, Mary, son William (standing, left) and son John (standing, right), pose for this 1879 photograph. Originally from England, the Pringles came to the Nehalem Valley in 1877. He was a carpenter, cabinetmaker, and a mason. He built a one-room schoolhouse on Stoney Point Road near the Pringle homestead along the Nehalem River. Mary was one of the first midwives in the area. (Pringle.)

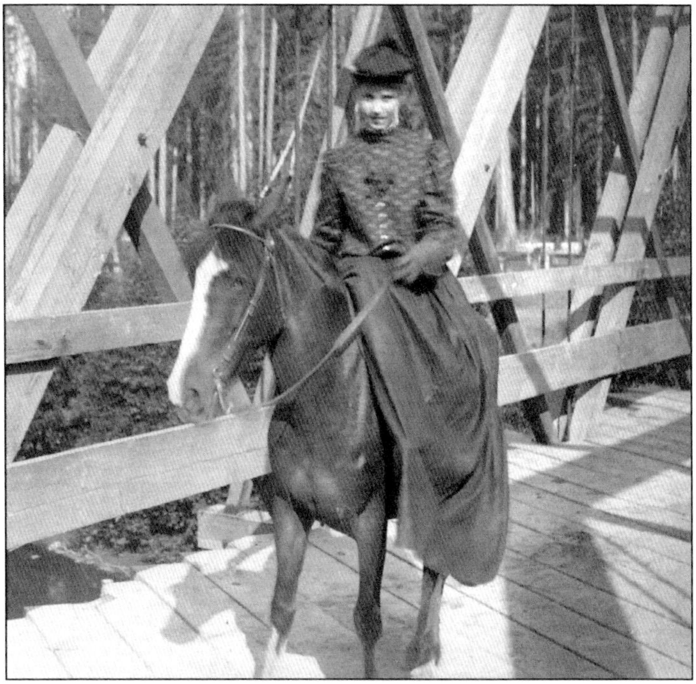

Bertha Detrick Keasey was photographed on the Pittsburg Bridge in 1890 while mounted sidesaddle on her horse, Flora. The town of Pittsburg, located about 5 miles down the Nehalem River from Vernonia, was homesteaded by the Detricks in the winter of 1877–1878. Named for the Pennsylvania city that was the home of Peter Brouse, one of the other homesteaders, the settlers dropped the "H" at the end when the post office was established. (Keasey.)

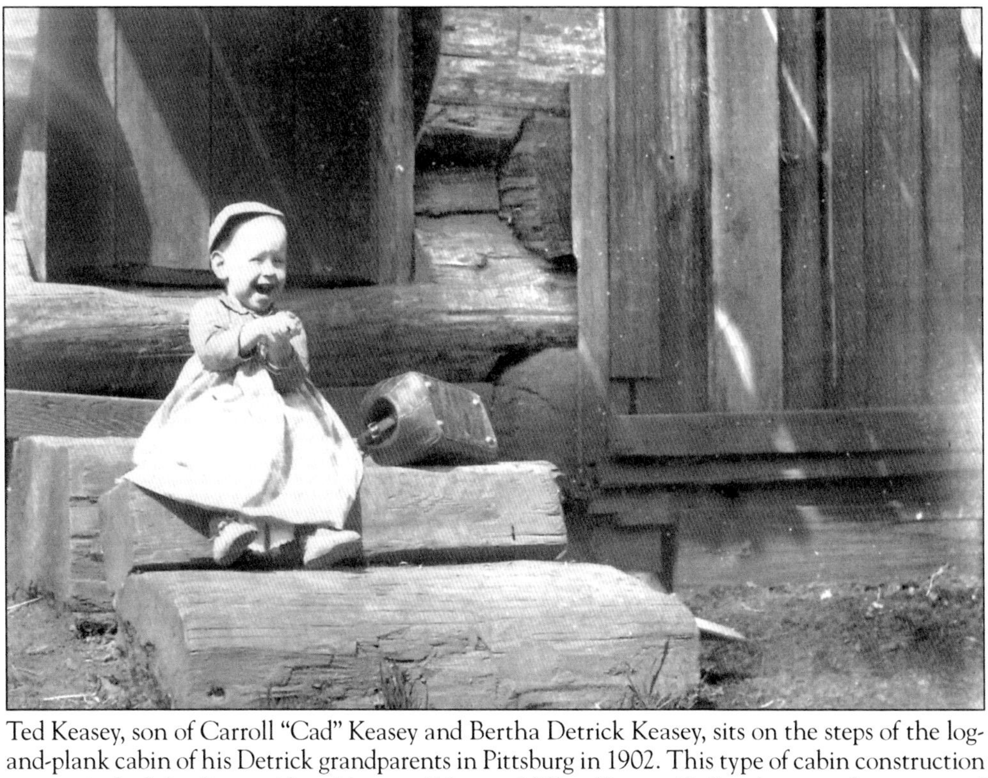

Ted Keasey, son of Carroll "Cad" Keasey and Bertha Detrick Keasey, sits on the steps of the log-and-plank cabin of his Detrick grandparents in Pittsburg in 1902. This type of cabin construction was typical of the first residents' homes. Eden and Ellen Keasey, Ted's other grandparents, and three of their five adult children—sons Cad, Dorr, and Dow—came to the Vernonia area from the Midwest in 1880. (Keasey.)

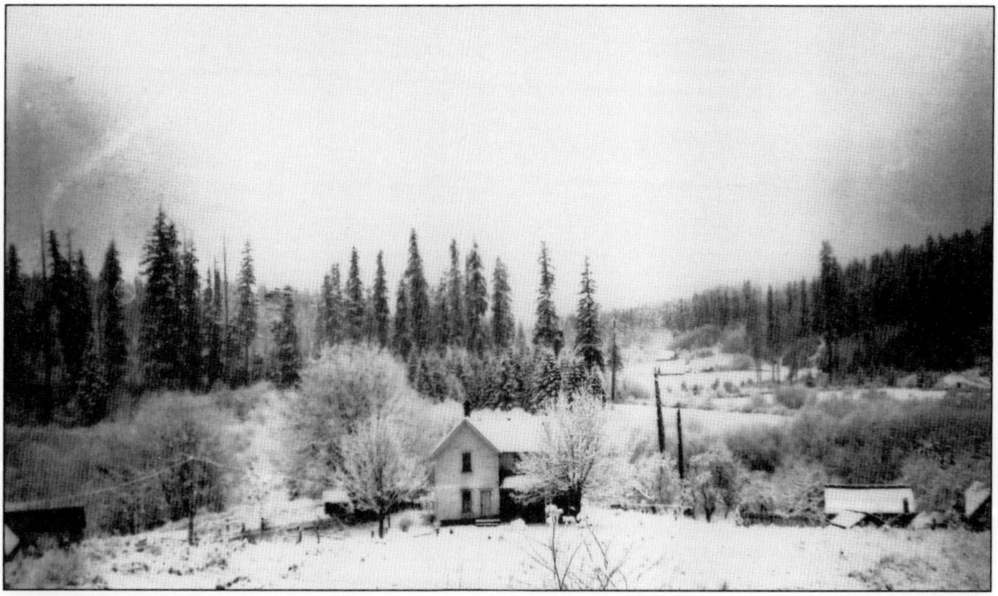

The Tucker homestead on Keasey Road was established in the 1870s about 1 mile north of Vernonia. The original cabin was replaced in 1901–1902 by the home in the photograph. The picture was taken in the 1930s while Walter and Eda Tucker Parker lived there. Part of the Tucker homestead is now Camp Cedar Ridge, formerly Perry's Sports Camp. (Keasey.)

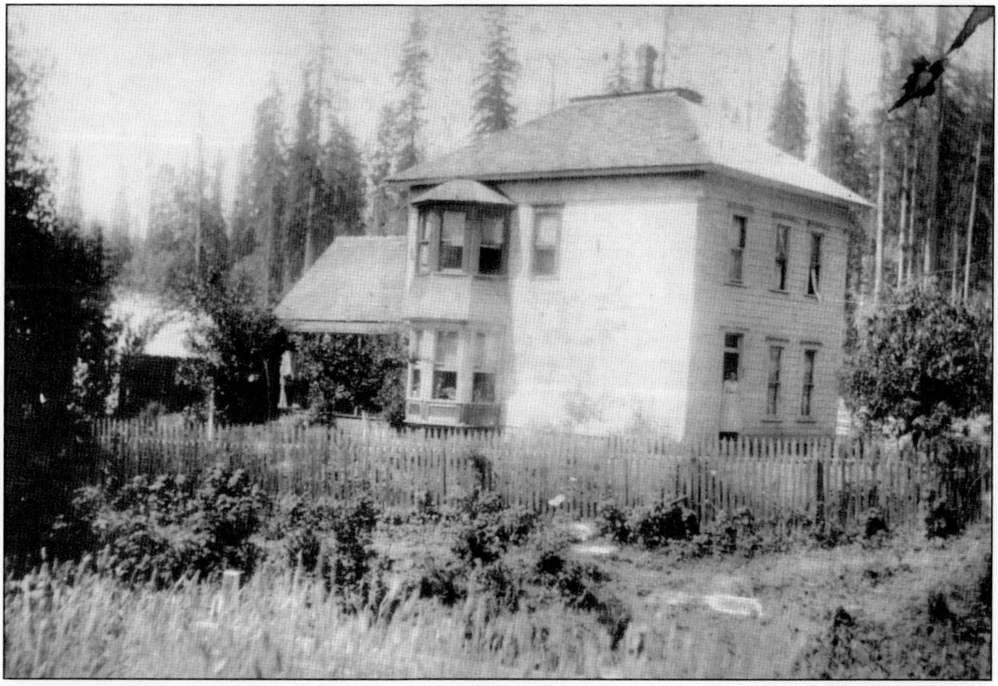

In the mid-1890s, Cad Keasey built the two-story addition to his father, Eden Keasey's, original homestead cabin. Located 5 miles outside of Vernonia on Keasey Road (then known as Rock Creek Road), it was considered one of the area's finer homes because of its bay windows and stained-glass front-door window. The lumber came from the Detrick Mill in Pittsburg, where Cad met his future wife, Bertha Detrick. (Keasey.)

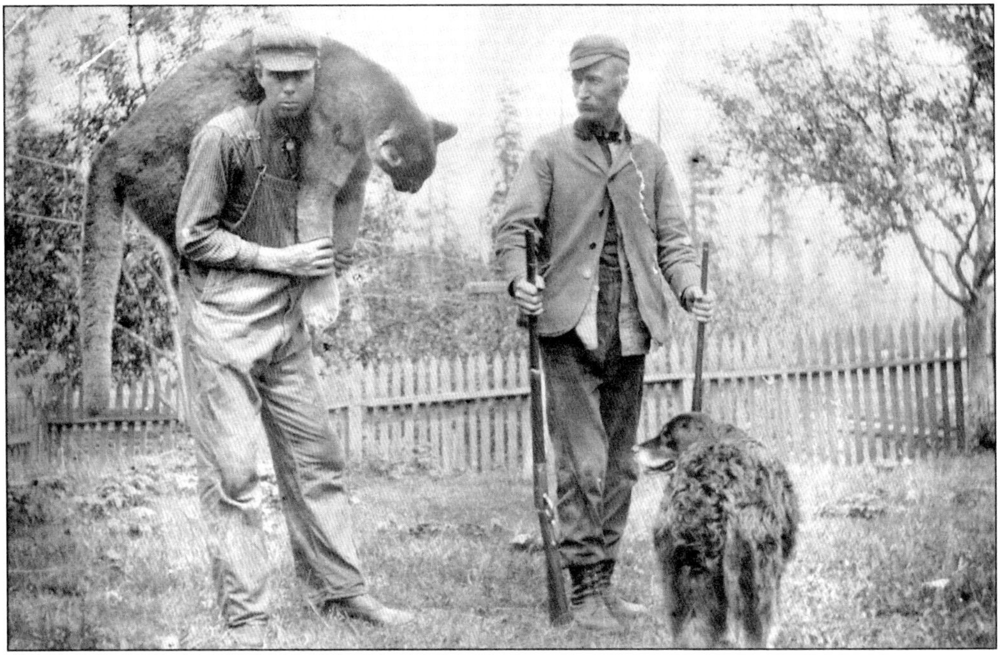

Cad Keasey carries home the cougar he and Charley Eichman (right) shot on the Keasey homestead c. 1906. The big cat had killed several Angora goats the Keaseys were raising before Charley's dog treed it. The cougar was 9-feet long from nose to tail and weighed 140 pounds. Early settlers often wrote of their fear of cougars when camping out on the three-day journeys to Forest Grove and St. Helens. Then, as now, coyotes, bobcats, and cougars were a serious problem for farmers who raised domestic animals in forested areas. (Both, Keasey.)

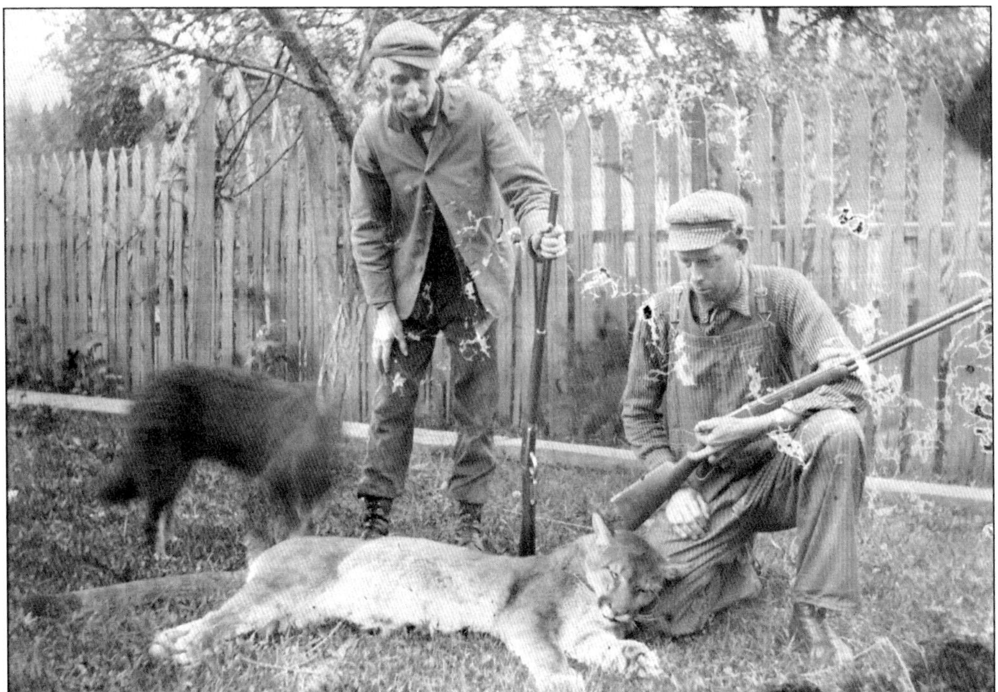

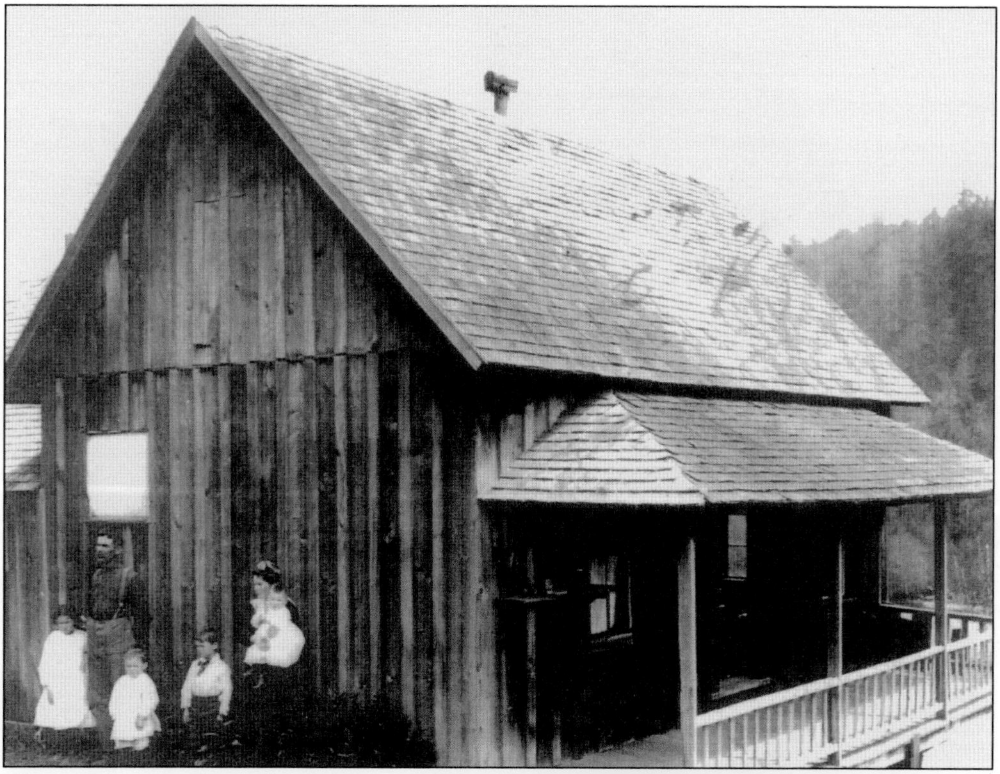

Thomas Anderson built this home on Timber Route south of Vernonia in 1898 with lumber from the Detrick Mill in Pittsburg. Thomas and Mary Huber Anderson raised six children there. Their son Willie inherited the home and lived there until his death in 1986. The house is still standing but is in ill repair. The above photograph was taken in 1911. Pictured from left to right are Helen, age 10; Thomas; Ted, age 5; Willie, age 8; Mary; and baby Chet. (Queen.)

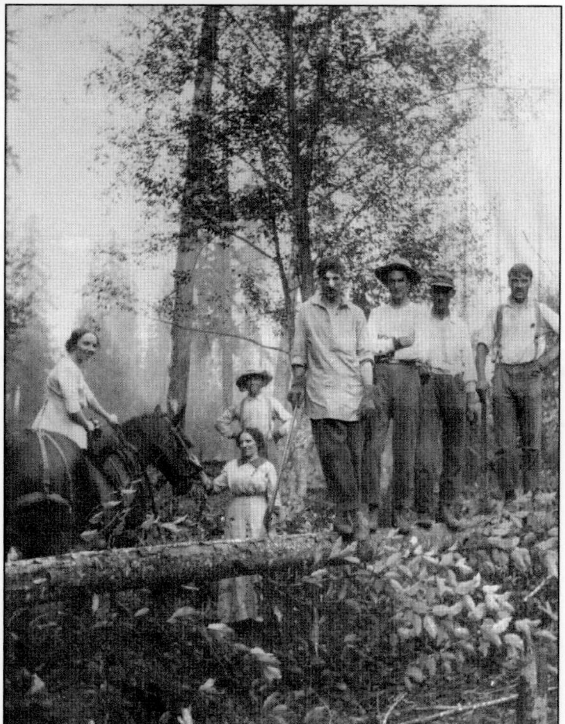

Lizzie Parker holds the horse for her sister. Her husband, Albert Parker, is standing behind the girls. Standing on the fallen log are, from left to right, Bob Spencer, Alden Johns, unidentified, and Vester Christensen. Bob Spencer, the oldest native Vernonian—age 102 at the time of his death in 1993, was the son of Israel Spencer. (Gwin.)

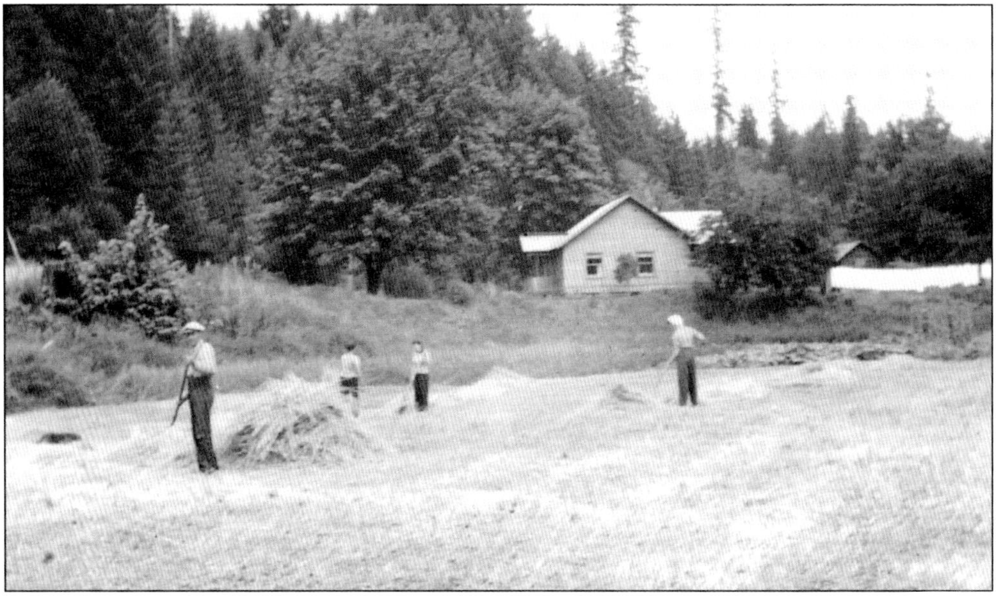

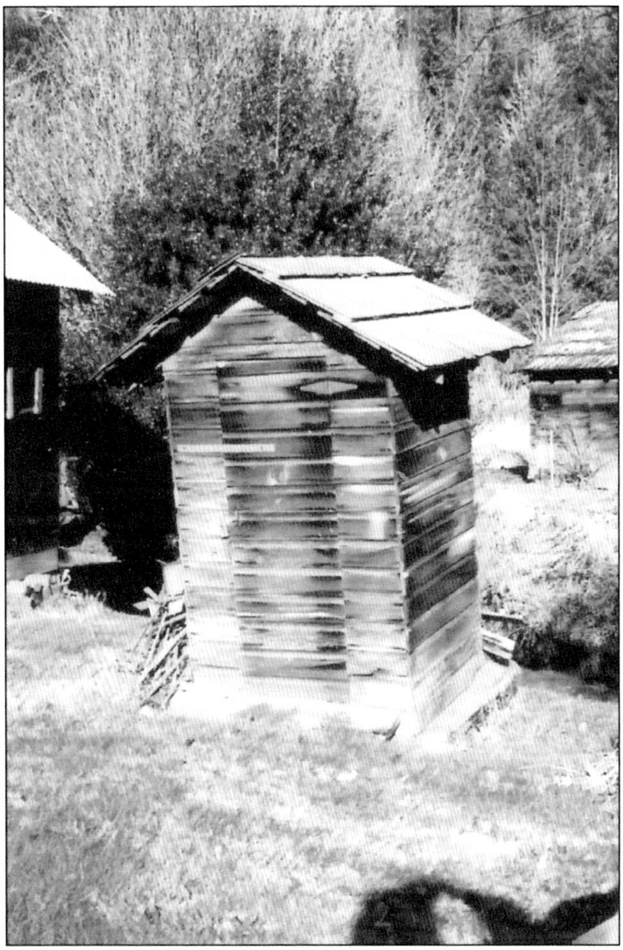

Hans and Anna VanBlaricom Christensen purchased this property from her mother, Hannah Bennett VanBlaricom Brand. It was originally part of her second husband's homestead. Anna sold it to her son Vester in 1929. He and his wife, Helen Anderson Christensen, lived out their lives there and raised four children: Ernie, Arvela, and twins Lesta and Vesta. The house pictured above replaced the original homestead cabin. The property remained in the family for more than 100 years, until it was sold in 1990. (Queen.)

A necessity of all homes in the days before indoor plumbing, the outhouse (also known as the backhouse) on the Christensen property on Timber Route still stands. When establishing a homestead, the barn, cabin, and outhouse were usually built in that order. The barn, however, was the most likely to be improved when finances allowed. (Queen.)

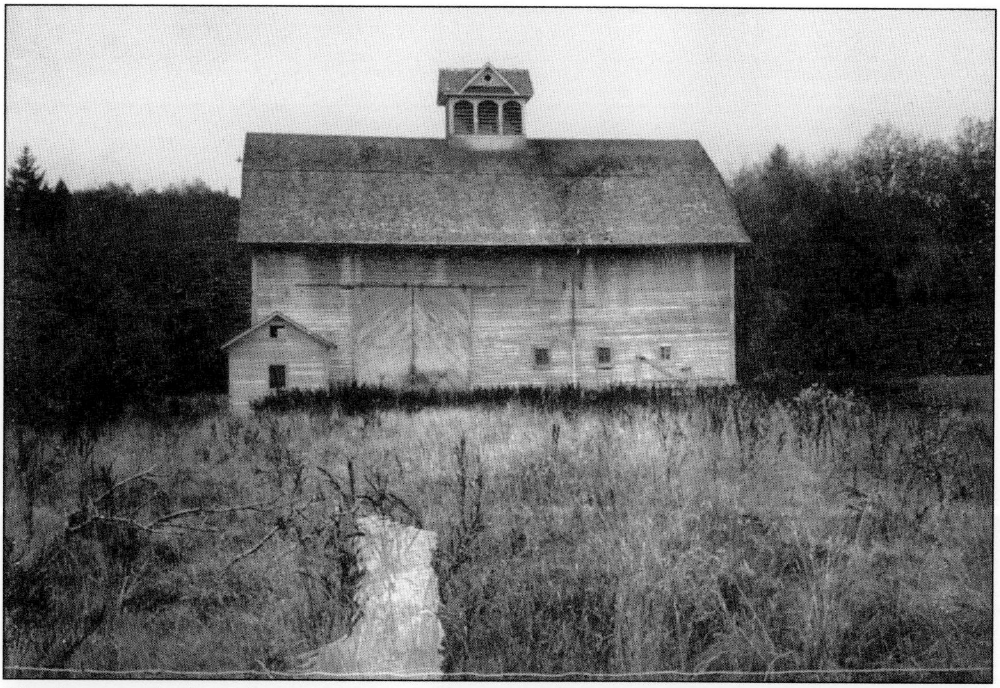

This barn was built in the early 1900s on Henry VanBlaricom's 160-acre land grant. Located on the east side of the Nehalem River, 1 mile downstream from Vernonia near the original Parker homestead, the barn survives to the present (as seen in the photograph below). The above photograph was taken several years after its construction. (Thomas.)

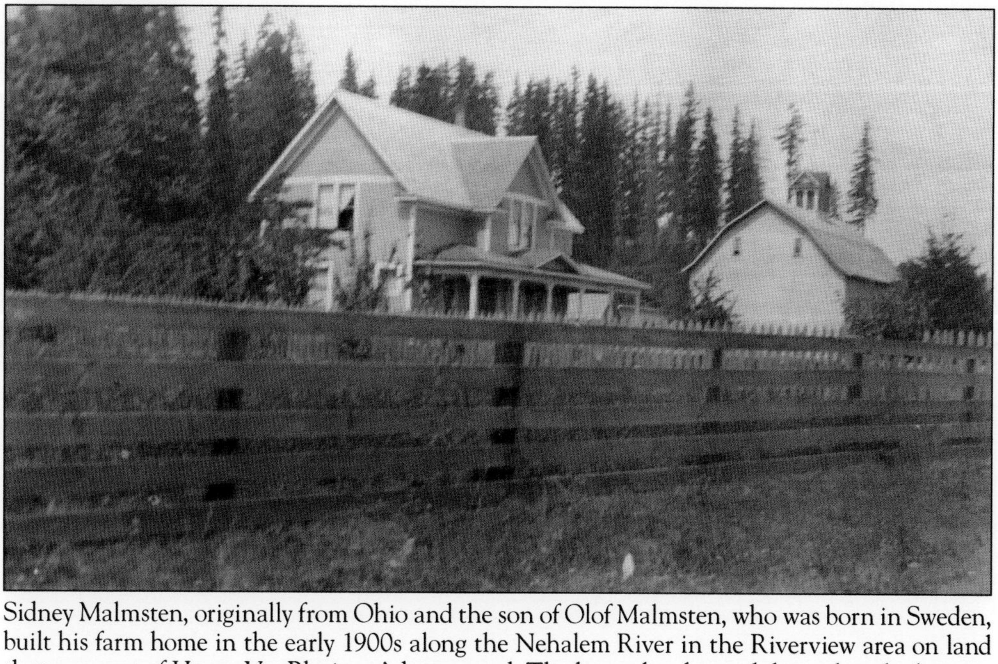

Sidney Malmsten, originally from Ohio and the son of Olof Malmsten, who was born in Sweden, built his farm home in the early 1900s along the Nehalem River in the Riverview area on land that was part of Henry VanBlaricom's homestead. The house has burned down, but the barn in the background survives. The Malmsten brothers established several homesteads in the Vernonia area and ran a small sawmill nearby. (Malmsten.)

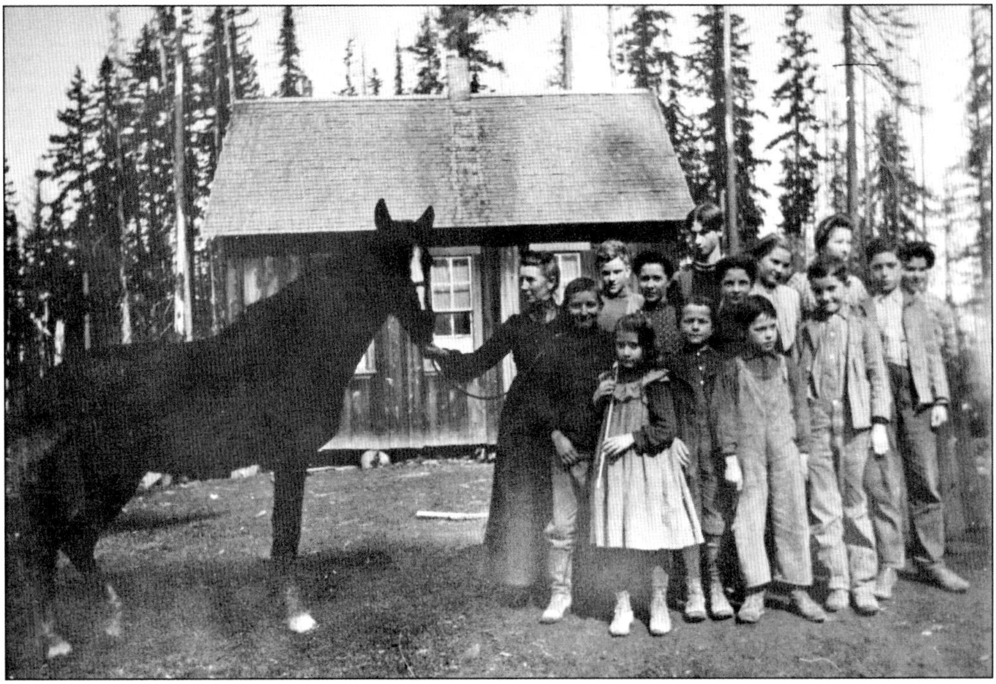

Students of the Tucker School on Keasey Road gather for this c. 1912 photograph in front of the school. Due to the distance between homesteads, some students rode horses to school, as did the teacher, Mrs. Cornelius (Mamie Woods) Hatfield, whose horse is shown in the picture. Eda Tucker is standing in the second row, third student from the left. She later married Clark and Melissa Parker's grandson Walter. (Gwin.)

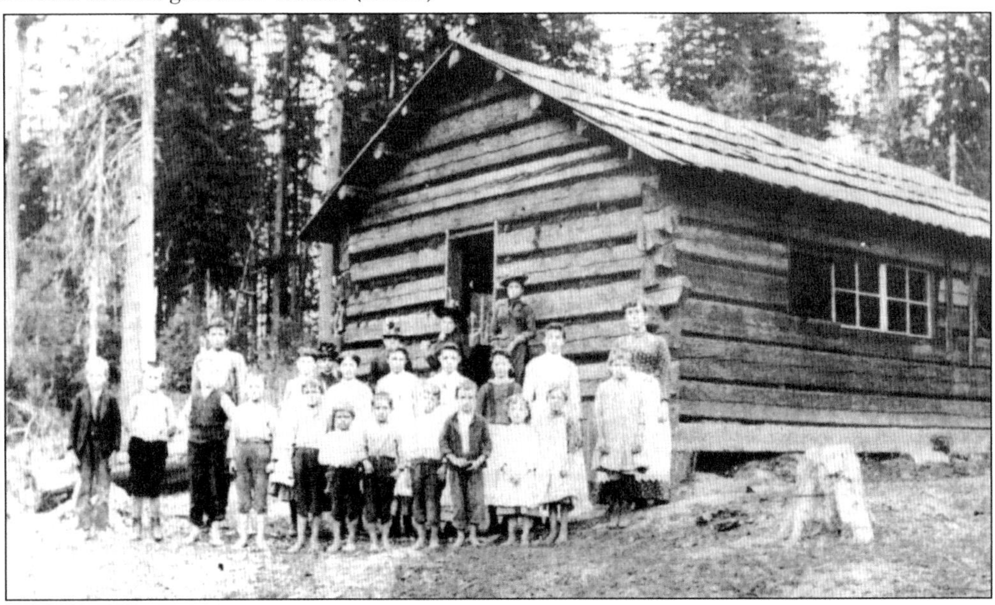

The Rock Creek School, the first school for children living in the town of Vernonia, was built in 1889 above Rock Creek near the intersection of Keasey and Stoney Point Roads on land donated by the Mellinger family. A Miss Lovelace was the teacher when this picture was taken in 1890. (Queen.)

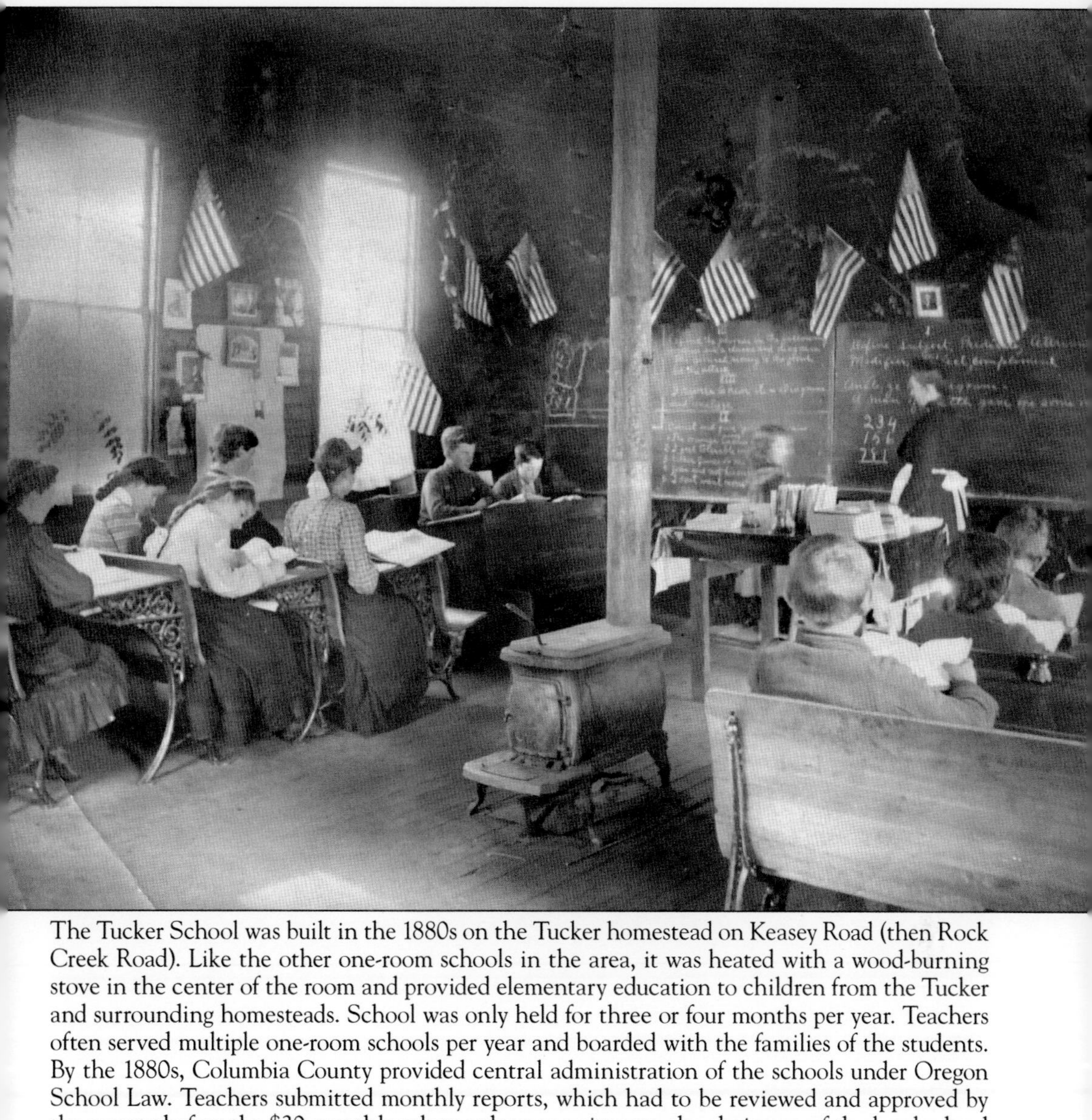

The Tucker School was built in the 1880s on the Tucker homestead on Keasey Road (then Rock Creek Road). Like the other one-room schools in the area, it was heated with a wood-burning stove in the center of the room and provided elementary education to children from the Tucker and surrounding homesteads. School was only held for three or four months per year. Teachers often served multiple one-room schools per year and boarded with the families of the students. By the 1880s, Columbia County provided central administration of the schools under Oregon School Law. Teachers submitted monthly reports, which had to be reviewed and approved by the county before the $30 monthly salary order was written to the chairman of the local school board. These orders were vouchers that would be presented for payment at the annual school meeting. Teachers were required to submit school-term summary reports to the county school superintendent in St. Helens. The teacher pictured above is Mamie Hatfield. (Keasey.)

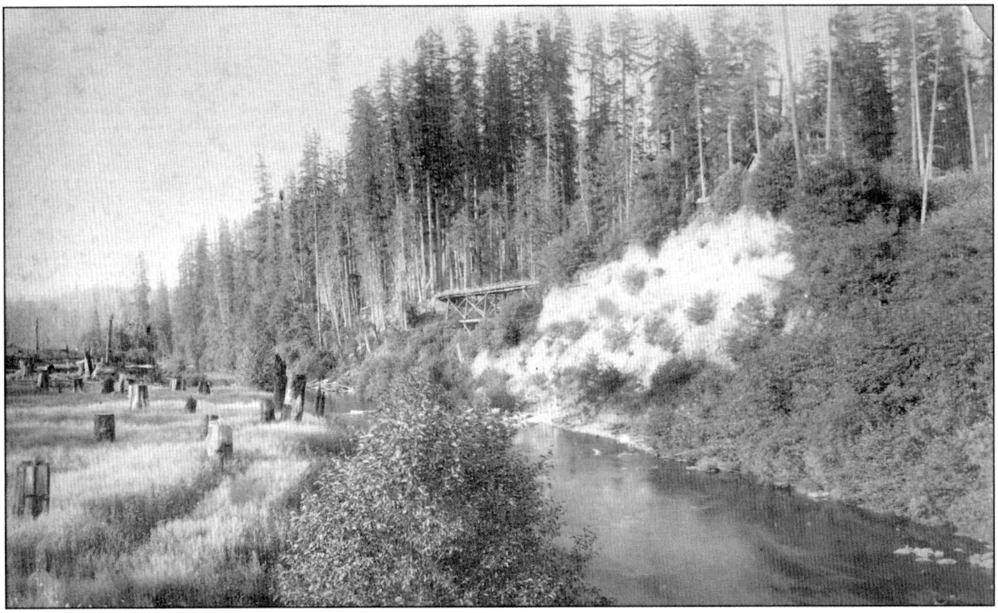

Taken in 1889 in Pittsburg just downstream from the Nehalem River's East Fork, this photograph shows the stumps remaining from the clearing of the limited flatland in this area. The Pittsburg School can be seen just beyond the stumps in the left of the picture. The trestle shown in the center of the picture was built for the road that went along the east side of the Nehalem. (Keasey.)

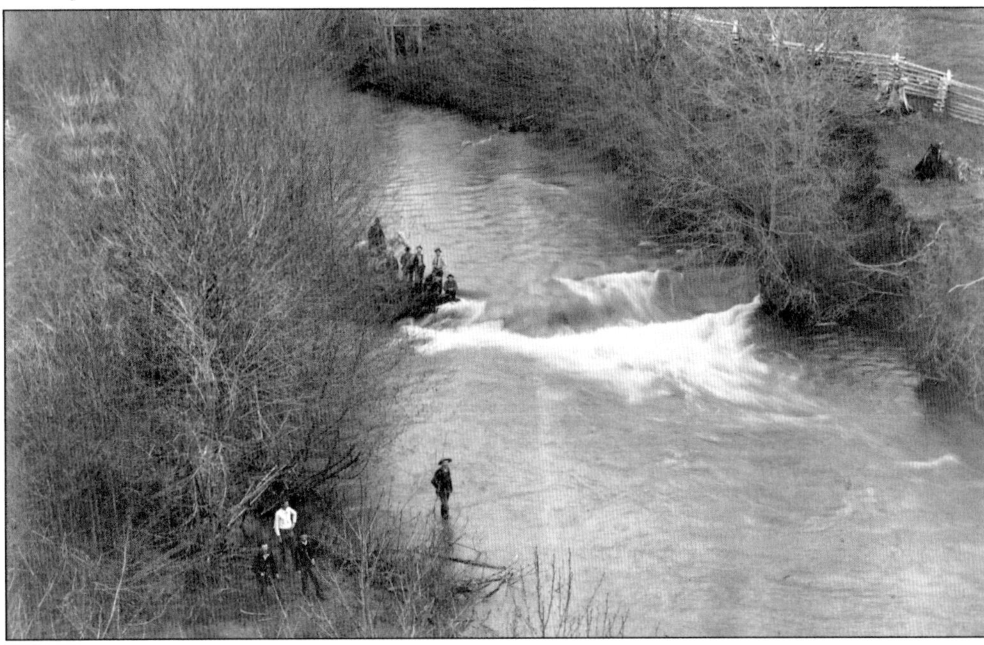

Taken in 1891, the year of Vernonia's incorporation, this photograph shows the falls on Rock Creek near its confluence with the Nehalem River. Beginning in Oregon's Coast Range, Rock Creek flows into the Nehalem in what is now Anderson Park. Each autumn, salmon return to their native spawning grounds in the river's tributaries, a major one of which is Rock Creek. As many as 10 salmon could be seen leaping the falls at one time in those days. The salmon still return each autumn but not in as great a number. (VPMA.)

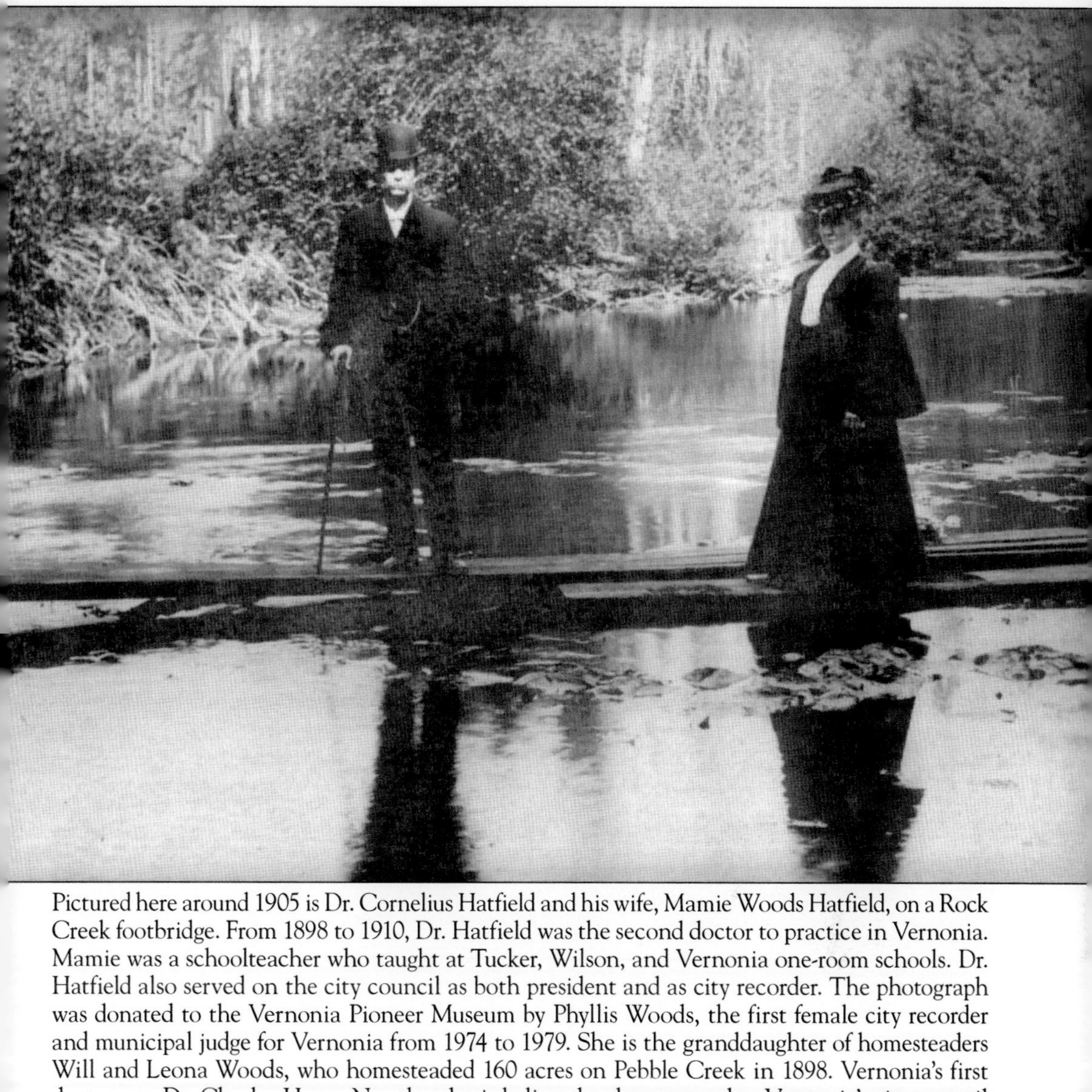

Pictured here around 1905 is Dr. Cornelius Hatfield and his wife, Mamie Woods Hatfield, on a Rock Creek footbridge. From 1898 to 1910, Dr. Hatfield was the second doctor to practice in Vernonia. Mamie was a schoolteacher who taught at Tucker, Wilson, and Vernonia one-room schools. Dr. Hatfield also served on the city council as both president and as city recorder. The photograph was donated to the Vernonia Pioneer Museum by Phyllis Woods, the first female city recorder and municipal judge for Vernonia from 1974 to 1979. She is the granddaughter of homesteaders Will and Leona Woods, who homesteaded 160 acres on Pebble Creek in 1898. Vernonia's first doctor was Dr. Charles Henry Newth, who is believed to have served as Vernonia's city council president (later titled mayor) from 1889 through 1899, but council records from 1891 to 1900 were lost long ago. (VPMA.)

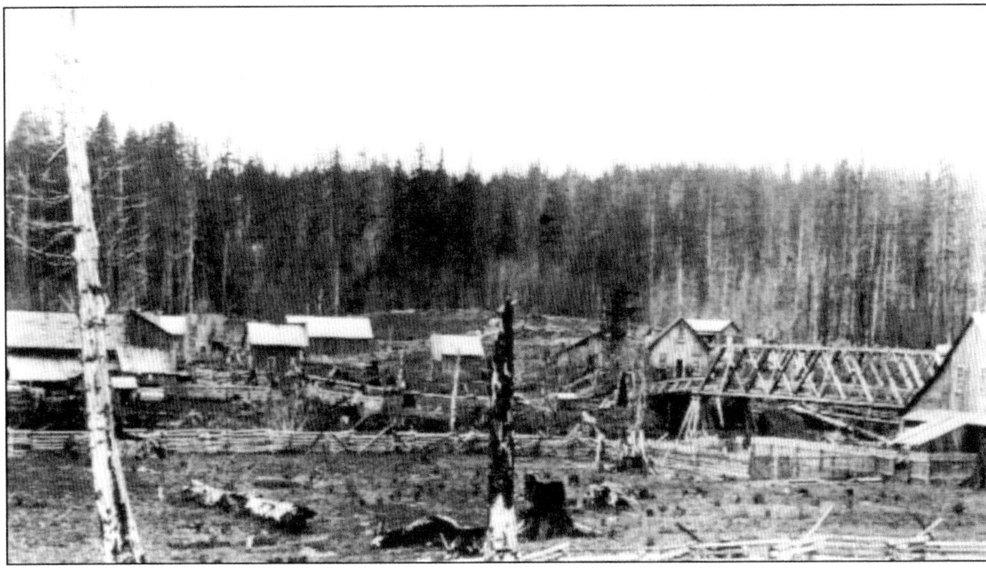

This 1894 photograph of Vernonia (above), taken from John VanBlaricom's homestead, shows the first bridge across Rock Creek. The bridge was built in 1889 and gave Bridge Street its name. It was replaced by a second bridge in 1916 and with the current concrete structure in the mid-1930s. Zilgitt's Store, built right on Rock Creek, is shown on the far right of the picture. The upstairs was known as Zilgitt Hall and was one of downtown Vernonia's first meeting places. McNutt's Store is visible behind the west end of the bridge. Vernonia's first hotel (pictured below) was built in 1879 of hand-hewn logs and split-cedar planks on what was to become Bridge Street. (Both, Queen.)

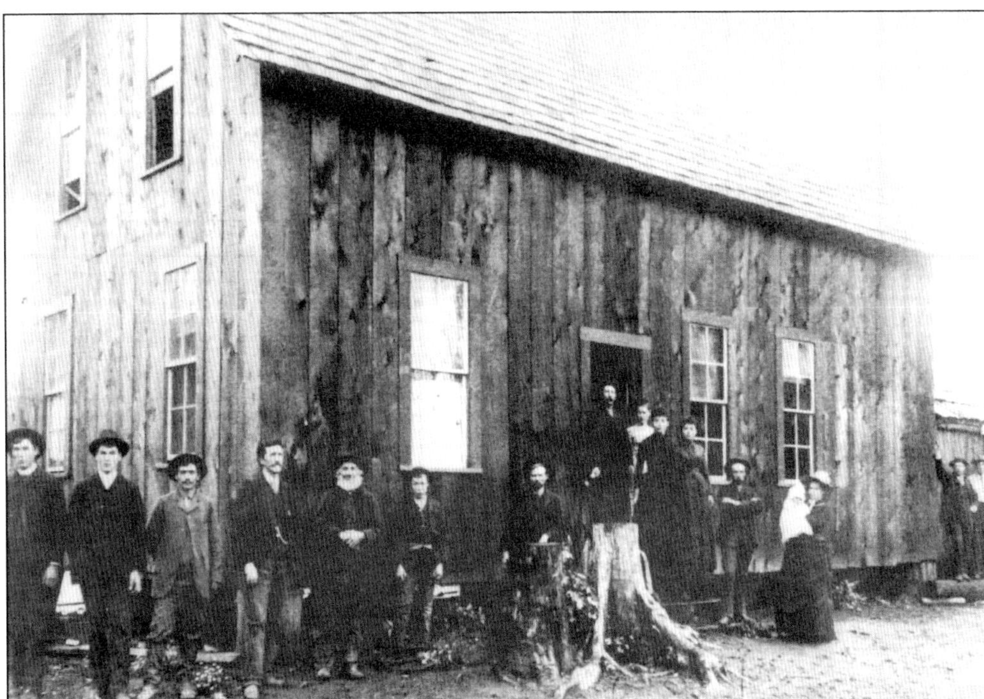

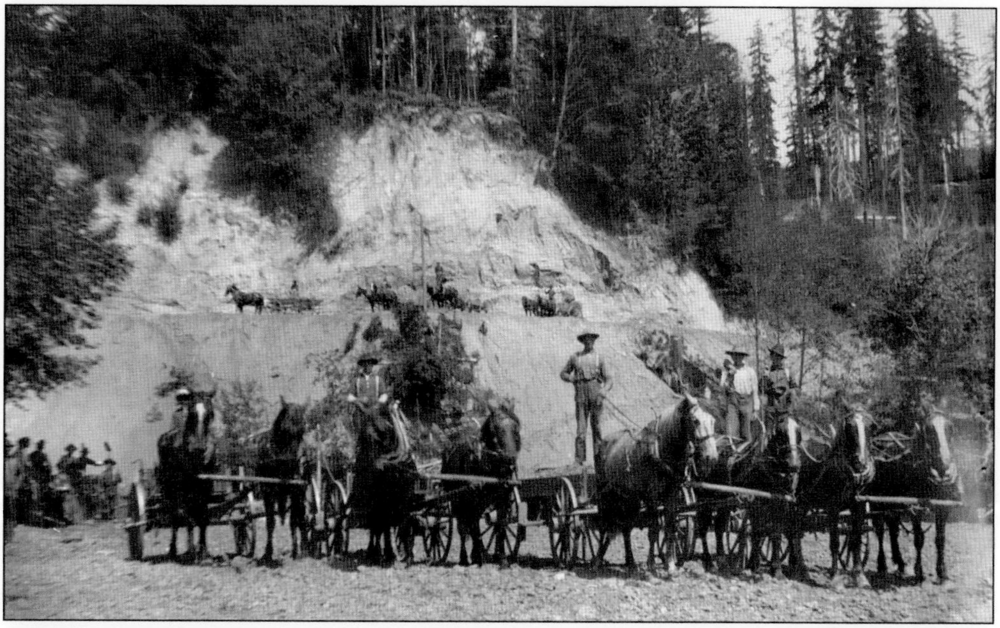

A road between Pittsburg and Vernonia was built in the early 1880s. At first, road construction was a task for the homesteaders so they could transport timber and farm goods to local markets. The real incentive for the men, however, was that they could credit their labor on the road to reduce or pay their property taxes. Trees were felled, and then teams of horses drew wagons carrying rocks and soil away from the cleared areas. Grading was done with a horse-drawn Fresno scraper. Heavier duty road-construction equipment, such as the dragline bucket shown in the photograph below with the road builders, was powered by steam donkeys rigged with cables to move dirt and level road grades. (Above, Keasey; below, VPMA.)

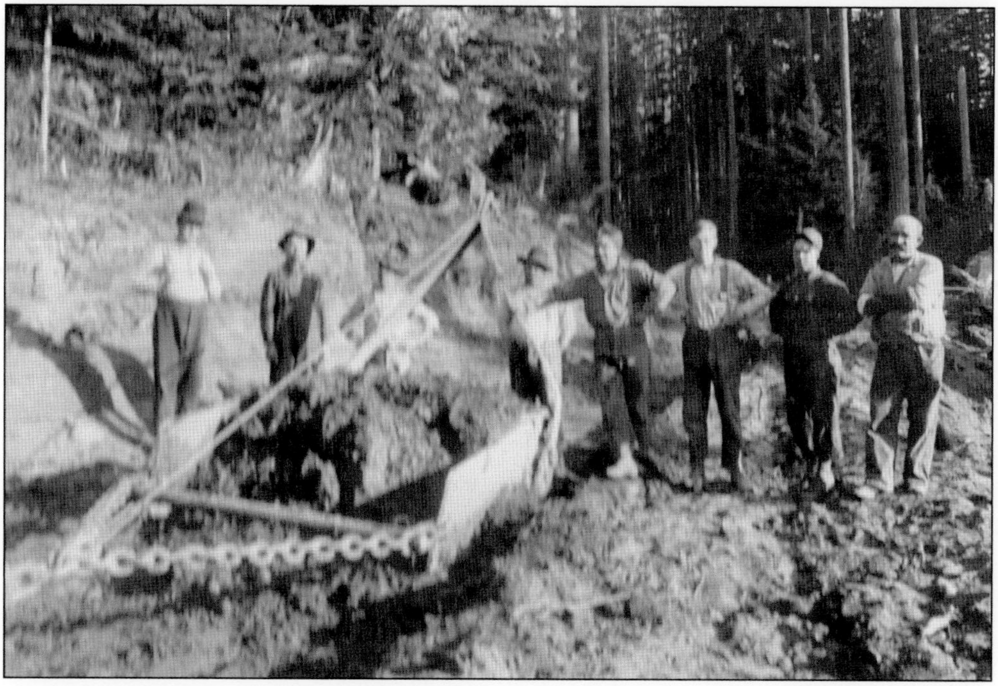

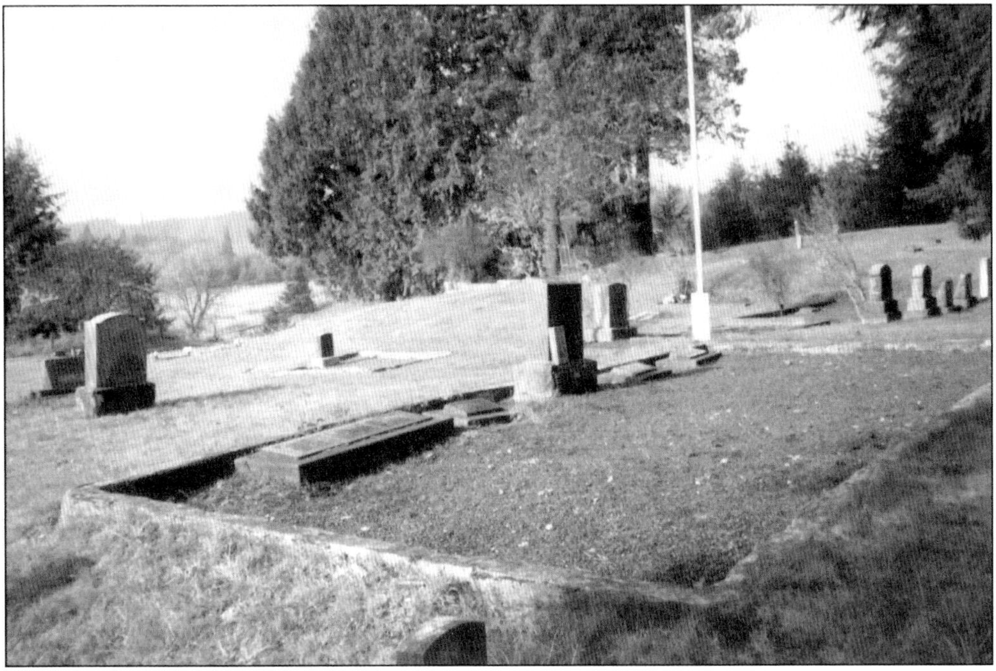

The Vernonia Pioneer Cemetery above Rock Creek on Keasey Road was established in the early 1900s with land donated by the surrounding landowners. The grave plots have all been sold for many years, but some families have vacancies, so there are still burials from time to time. The Vernonia Pioneer Cemetery Association, comprised of descendants of the early families, maintains the site. Headstones contain the names of many of the first families to settle in Vernonia. Below, Colton Patton stands by the new sign. Colton worked to get a new fence around the cemetery as his Eagle Scout project. (Above, Meyer; below, VPMA.)

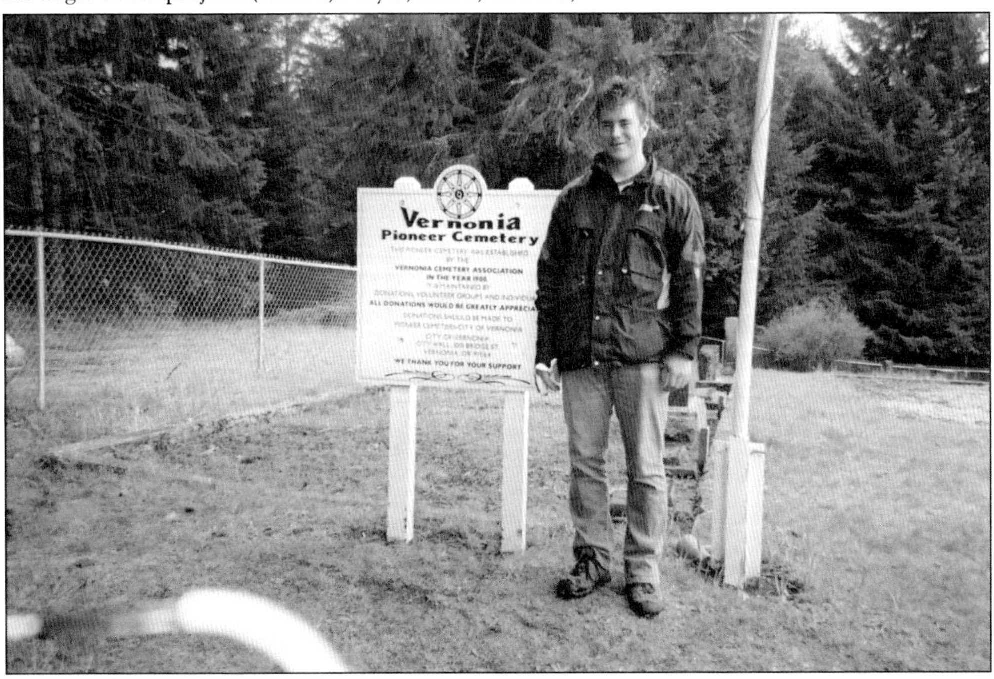

Two

Early Town and Farm Life

The hardy pioneering families stayed on and began to use the timber that was so abundant. Small dairies and sawmills were established as a source of income. Rumors of a railroad through the area started a temporary land boom and growth spurt that brought many new commercial enterprises and settlers to the area. The earliest logging in Columbia County took place along the Columbia River, where transportation of the logs to market was not such a challenge. As the supply of easy timber near the river diminished, logging railroads spread inland toward Vernonia around the time of its 1891 incorporation as a city.

Joseph VanBlaricom and Robert and Martha McNutt platted 18 blocks in 1888. Three more additions were platted in 1891 due to the growth. The first town school was built in 1889. Hotels, churches, theaters, social halls, stores, and other commercial businesses gradually appeared along or near Bridge Street, the main thoroughfare. The streets remained unpaved until the mid-1920s. Plank sidewalks helped pedestrians negotiate the often-muddy streets.

A small dam on Rock Creek brought electric power to Vernonia in 1923. Rural electrification did not occur until the 1930s. Cad Keasey and his brother, Dow, put in the first ground circuit telephone between Pittsburg and St. Helens in 1902. The first telephone exchanges started around that same time. A telephone and telegraph office, built in 1920, was staffed by a single operator who lived in the building.

The Grand Army of the Republic and the Women's Relief Society provided patriotic celebrations and took care of local Civil War and World War I veterans. Organizations such as the Vernonia Literary Society reflected the growing sophistication of the town. Grange dances, church socials and picnics, holiday festivals, dramas and musical performances, and hunting and fishing provided entertainment for hardworking farmers and town dwellers. On Saturday nights, loggers came in from the surrounding camps to attend the dances and partake of the less genteel activities in the taverns and brothels on Bridge Street.

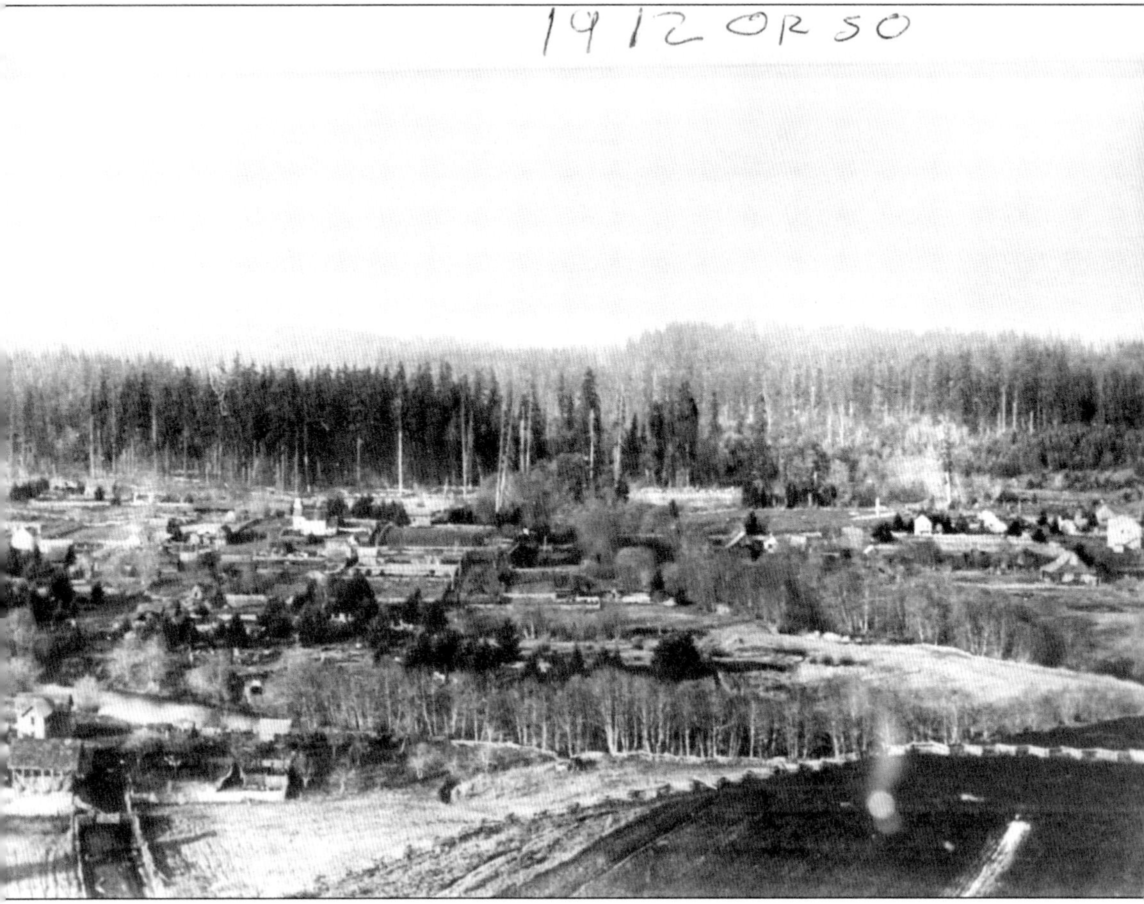

This photograph was taken from the second Alexander Sword homestead in 1912. The town of Vernonia with its lone church steeple has grown back to a population of around 100. After the city's incorporation in 1891 and a period of growth following speculation on a coming railroad, the Panic of 1893 started an exodus of more than half the town's population. By 1912, new businesses had come, and people were once again moving back to the area. The Vernonia Grange Hall, built in 1907, is the big white building in the center background on the far right. The Evangelical Church with its tall steeple is in the center left background. Joseph VanBlaricom donated the land for both edifices. VanBlaricom's original homestead covered most of the land that was then within the city's boundaries. The house on what has been known for more than 100 years as "the Sword Place" is seen in the lower left. (Sword.)

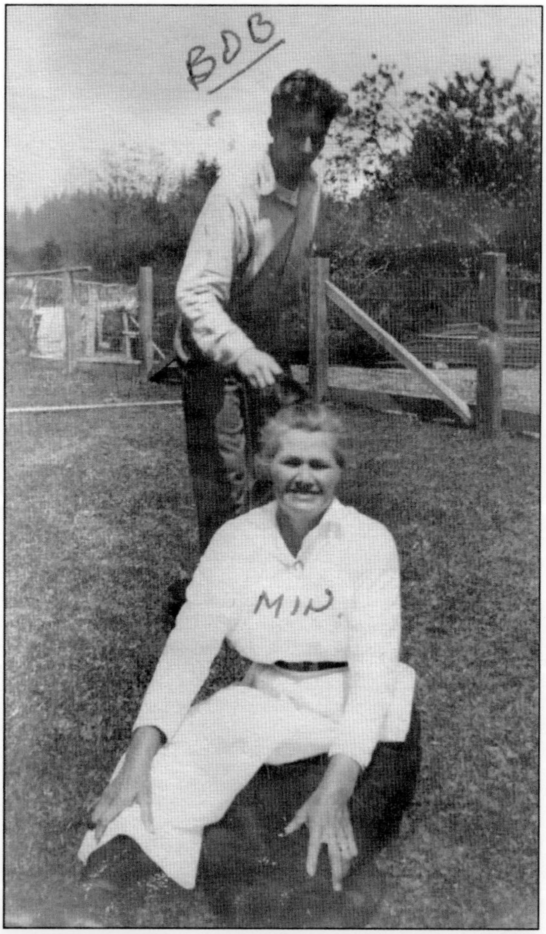

Alexander Sword, born in Scotland, came to Vernonia 1887 from Illinois. He and Hermione "Minnie" Wockener Sword first homesteaded 160 acres that he later sold to McPherson Lumber Company. The land was later acquired by Norbert Pelster. Alexander Sword purchased his second homestead from Alexander Eastlick for $750 in 1887. His son Bob (seen in the photograph at right pulling his mother, Minnie's, long braid) raised his family on the homestead. In 1968, Bob's son Bill and his family moved in. The 1918 photograph below of Minnie Sword (left) and an unidentified friend shows the back porch of the Sword home and its hewn cedar-log construction. (Both, Sword.)

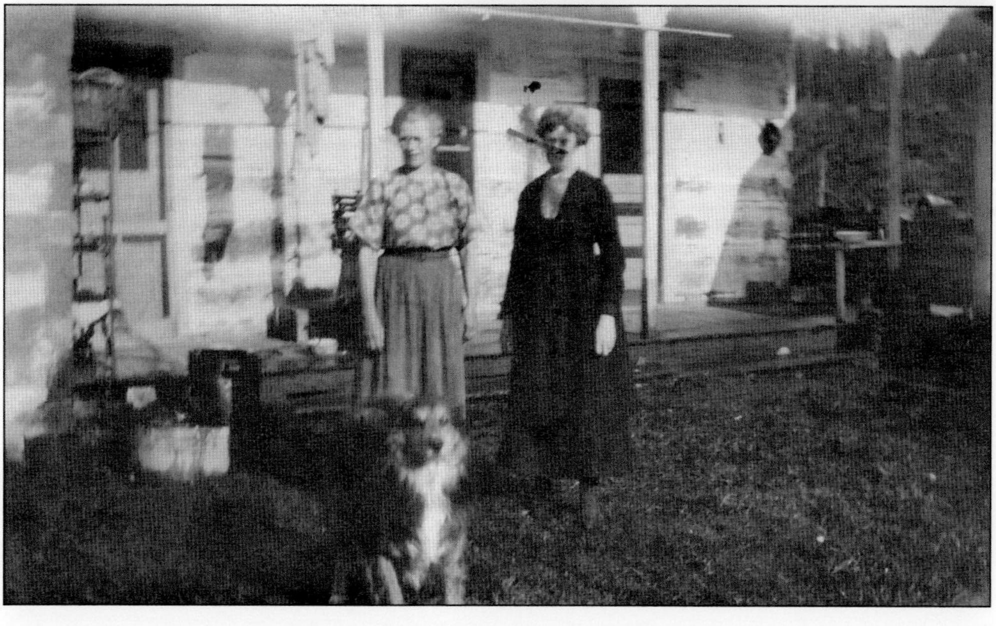

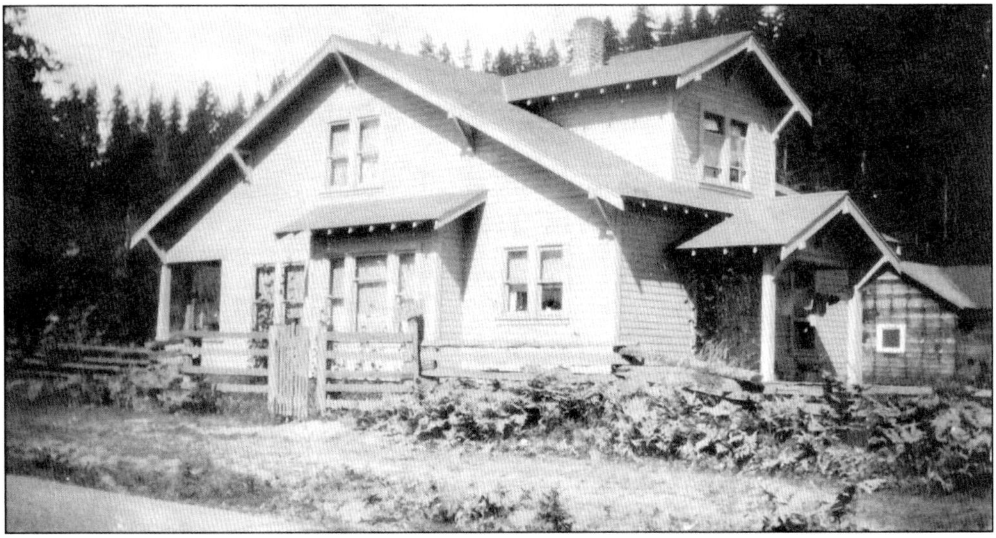

Olof Malmsten and his oldest son, Otto, came to Vernonia in 1889. The other adult children followed, and soon there were multiple Malmsten homesteads around Vernonia. The Charles Malmsten homestead of 160 acres was established in 1898 with land on both sides of Bridge Street, the main thoroughfare. In the early 1900s, he built the home pictured above. The orchards of the Malmstens were planted south of Bridge Street in the area currently occupied by Vernonia High School. The Charles Malmsten home still stands on the corner of State Avenue and A Street. Charles's father, Olof, lived in the home pictured below. It was also on State Avenue but has since been torn down. The first Washington Grade School can be seen to the right of the house. Olof's son Franklin sold part of his homestead to the Oregon-American Company for its mill site. (Both, Malmsten.)

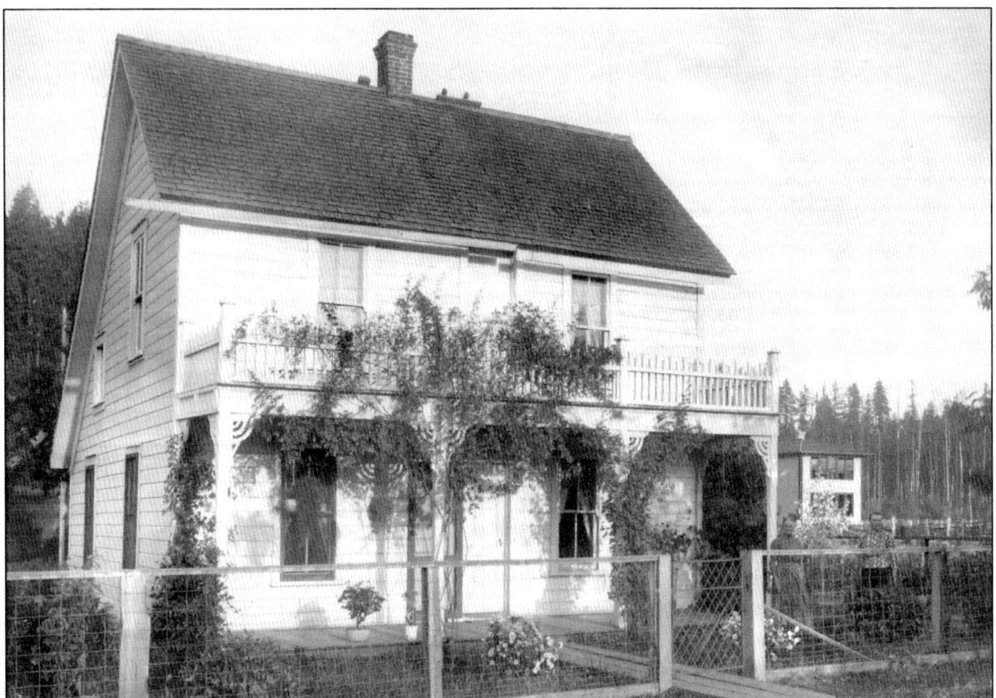

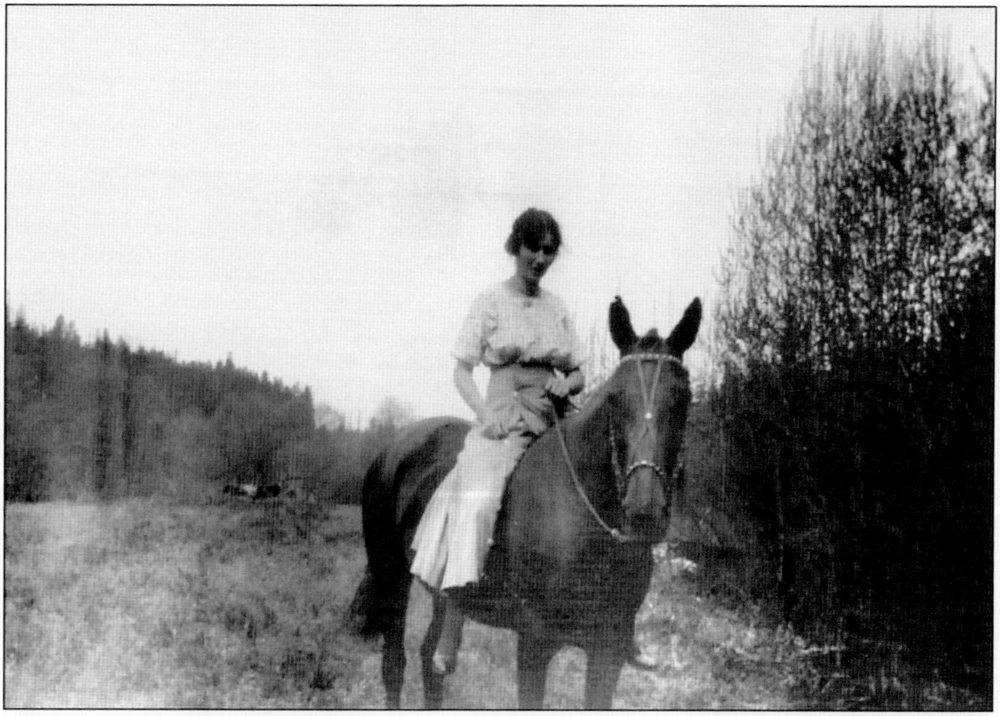

Helen Anderson Christensen rides her horse on the Anderson farm on Timber Route. At right, Helen is shown with her brother Willie in front of the Anderson home. At the time this picture was taken, Helen was about 18 years old, and Willie was 15. The Anderson and Christensen farms were close to each other. Thomas Anderson and his brother, Harve, came from Ohio to Oregon in 1880. In 1897, they bought property on Timber Route from Harve VanBlaricom and built a house a year later with lumber from the Pittsburg mill. Thomas married Mary Huber and spent the rest of his life in that house. (Both, Queen.)

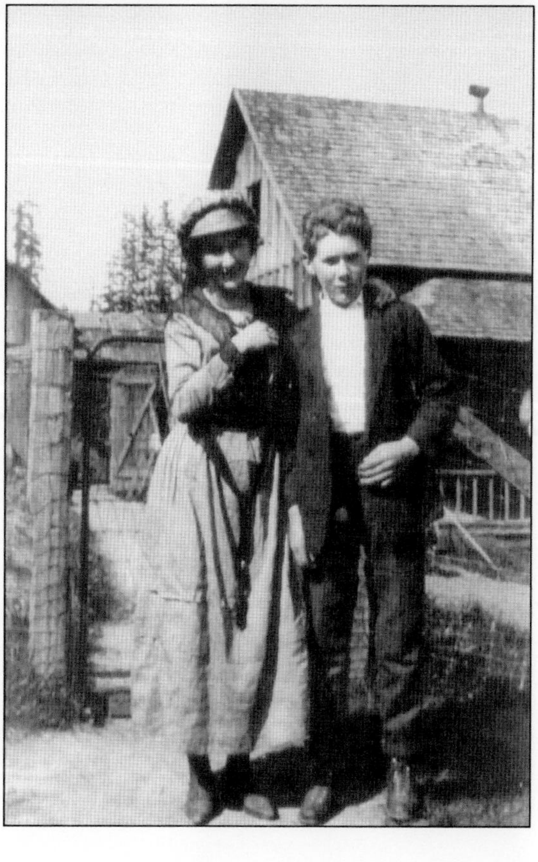

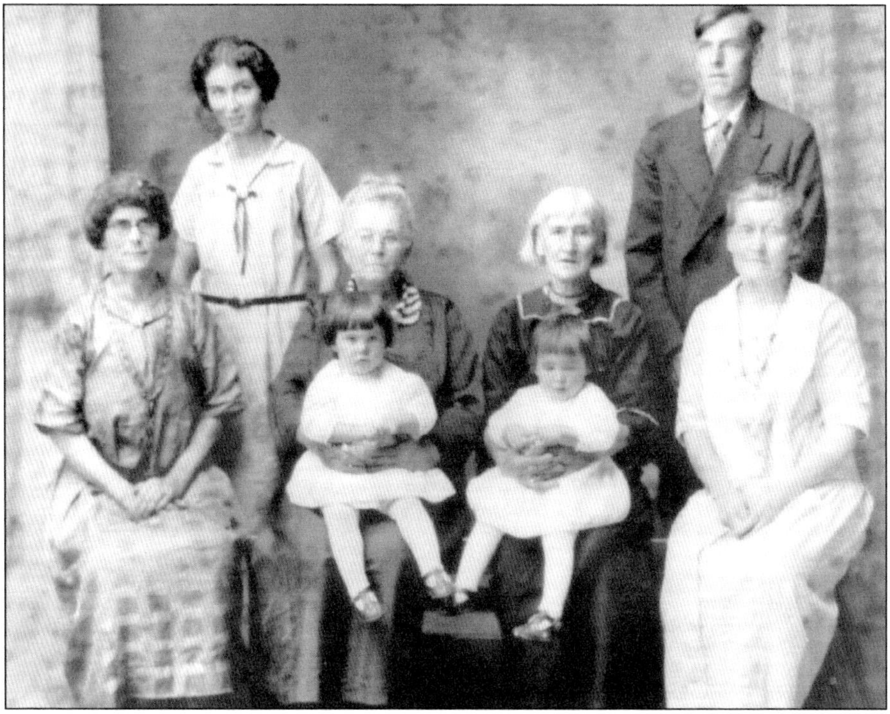

This multigenerational family photograph was taken in 1926 or 1927. In the first row are, from left to right, Mary Huber Anderson, Olive Staley Huber, Hannah Bennett VanBlaricom Brand (John VanBlaricom Jr.'s widow, who married Edgar E. Brand), and Anna VanBlaricom Christensen. Standing in the second row are Helen Anderson Christensen and her husband, Vester. Helen's twin girls, Lesta (left) and Vesta Christensen, are held by Olive and Hannah. Pictured below are the Christensen twin daughters, Lesta (right) and Vesta. Born on January 22, 1925, at their maternal grandmother's (Mary Huber Anderson) home on Timber Route, they were quite a surprise to 24-year-old Helen. Lesta was born at 10:55 a.m., and Vesta followed at 11:25 a.m. Each girl weighed 8 pounds. (Both, Queen.)

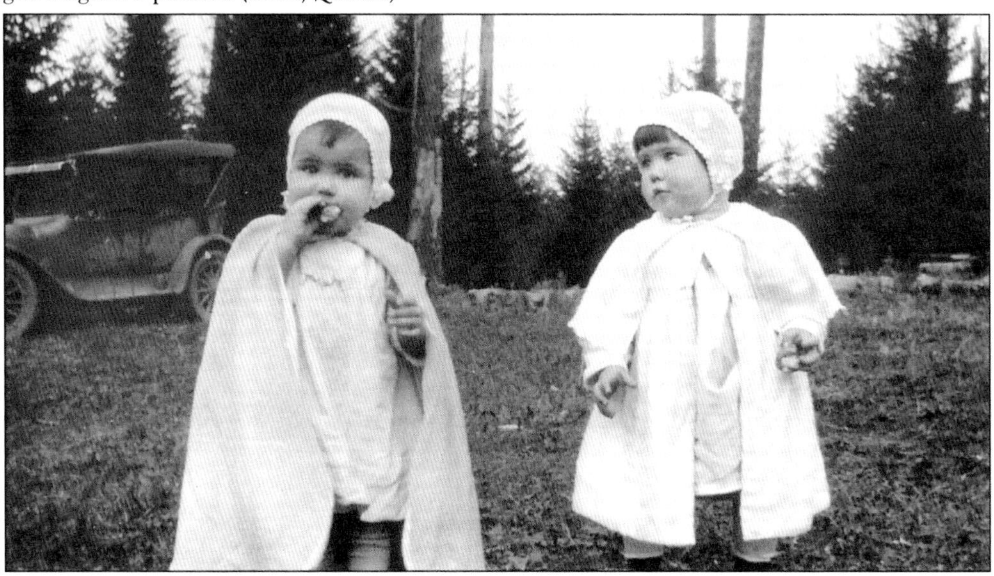

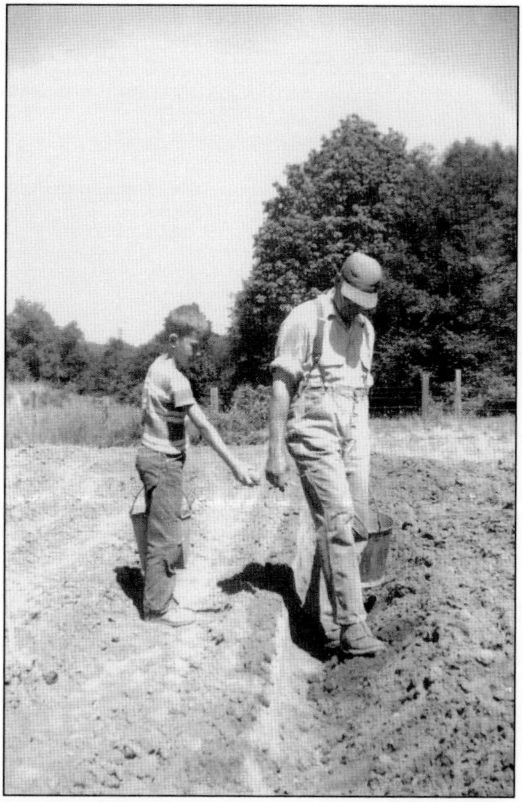

An unidentified boy and Vester Christensen plant potatoes on the Christensen farm on Timber Route in the 1940s. Vester and his wife, Helen, were married at the nearby home of her parents by a Vernonia cousin of Vester's, justice of the peace Lester Sheeley. Vester had to ride a horse to St. Helens, a 70-mile round-trip, to get their marriage license from the county courthouse. In the photograph below, another summer's hay is loaded for the barn with daughters Lesta (left), Vesta (center), and Arvela seated on the John Deere tractor. In addition to farming, Vester made a living by logging, as did many Vernonia farmers. (Both, Queen.)

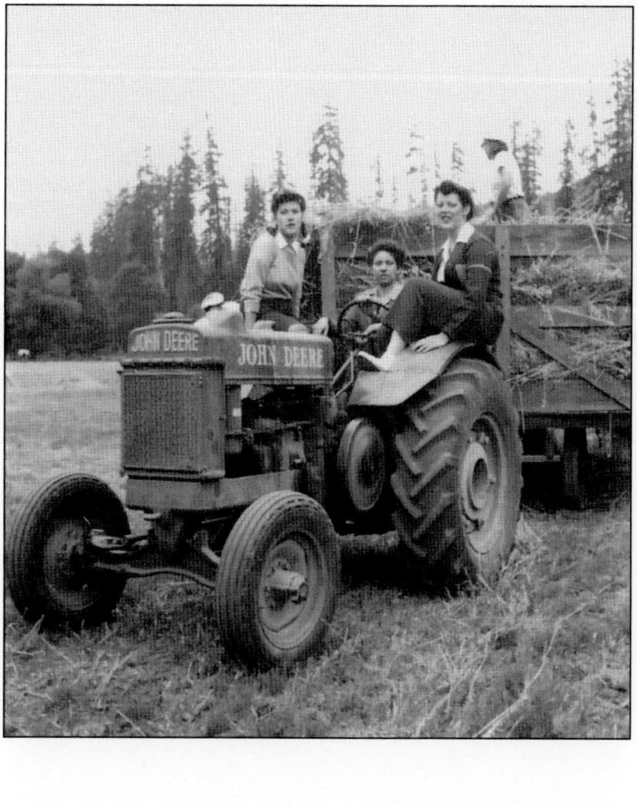

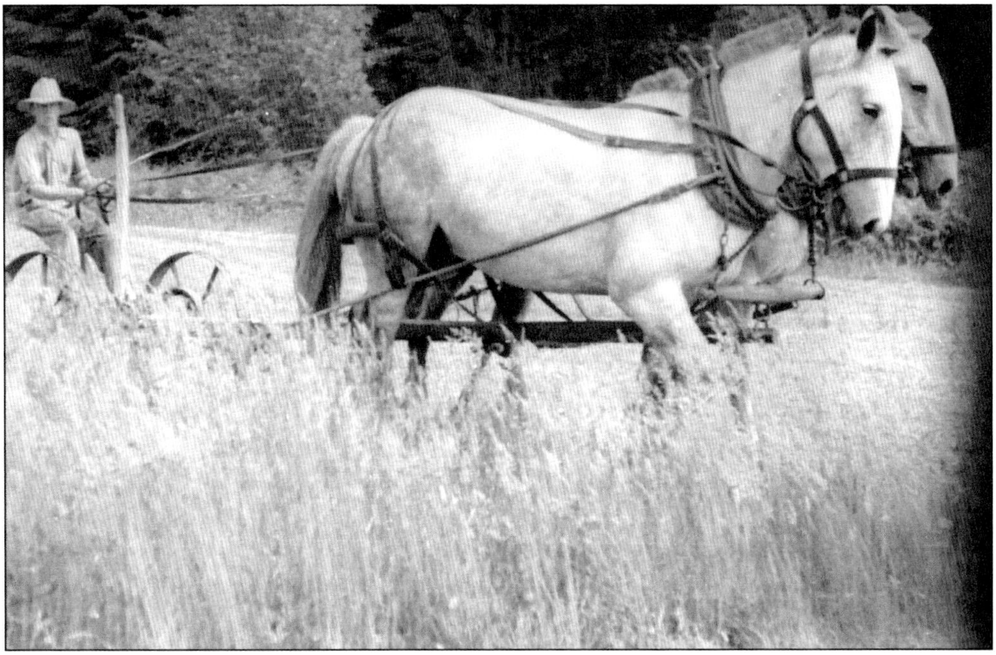

Hay was an important crop for farmers who raised cattle and horses, and the hay-and-animal barn was often the first structure built on a homestead. Although some of these photographs were taken in the mid-1940s, horses were still used to mow, rake, and haul the hay. Above, Ralph Keasey drives the horse-drawn mower to cut the hay. His father, Ted Keasey, (below) drives the hay rake. Before modern cutting and baling equipment was widely used, hay making required many hands. Haying and grain harvesting were usually extended family and even community affairs. (Both, Keasey.)

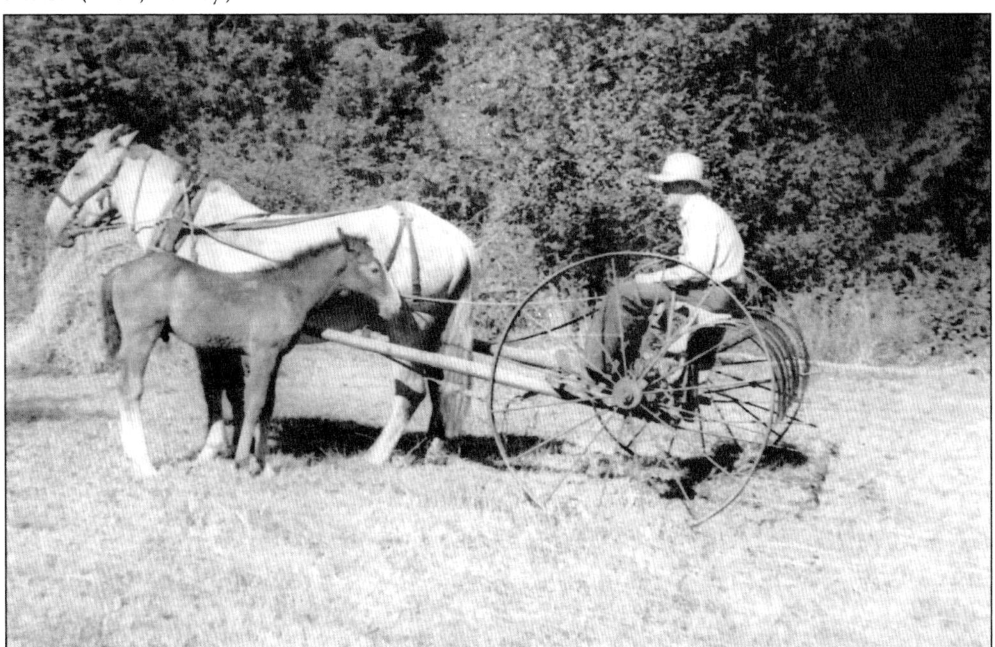

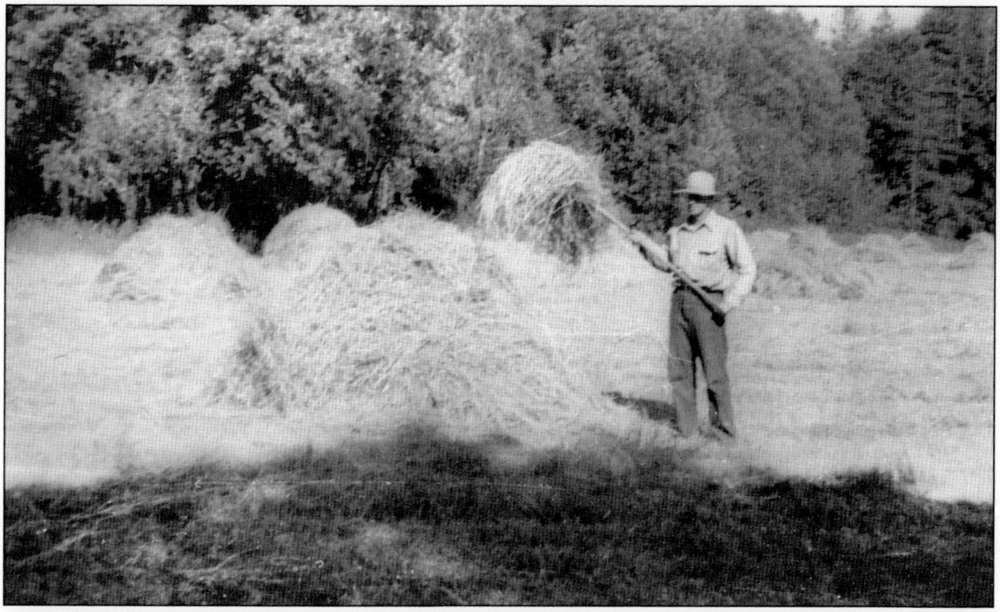

After the hay has sufficiently dried, it is gathered into stacks, which are then loaded into wagons to take to the barn. Ted Keasey is seen above with pitchfork in hand, gathering the hay. The picture of the hay loading below was taken in the early 1900s. Cad Keasey and other family members provide the manual labor. The Keasey homestead was located 5 miles outside of Vernonia, and when the railroad came, their stop was called Homewood, as was the one-room school there. The town of Keasey, several miles beyond Homewood, was the major rail yard between Vernonia and the O-A lands beyond. (Both, Keasey.)

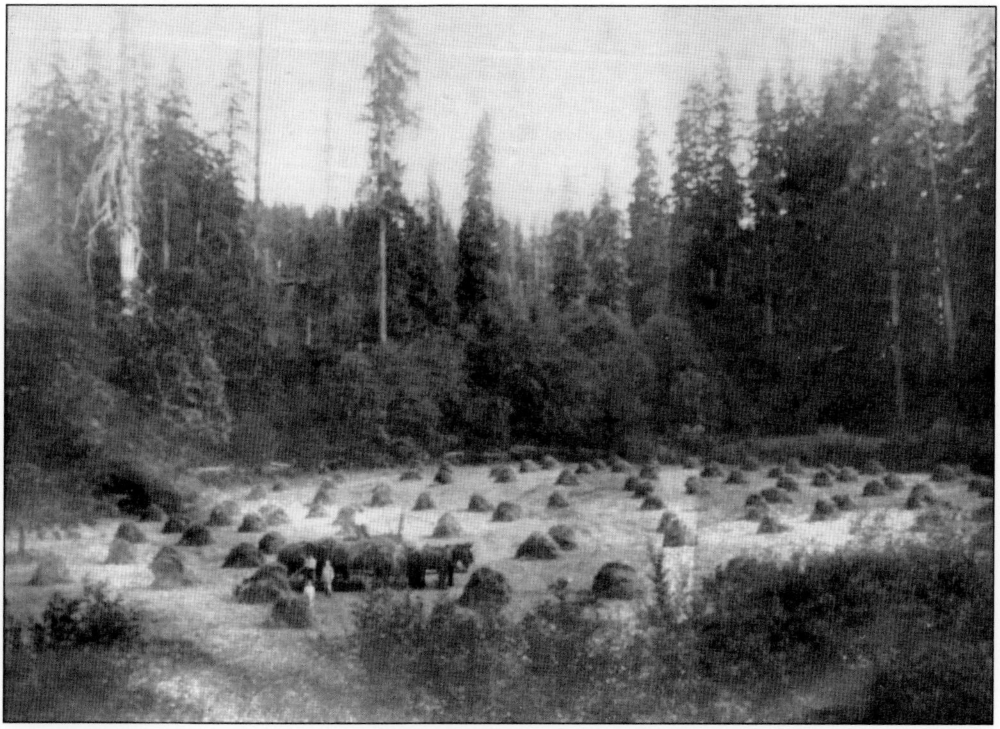

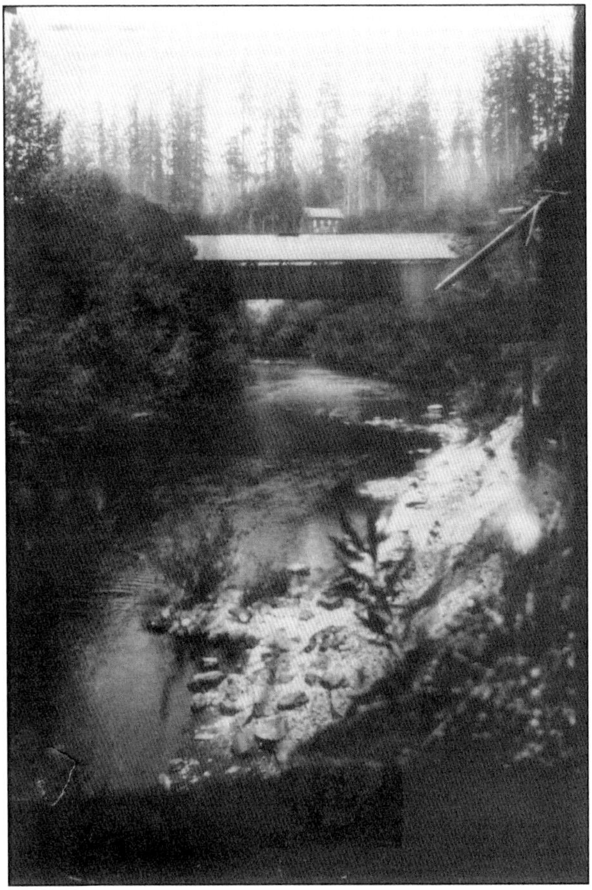

Covered bridges were common throughout western Oregon in the late 1800s and early 1900s. Due to the rainy climate and winter snows, covered bridges prolonged the useful life of these wooden structures. The Pittsburg School can be seen in the background. This covered bridge at Pittsburg on the east fork of the Nehalem River lasted until the 1970s. (VPMA.)

The empty water tank being delivered by a horse-drawn cart from Pittsburg is headed to a logging or road-construction operation nearby. A ready supply of water was needed to operate the steam donkeys that provided pulling and lifting power to move large logs and drag line buckets full of dirt and rocks or other heavy objects. (VPMA.)

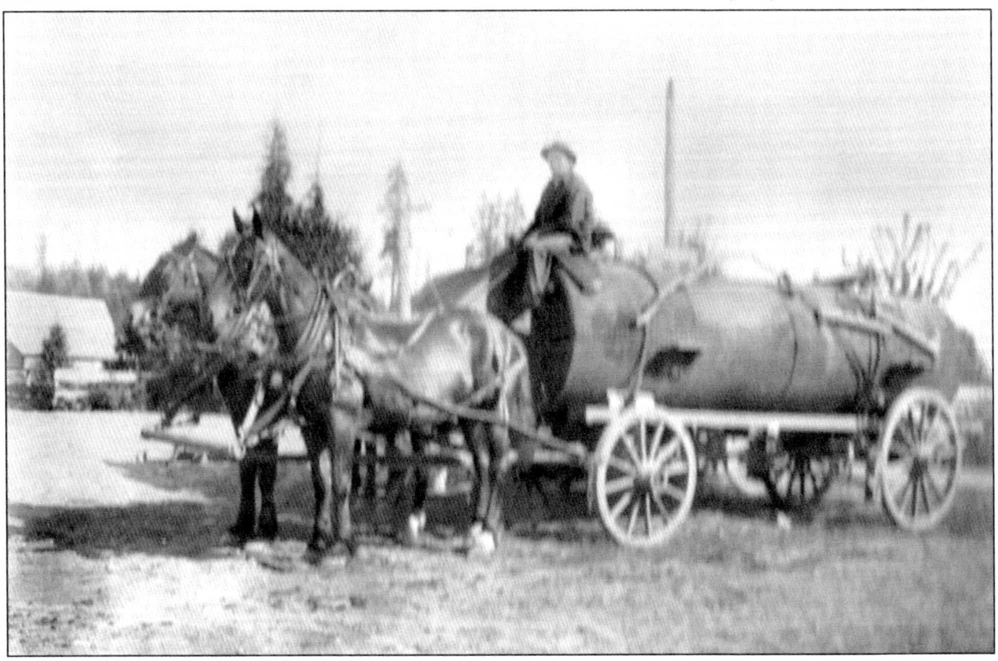

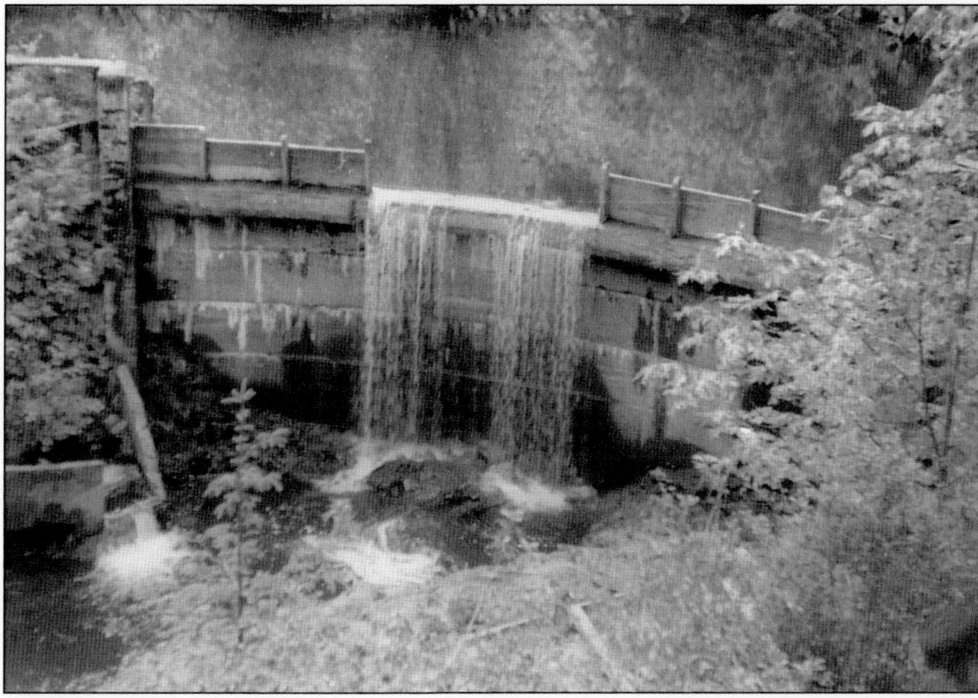

The Vernonia Power and Light (VP&L) Company was started and owned by George Burdick. VP&L built the Keasey Dam on Rock Creek in 1922–1923. It started producing electric power for downtown Vernonia in 1924. This photograph was taken from the nearby railroad bridge. Water from the dam came downhill through the wooden penstock to a small powerhouse. The penstock can be seen on the trestle in the background of the picture below, where Deale Hanson is fishing. VP&L was later acquired by the Oregon Gas and Electric Company, which served the area until 1945, when it was sold to West Oregon Electric Cooperative. (Above, Keasey; below, Meyer.)

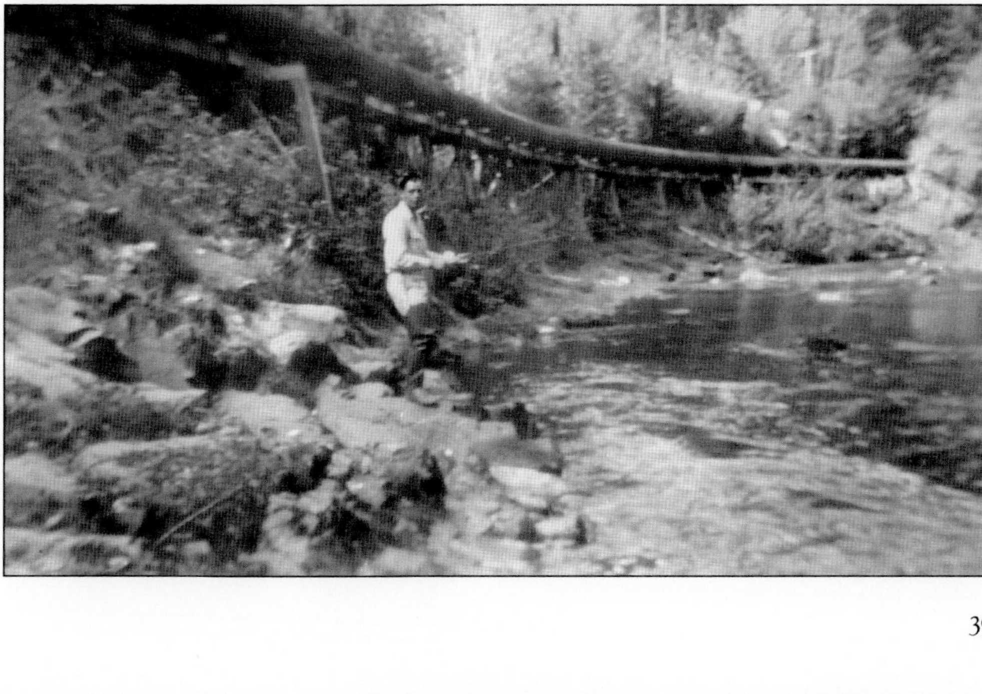

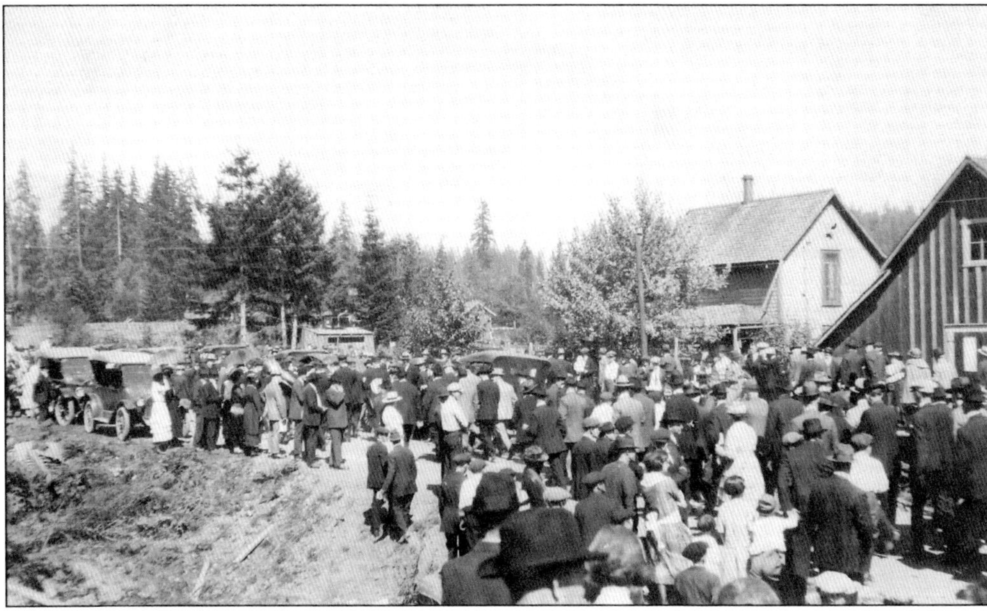

For years, Vernonians had waited for passenger-train service to the area. The arrival of the first train on September 9, 1922, was eagerly anticipated by the townspeople as they gathered near the tracks in the picture above. A special Vernonia Day celebration was held to celebrate the occasion. The celebrations included a program with speeches by visiting dignitaries, ball games, dancing, concerts, parades, and a greased pig contest. Seen below, the Spokane, Portland and Seattle Railway (SP&S) special excursion train from Portland arrived with four passenger cars attached. It was now possible to go outside without a half-day's journey on unpaved roads, and freight could be brought in by train to serve the growing population. (Above, Keasey; below, Pringle.)

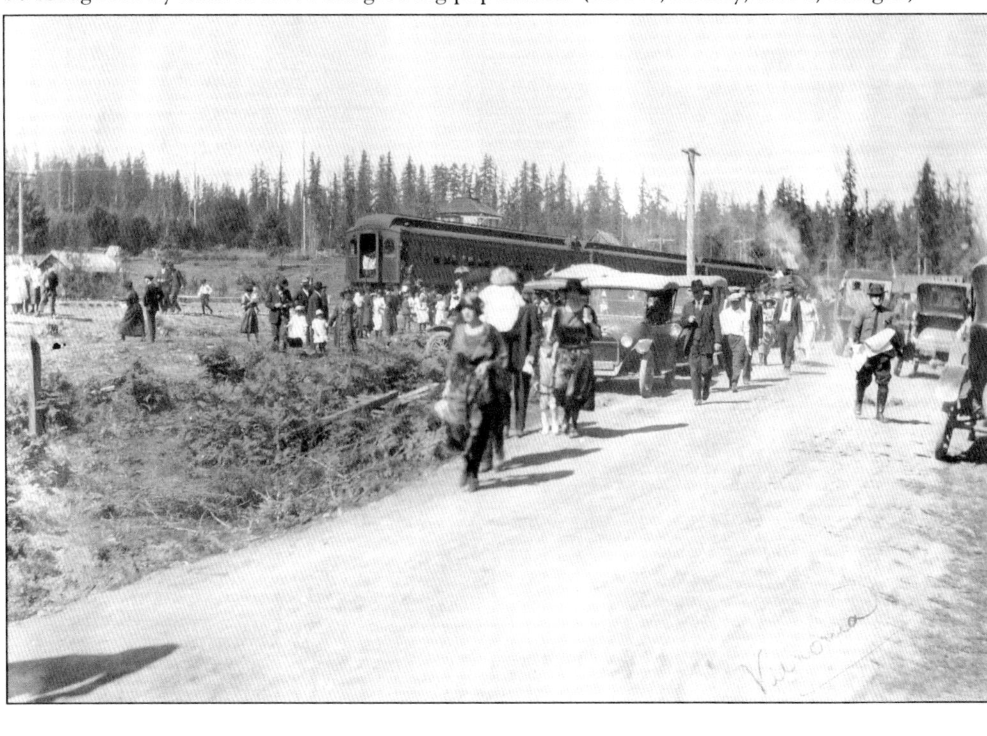

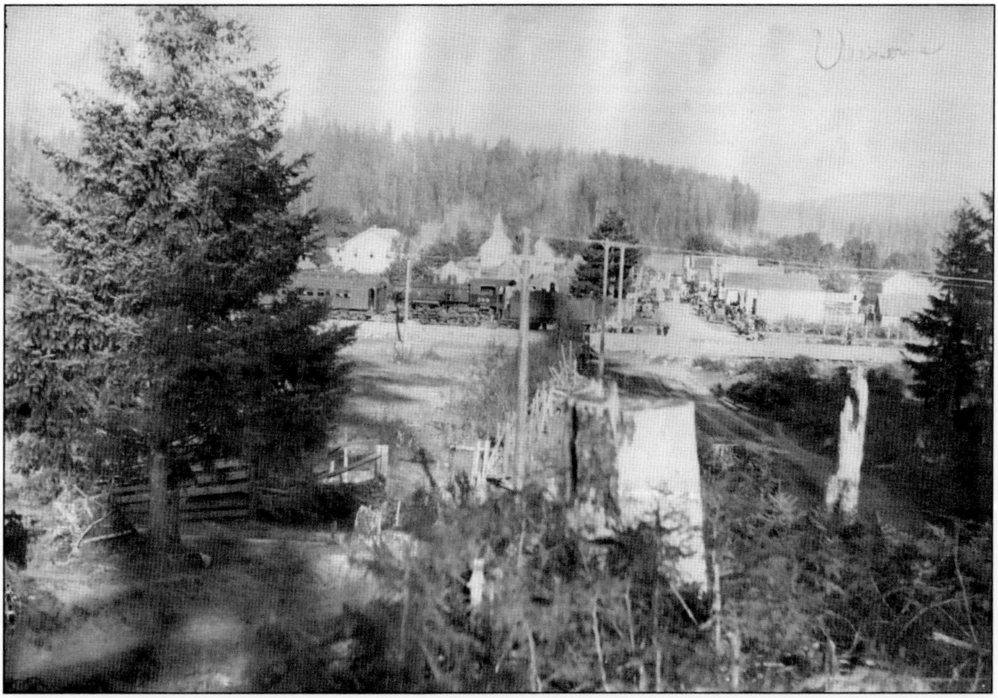

Taken shortly after the arrival of the first train, this photograph shows the main street of Vernonia, Bridge Street, from a vantage point on Corey Hill. The streets will not be paved for three more years. The tree-covered hill in the distance would soon be known as O-A Hill for the houses of the mill workers that were being built there. The mill, which was also under construction at the time, would lie in the clearing seen in the upper right corner. The new Vernonia depot and telegraph office in the photograph below were built in the early 1920s to serve the new rail line. (Above, Pringle; below, Malmsten.)

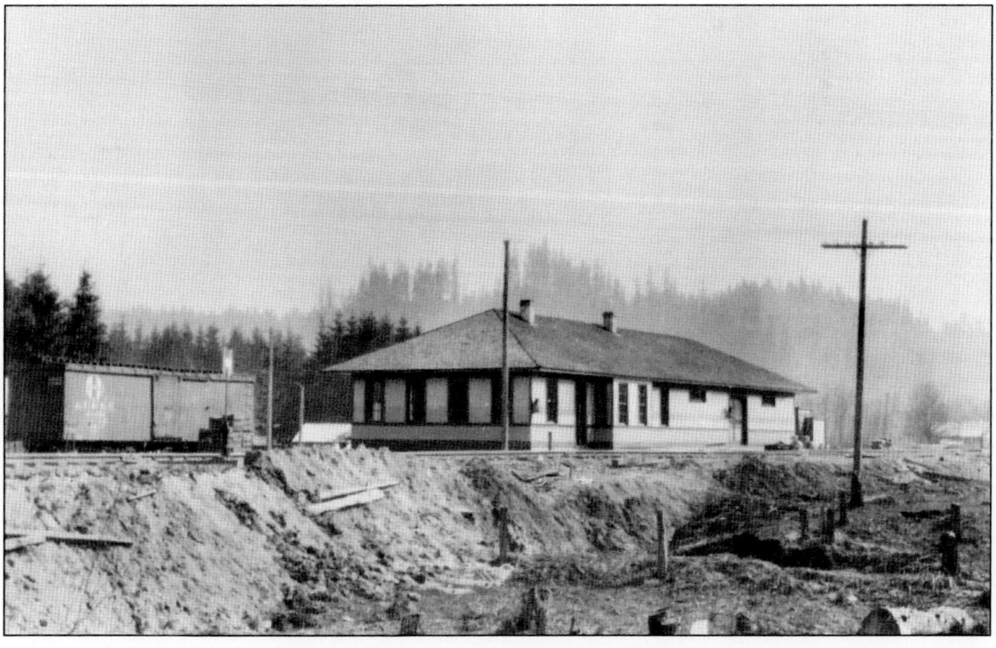

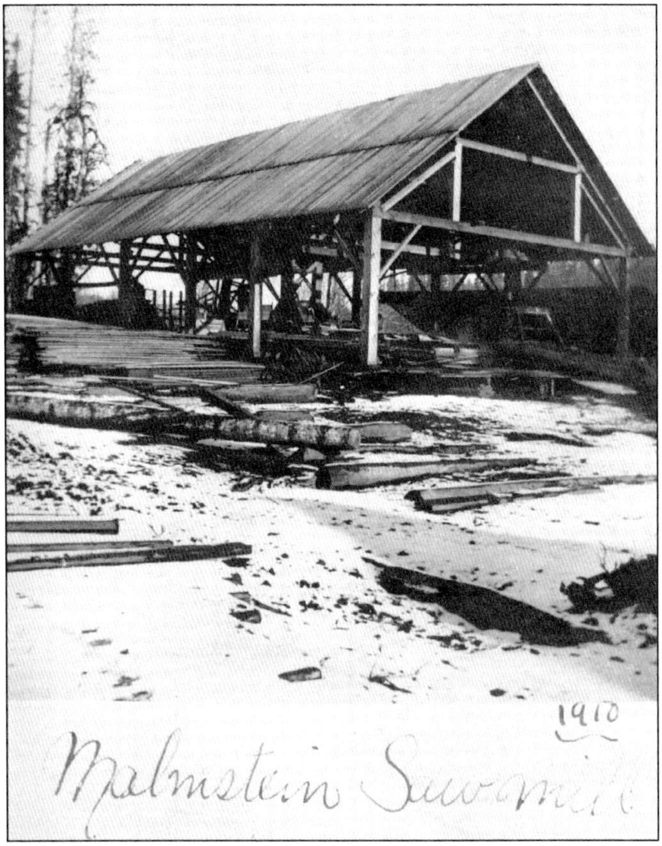

Small sawmills were common sights around Vernonia. Powered at first by steam engines and later by gas, diesel, and electric motors, they provided the fir for lumber and cedar shingles for roofs and the siding of houses and businesses in the growing town. The Malmsten brothers, Sidney, Charles, and Franklin, built and operated a sawmill on the west bank of the Nehalem River across from Riverview. The photograph at left was taken in 1910. In a much later photograph below, Ted Keasey's sawmill is shown. (Left, Malmsten; below Keasey.)

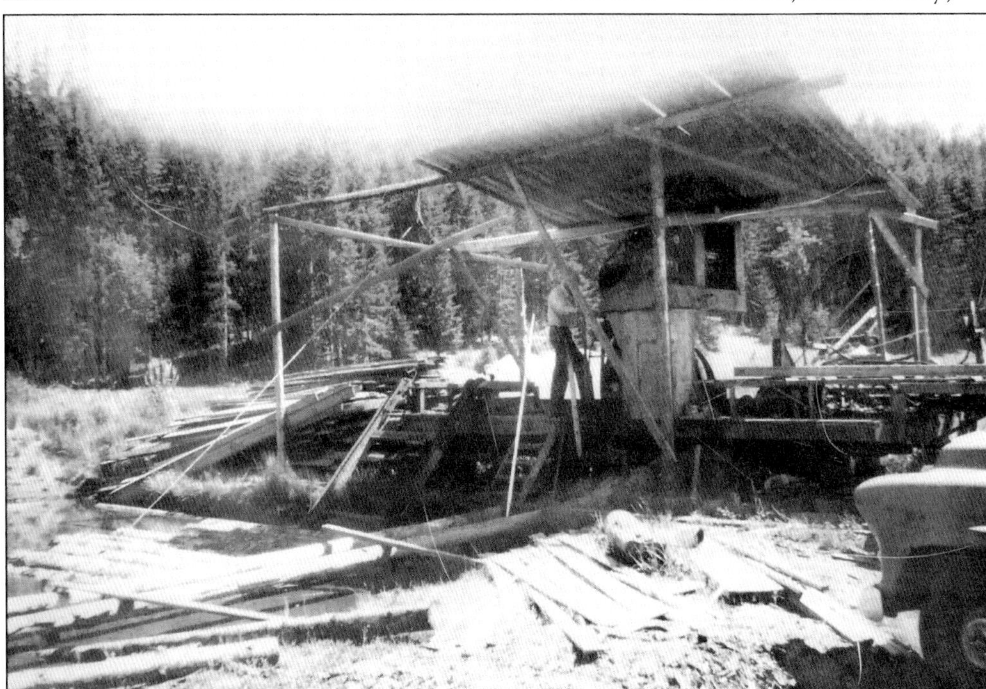

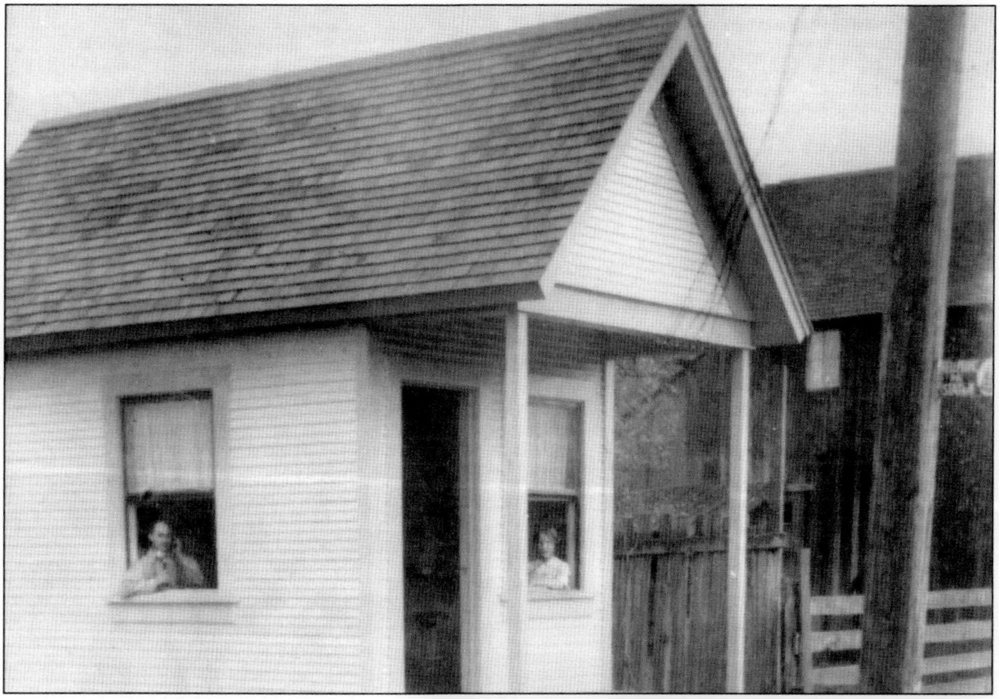

Cad Keasey and his brother, Dow, set up a telephone connection between Pittsburg and St. Helens in 1902. The Wood brothers established an exchange between their homes on Stoney Point Road. The Malmsten brothers set up a family telephone exchange that became the Nehalem Telephone Company. A telephone office was built in 1922. Above, Louis Vadney is making a call. The resident operator, Olga Holmstrom, can be seen in the front window. (VPMA.)

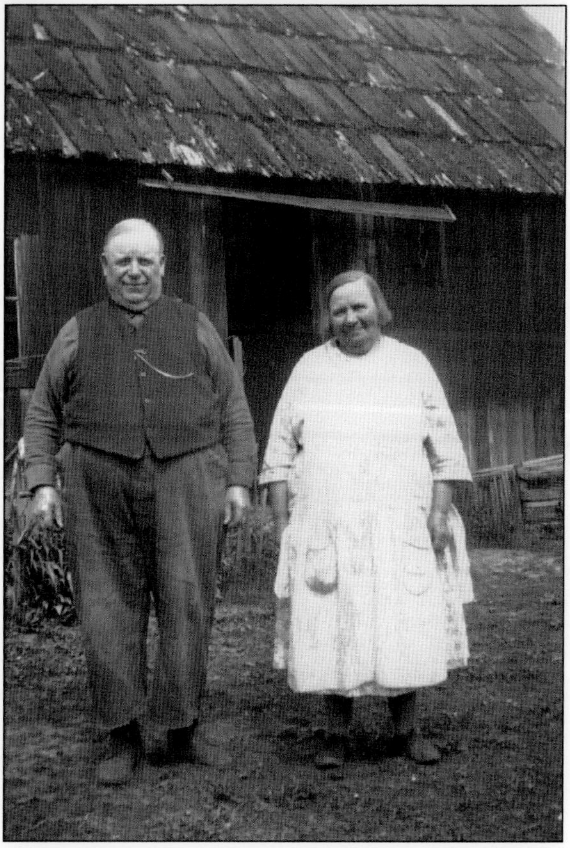

Matt Johnson and his sister, Jennie Johnson Shauer, stand in front of their home on Burn Road in the 1930s. As a child, Ellen McDonald Meyer and her siblings used to walk the mile or so to visit these nearest neighbors. Jennie always gave them a silver dollar when they visited. (Meyer.)

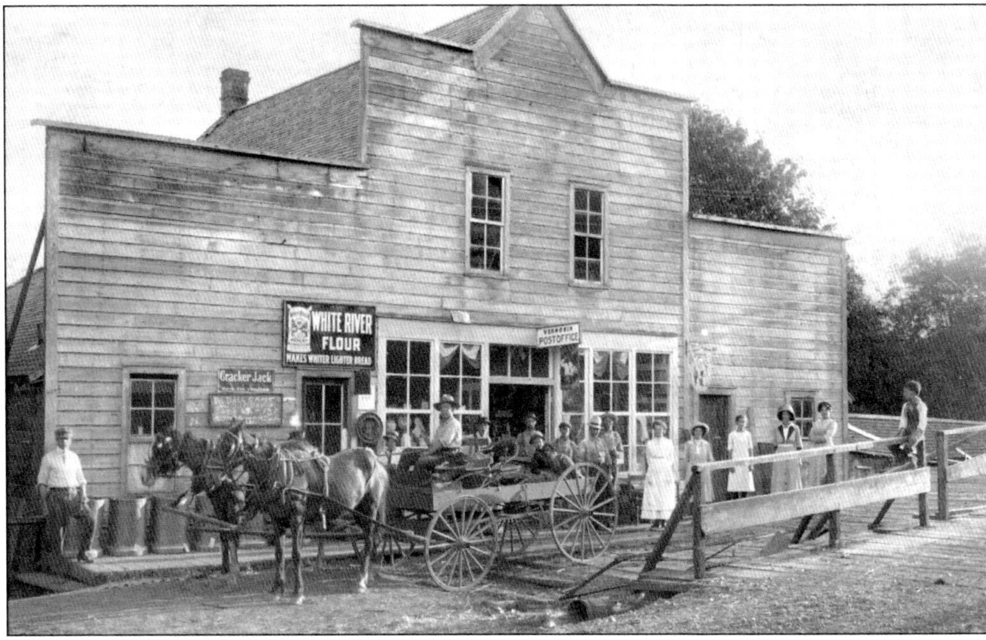

David "Frank" Baker, Drucilla VanBlaricom's husband, was Vernonia's first postmaster. His home served as the post office. He received his appointment on January 11, 1878, and served until June 29, 1886. In October 1879, Hiram VanBlaricom got a four-year contract to deliver mail between Vernonia and St. Helens on horseback. During a terrible windstorm in January 1880, Hiram was stranded in the woods overnight. By 1913, the post office for the city was in the Zilgitt Mercantile on Bridge Street. In 1923, the post office was in other quarters, pictured below. The men in the photograph are, from left to right, Curley Buffmire, Tom Bateman, Emil Messing (postmaster from 1914 to 1955), Jack Nance, and an unidentified person. (Above, Gwin; below, Queen.)

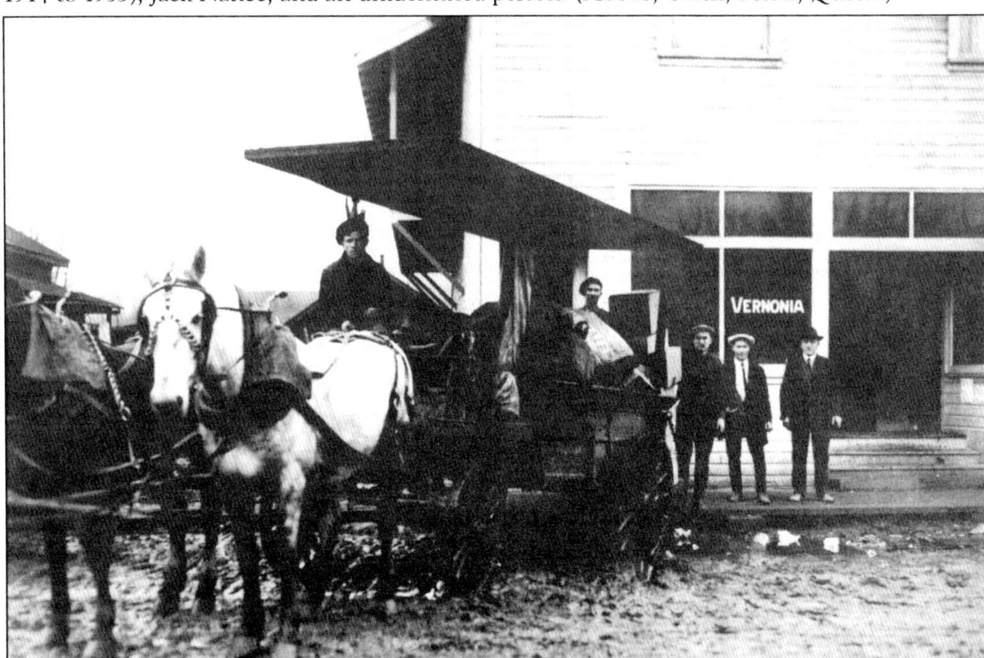

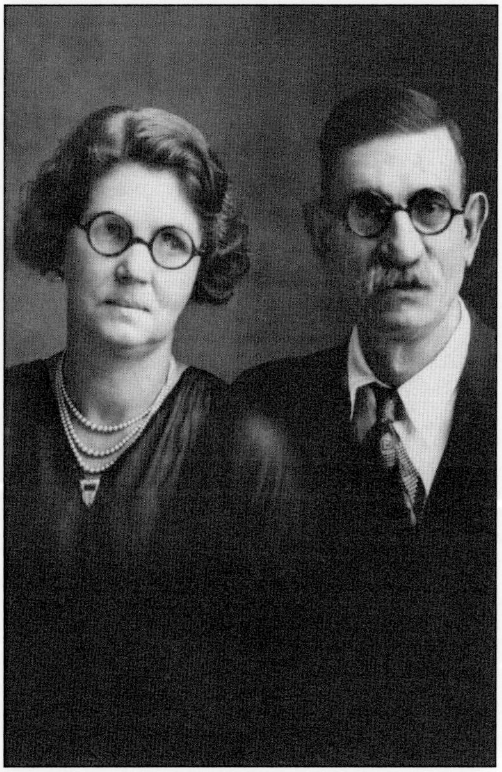

Benjamon and Myrtie Howell Cline were married in 1900 in Olive Hill, Kentucky, where he worked in a brick factory. They came to Vernonia in 1919 after trying farming in Idaho for a few years on their way west. Myrtie's family owned a furniture store on the block where the post office, built in 1953, stands today. The whole block burned in the 1920s. Due to the many fires in downtown buildings in the early years, a city code was written after this fire to require future buildings to be constructed of brick. Many of the original wooden buildings still stand however. Benjamon ran the only shoe repair shop on Bridge Street in the 1920s and 1930s. His son, Merle, later opened a shoe repair shop in another location. (Both, Cline.)

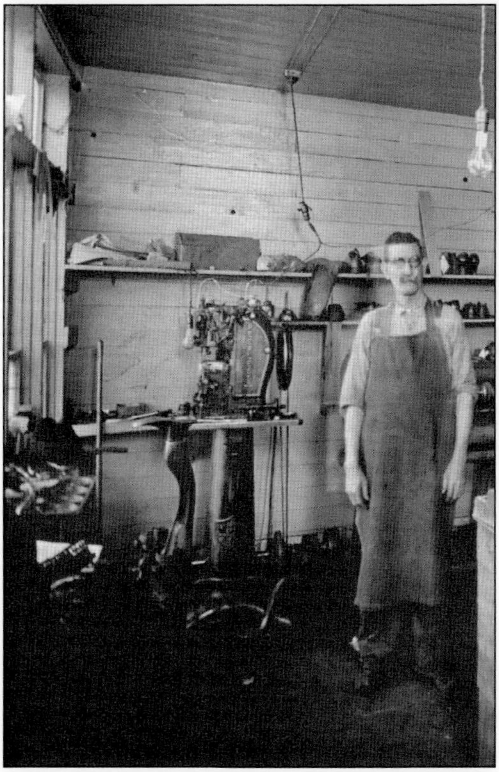

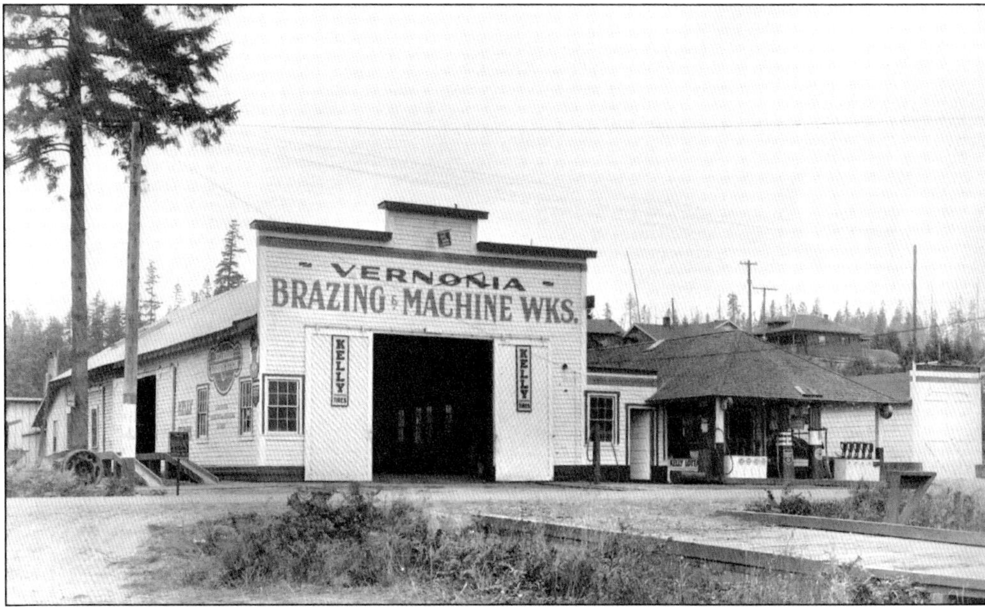

One of the first businesses to be located at the west end of town was Ed Salomonsen's Vernonia Brazing and Machine Works. As shown by the above photograph, the store also sold tires and gasoline. Herb Sturdevant bought the building in 1939 and opened it as the Rose Avenue Garage. His son, Ralph, purchased the business in 1960 and renamed it Ralph's Service. The right half of the structure remains today as Randy Shaw's Triple S Service. (VPMA.)

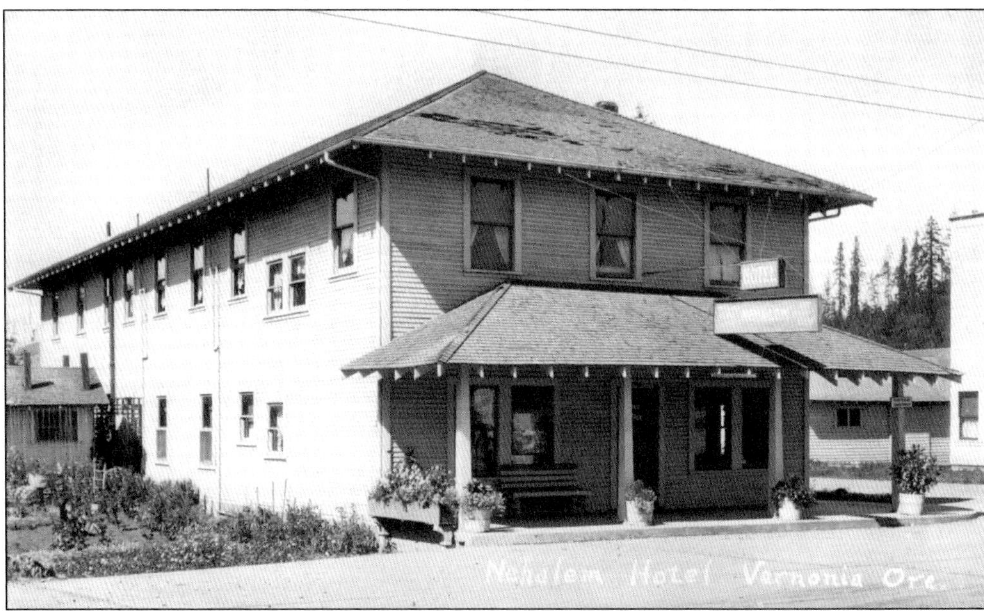

The Nehalem Hotel, built by William Pringle in 1924, was located at the corner of Grant Avenue and Bridge Street. A corner of the Vernonia Hotel can be seen on the right. It was the first hotel in town with electric lights and running water. It was built by Franklin Malmsten in 1920–1921 and run by his wife, Bessie, until they leased it in 1924. In the 1940s, the Nehalem Hotel was run by Fred and Sigrid Ovesen. Sigrid Ovesen was known for her excellent meals and coffee. (Malmsten.)

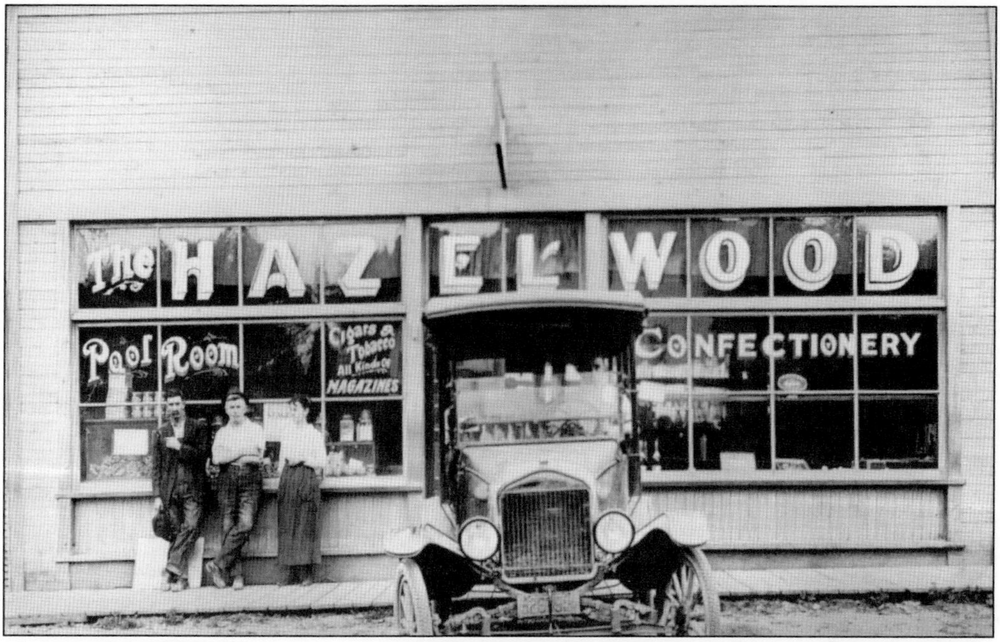

The Hazelwood Confectionery opened in the 1920s. In addition to candies, ice cream, and soda fountain items, the store sold cigars, cigarettes, and tobacco. It also had a pool table or two. It was one of the first businesses in town to have electric lighting once the Rock Creek Dam was completed in 1923. The electric lights eliminated the daily routine of cleaning and filling kerosene lamps. Owners Jack Nance (left) and Lloyd Thomas stand in front of the store with an unidentified woman. In the photograph below, the proprietors stand behind the soda fountain's counter. The Nances owned other businesses in town, including a pharmacy. (Both, Malmsten.)

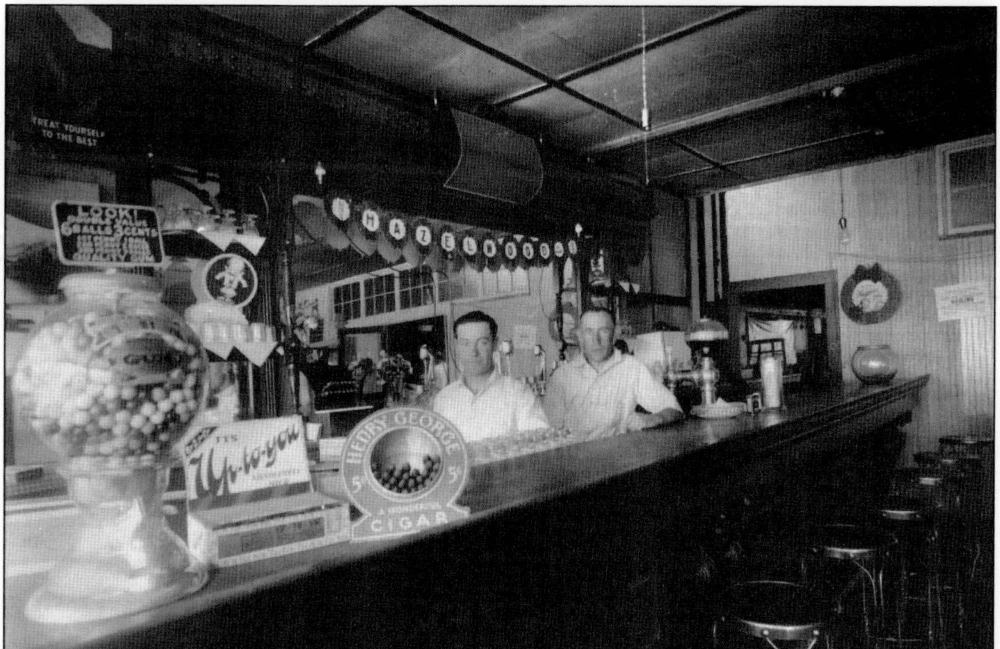

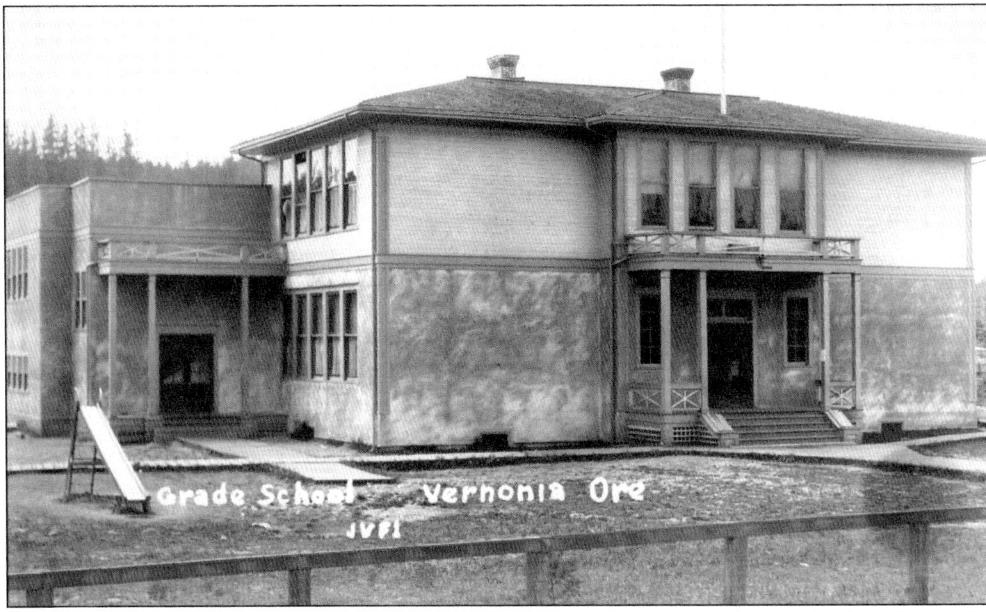

The first multiroomed school in Vernonia was the Washington Grade School, built in 1913. The annex on the left was added years later with the influx of the children of mill workers in the 1920s. In 1930, it was torn down and salvaged by the members of the Natal Grange to build their new hall 9 miles north of Vernonia. The remainder was given to local residents to build additions to their homes, chicken coops, and other structures. It was replaced by the new Washington School (seen below), a brick structure that opened the following year. It was built at a cost of $90,000—around $15,000 over the initial bid. It is still being used as the main grade school until a new school complex can be built on higher ground. It endured two severe floods in 1996 and 2007. (Above, Anderson; below, Malmsten.)

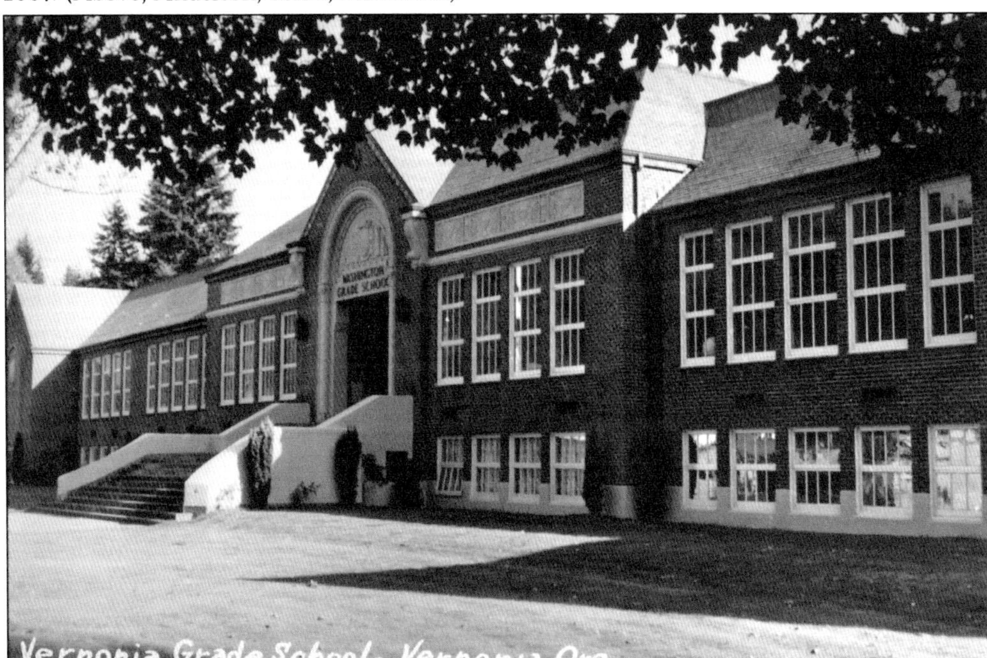

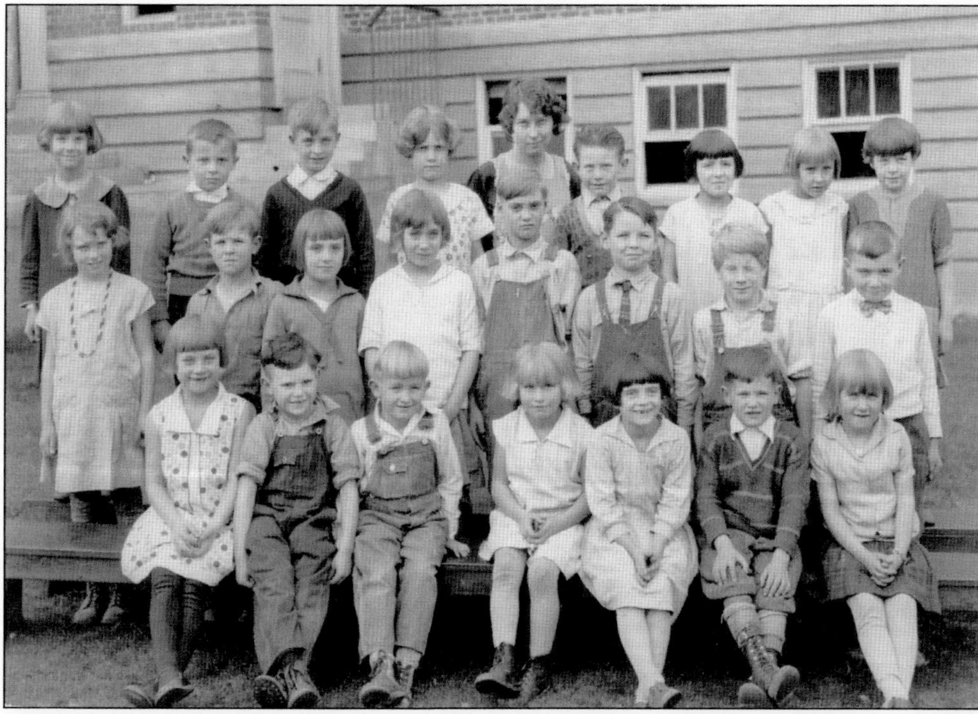

Charles Minger (third row, second from the left) attended first grade in 1929 at the Lincoln School. A four-room, brick building, the Lincoln School was built in 1923 and served the Vernonia School District until 2004, when a middle school was built and all elementary students—except for those attending the remaining one-room school in Mist—were consolidated at Washington. Charlie Minger began work at the O-A mill in 1940. (Minger.)

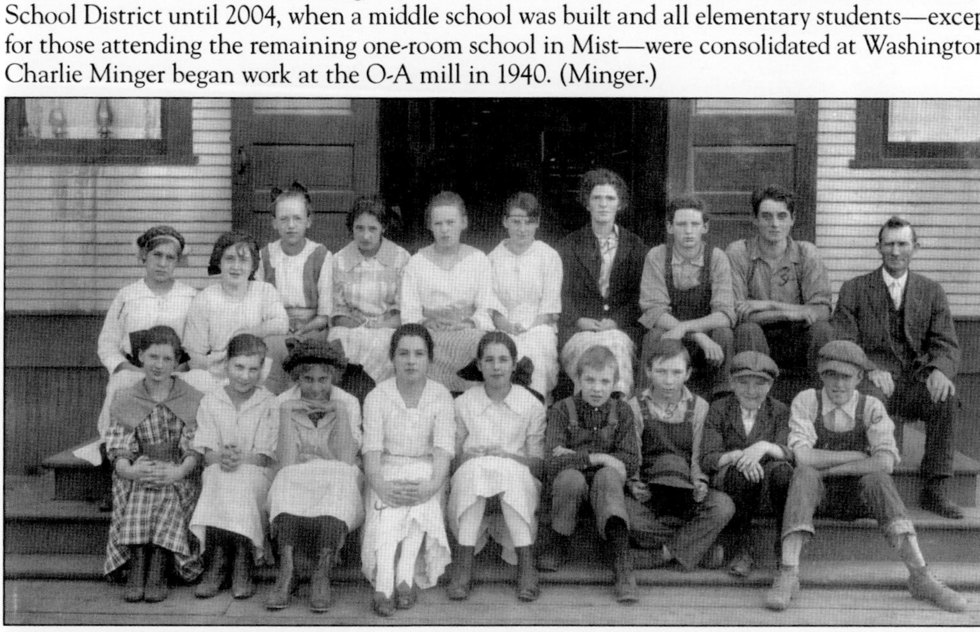

The first Vernonia High School was built on A Street in 1923. The class of 1952 was the last to graduate from there because a new brick high school had been built two blocks south on Bridge Street. Among the students pictured in this photograph are Blanche Bergerson, Laura VanBlaricom, Harold "Smokey" Parker, Oscar Enstrom, Herb Counts, and Hilda Tucker, who later married Ted Keasey. (Keasey.)

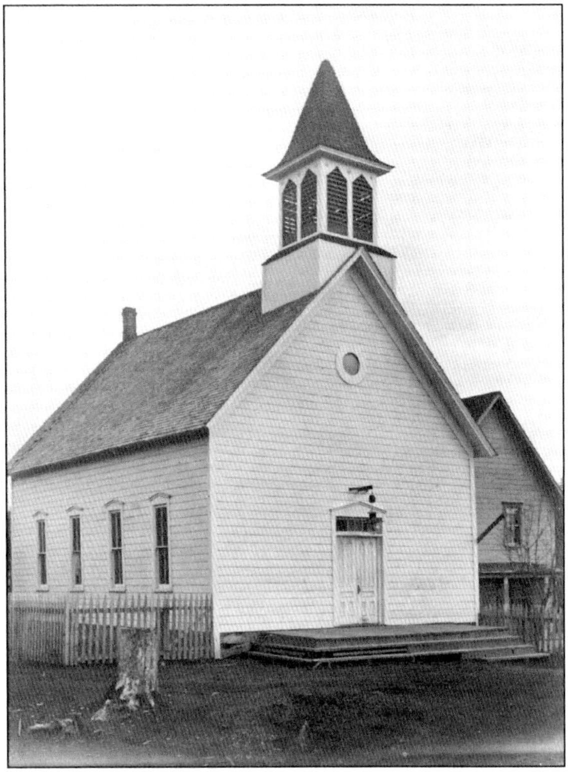

Before the Evangelical Church was built in 1890, Vernonians worshipped in various places, including schoolhouses and homes. The church parsonage can be seen in the background on the right of the church. The Evangelical Church merged with the United Brethren Church, forming the Evangelical United Brethren Church. When the new, much-larger Evangelical United Brethren Church was completed on State Avenue, the congregation held a ceremonial march as they moved from the old structure to the new. The old church and parsonage were later converted to apartments that stand today. (Keasey.)

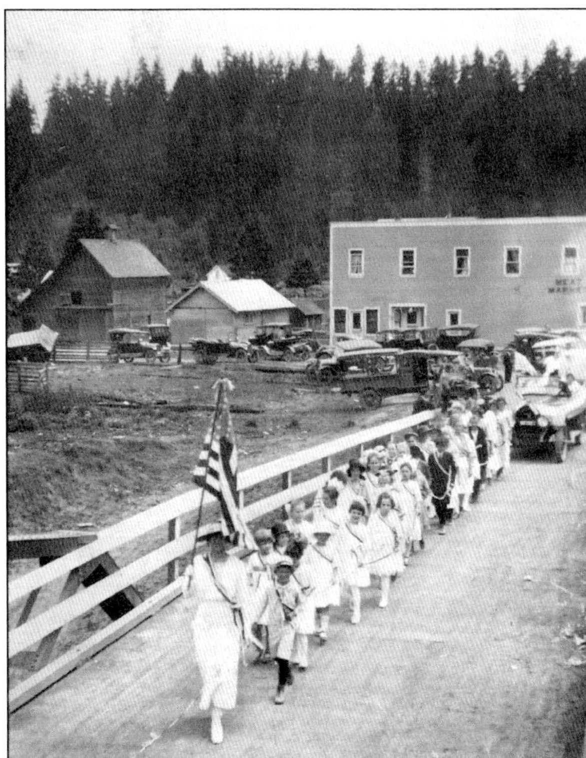

A Sunday school group from the Evangelical United Brethren Church led the Fourth of July parade in 1921. They are crossing the Rock Creek Bridge in the center of town. The Vernonia Hotel and Market can be seen in the background with Spencer Hill (soon to become known as O-A Hill) in the distance. (Keasey.)

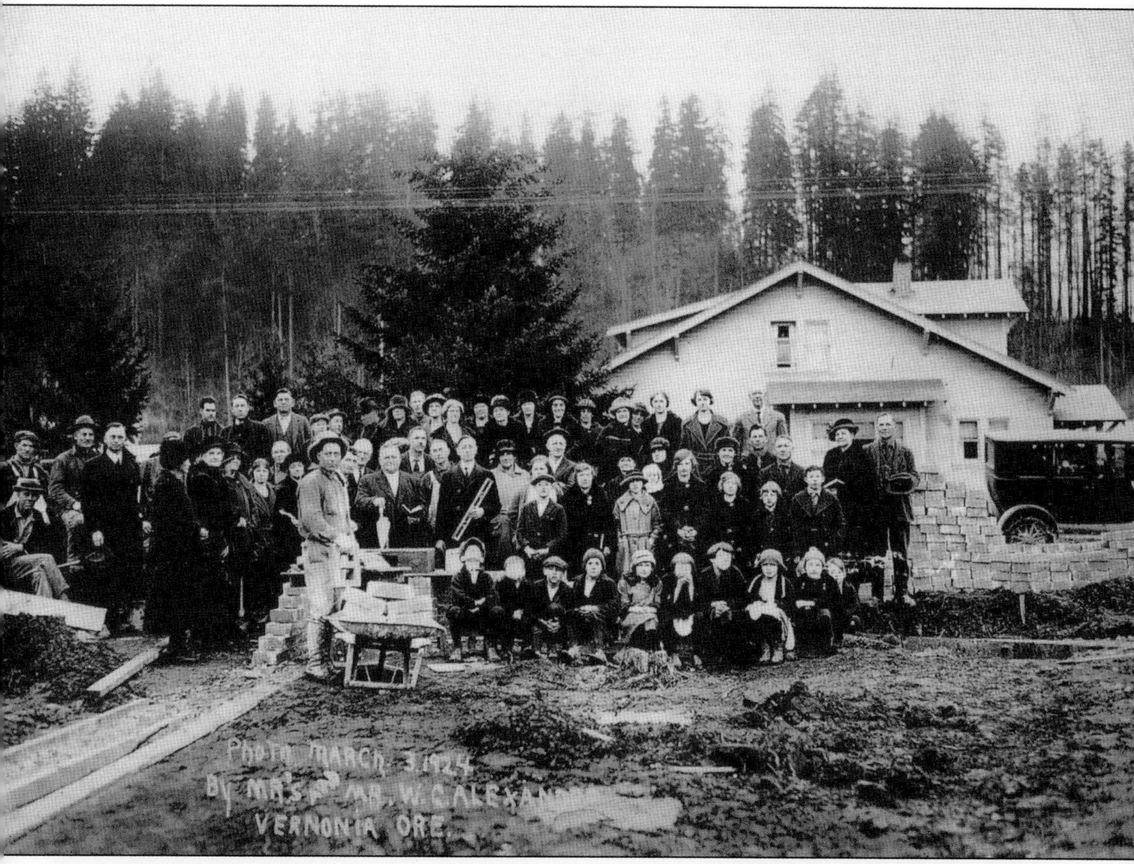

On March 3, 1924, the ground-breaking ceremony for the new Evangelical United Brethren (EUB) Church was held. Due to the rapid increase in population caused by the new lumber mill, the old church was too small to accommodate the growing congregation. Among the church members in this photograph are Emma VanBlaricom Weed (Oscar Weed's mother) and Bessie and Oscar Weed, along with their children Chester, Melvin, Oren, and Mildred. Members of the Keasey and Malmsten families were also in the group. Charles Malmsten's home can be seen in the background. His daughter, Louise Malmsten Thomas, played the organ at the EUB church for many years. The building with its 1924-dated cornerstone endures as the Vernonia Community Church. During the 1920s, the growth in Vernonia was accompanied with the establishment of a number of new churches, including the Christian, Latter Day Saints, and St. Mary's Catholic Churches. (Condit.)

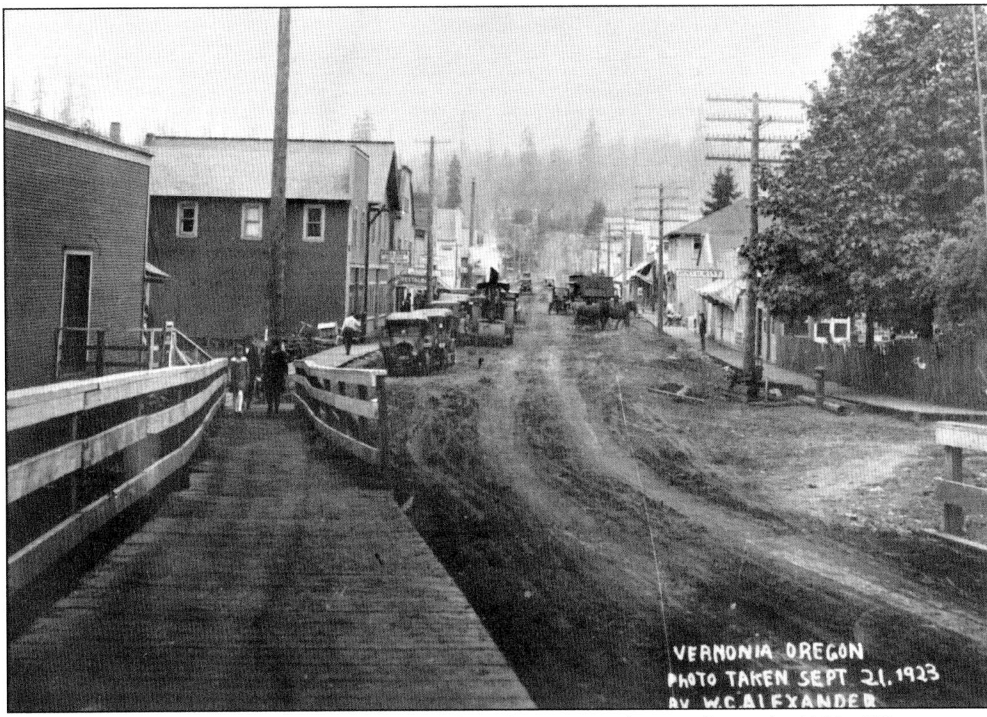

W. C. Alexander took numerous photographs of Vernonia during the early 1920s. This view of the main downtown business district was taken in September 1923 from the Rock Creek Bridge. The streets were still unpaved and would remain so for two more years. The road as it continues up Corey Hill can be seen in the distance. The photograph below was taken from muddy Bridge Street on Corey Hill in the mid-1920s as a freight train passed. The new lumber mill is barely visible in the background beyond the downtown area and to the right of wooded O-A hill. (Above, VPMA; below, Malmsten.)

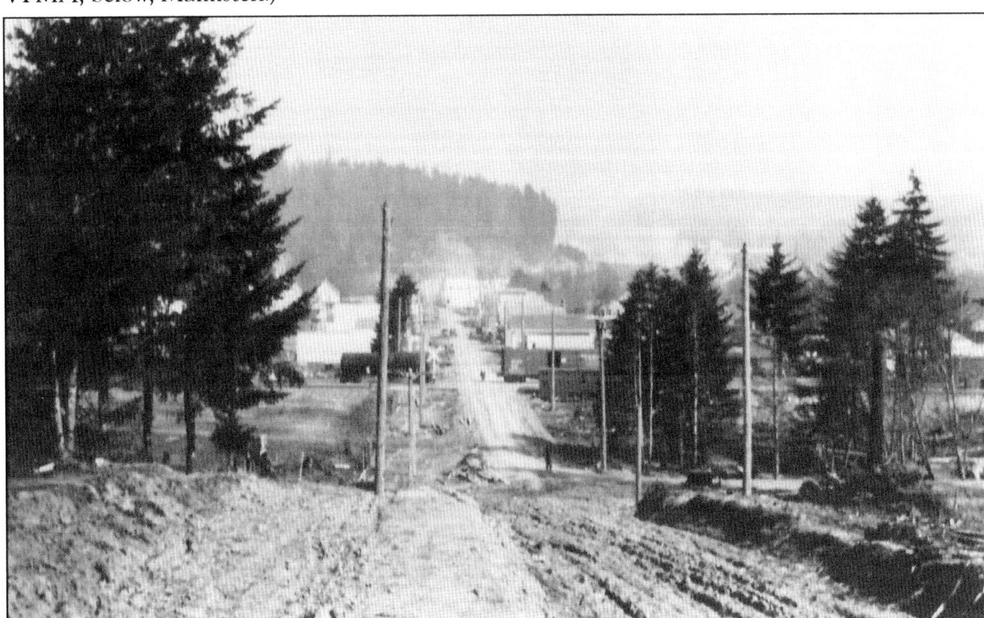

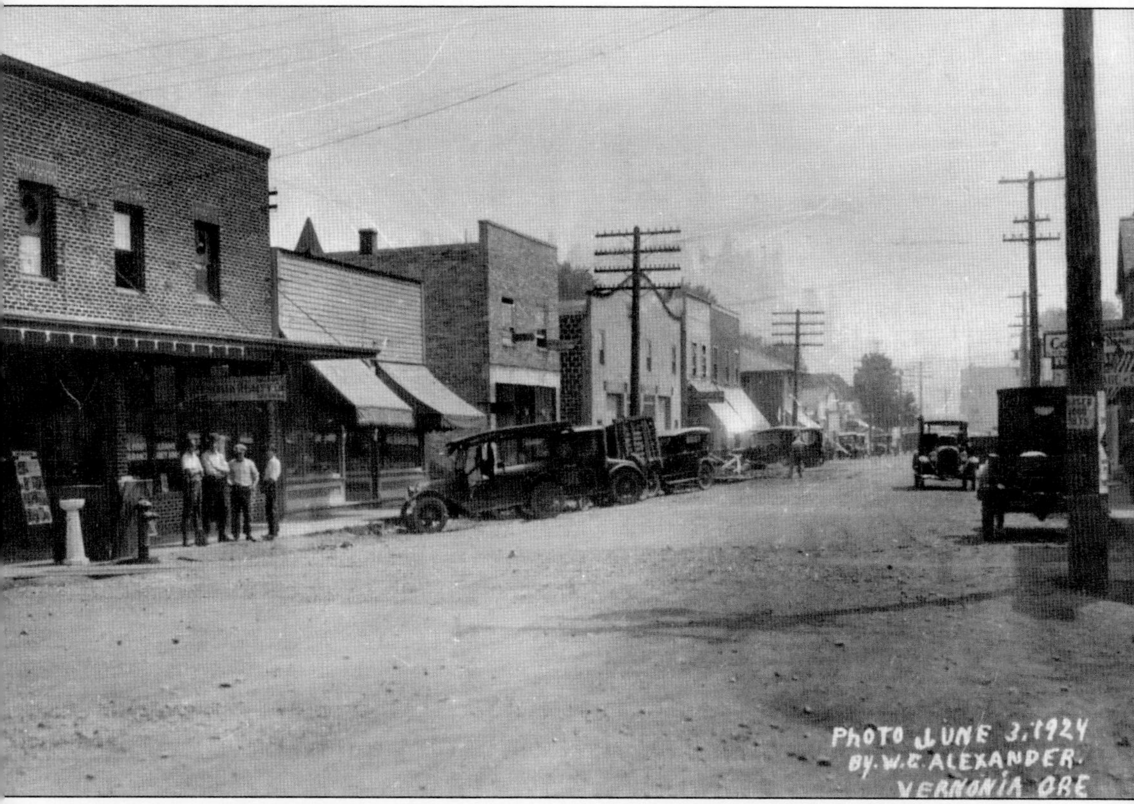

Another Alexander photograph shows some of the downtown businesses on Bridge Street in June 1924. The brick building on the left, known as the Lusby Building, held Vernonia Realty at the time. Behind the utility pole on the right, part of the Hazelwood Confectionery sign is visible, as is that of the Oregon Stage (bus) Depot. The brick J. C. Penney store would be built on the north side of the street in 1930, but it closed in 1934 because of the business slowdown during the Depression. J. C. Penney leased the building to the Miller Mercantile Company, a clothing store that operated in that location from 1934 through 1961. Les Dewey was the manager in the 1930s. Cecil Johnson succeeded him as manager and worked there from 1941 until its closing. (VPMA.)

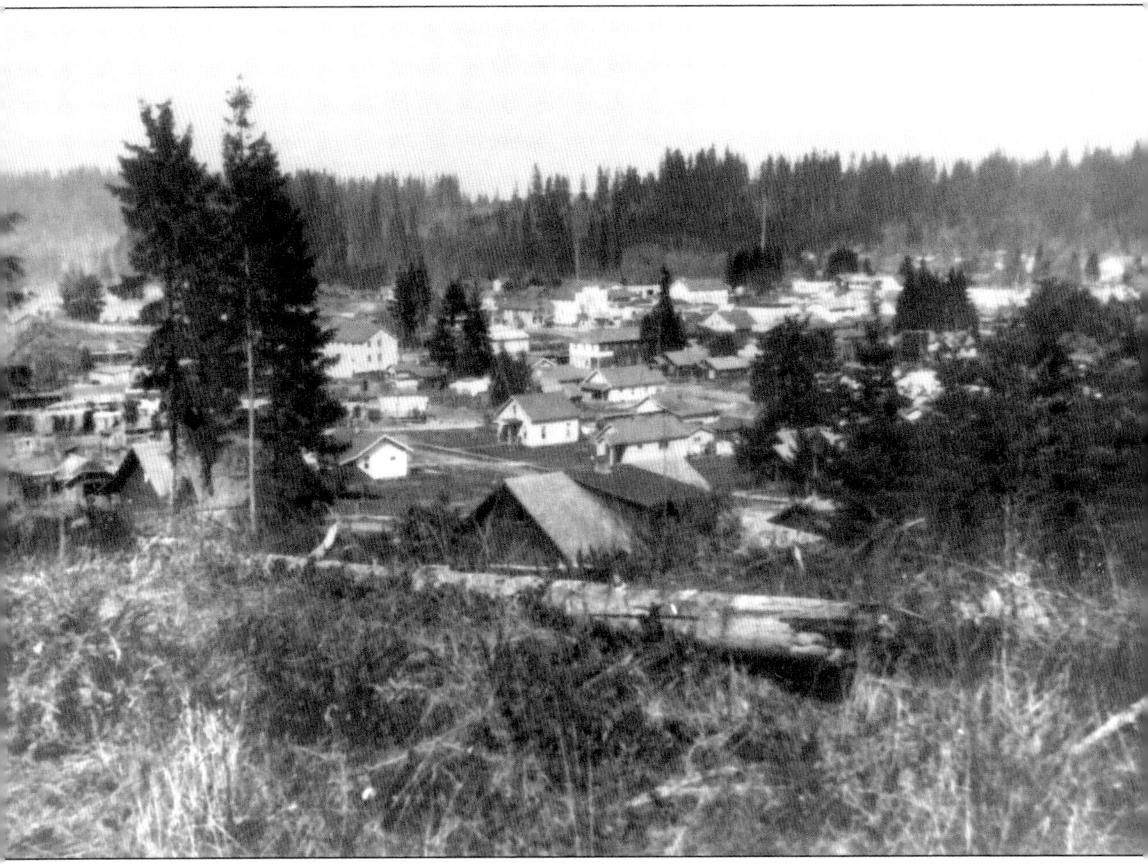

Helen Christensen took this photograph in 1923 from Capitol Hill, which is just south of Corey Hill at the west end of town. The Bennett sawmill is visible in the left center of the picture just beyond the two big trees. The new railroad tracks and water tower are not easily seen in this picture, but they ran just beyond the trees in the right center foreground. With the arrival of the railroad and the completion of the new Oregon-American Lumber Mill, many new businesses, homes, hotels, and churches were being built. Things looked bright for Vernonia this year. It was going be a "big payroll" town at last. (VPMA.)

Three

The Oregon-American Mill

By 1922, the long-awaited railroad from the greater Portland area finally arrived, and construction of the Oregon-American Lumber Mill (O-A) began. The O-A mill was a state-of-the-art electric-powered sawmill. The burning of wood waste provided the steam to power the mill's huge generators. When the mill opened for operation in 1924, a supply of logs from Camp McGregor was ready to ship. For the next three decades, trainloads of logs came in from timber camps on lands surrounding the town.

Typical of other mill towns around the Pacific Northwest, many of the managers and workers lived in company-built housing, but Vernonia was not strictly a company town. The company was instrumental in building the first high school in town and had its own sports teams. The mill caused a population boom so great that Vernonia became the fastest growing city in the state and was called the "Biggest Little City in Oregon."

With the influx of both white and black workers brought in from the South by the mill owners, Vernonia also became known as the "Most Southern City in the North." Other ethnic groups, including Japanese, Filipinos, and Hindus, were also represented in the segregated housing on mill property (designated as "colonies" by the mill owners) and in separate logging camps. The Great Depression and the closure of the mill from 1933 to 1936 forced many people to look for work elsewhere.

When World War II caused major changes in the population, women were temporarily allowed to hold mill jobs formerly restricted to men. There was a postwar boom due to escalating demand for timber products, but by 1957, the last of the nearby old-growth trees was gone, and the O-A mill, now owned by Long-Bell, ceased operations. Except for the office and empty fuel bunker, the mill buildings were soon gone. The office became the Vernonia Pioneer Museum, which houses artifacts from those days. There is little physical evidence of the company that, over the course of its lifetime, processed 2.5-billion board feet of timber.

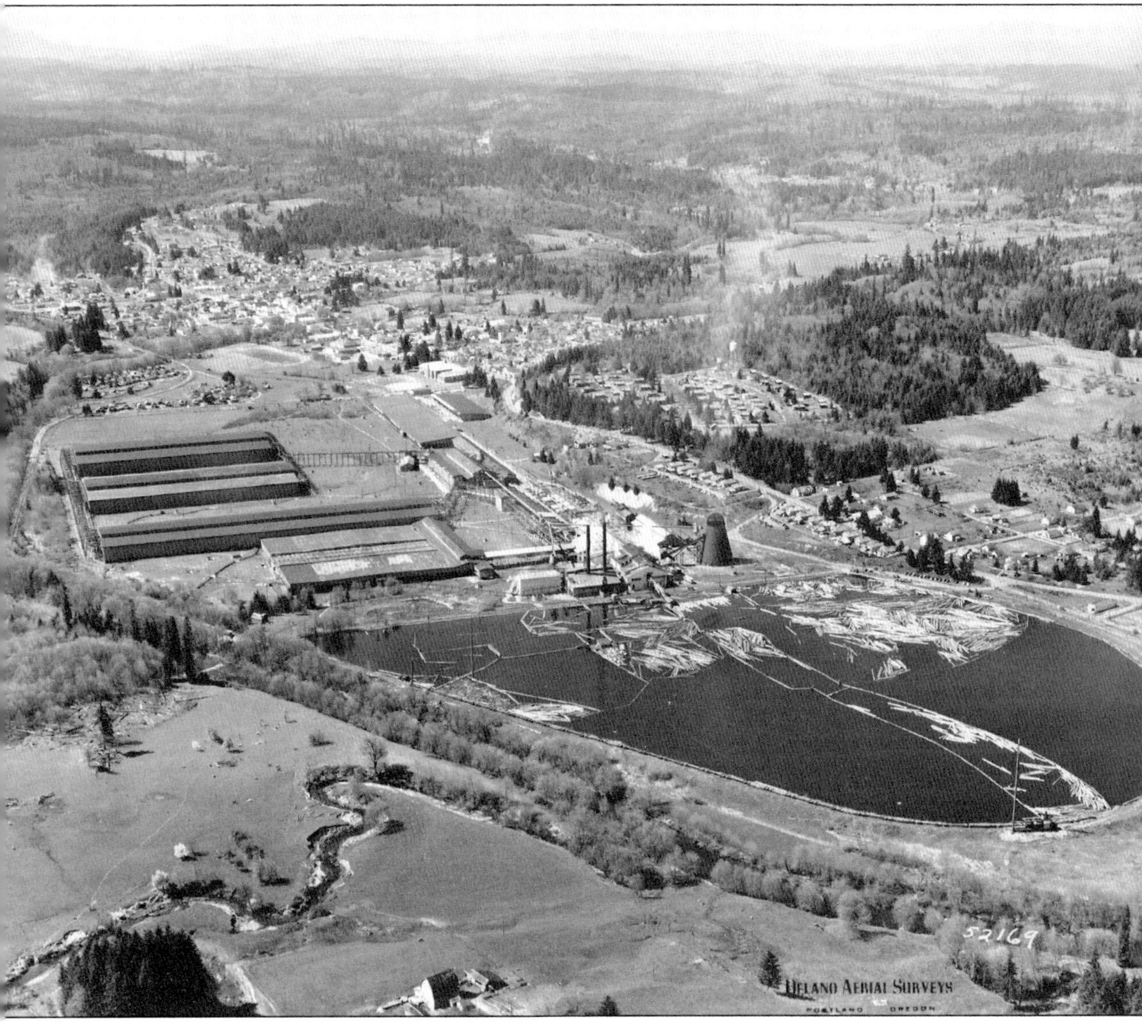

Although this aerial photograph was taken many years after the Oregon-American Lumber Mill was opened in 1924, the size of the operation and the company-built housing can plainly be seen. The original town of Vernonia is visible in the background. The mill covered more than 200 acres on what had been part of several homesteads. Housing for the married white workers and managers was located on a tree-covered hill on 30 acres of Israel Spencer's original homestead. A bowl of land was deepened and water was diverted from the Nehalem River (seen in the lower part of the photograph between the two lines of trees) to create the 36-acre millpond. Construction of the mill began in 1922. By 1928, the population of Vernonia was more than 1,500, ten times its 1920 population. The electric-powered concrete-and-steel lumber mill was one of the first to kiln-dry lumber. The long drying sheds and steam-powered drying kiln can be seen in the left center. The ethnic "colonies" lie beyond the drying sheds near Rock Creek. (East.)

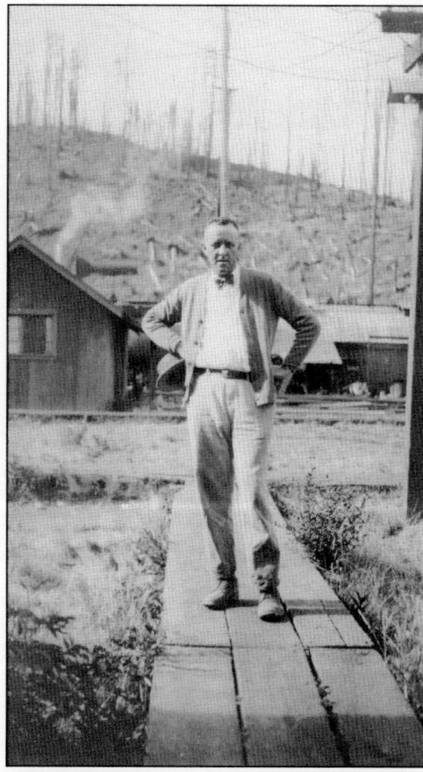

Judd Greenman, general manager of the Oregon-American (O-A) Lumber Company from 1925 to 1955, visits Camp McGregor. Sixteen miles up Rock Creek on O-A timberland, Camp McGregor was the first O-A logging camp. It was built in 1922 while the mill was under construction. This photograph was taken during its 1936 reconstruction after being completely destroyed in the Wolf Creek fire of 1933, a separate but concurrent fire with the first monstrous Tillamook Burn. (Anderson.)

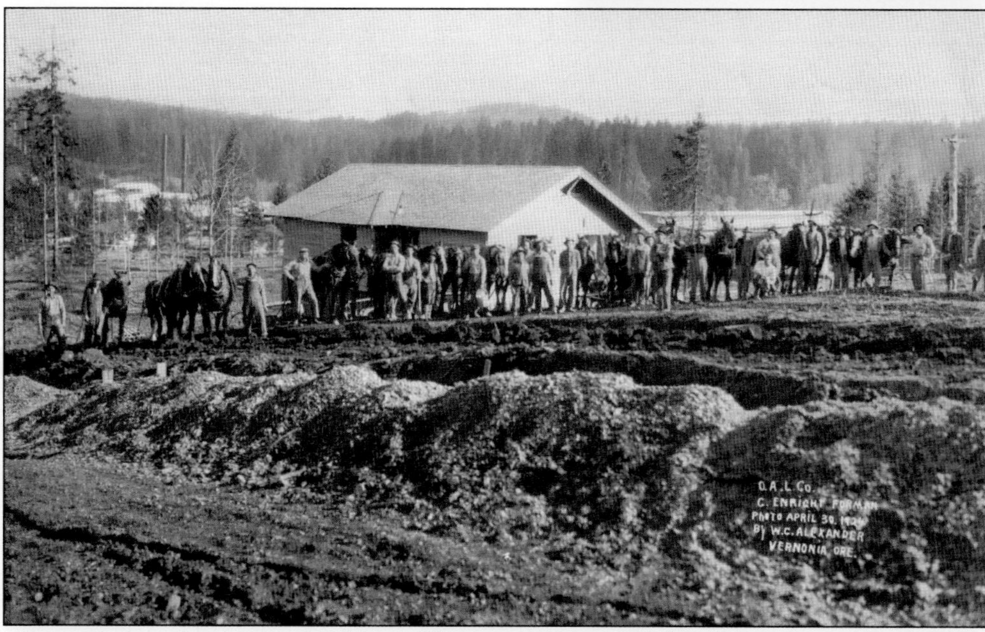

Men and horses clear land in 1924 for mill houses on Spencer Hill and along Bridge Street. Bruce McDonald (sixth from right) and his horses, Maud and Nell, are among those pictured. Due to the population explosion caused by the new mill, housing was scarce. O-A built homes for managers and mill workers with families to alleviate the housing shortage. Homes could be rented for $10 to $12 per month or purchased. All had inside plumbing and electric lights. (Meyer.)

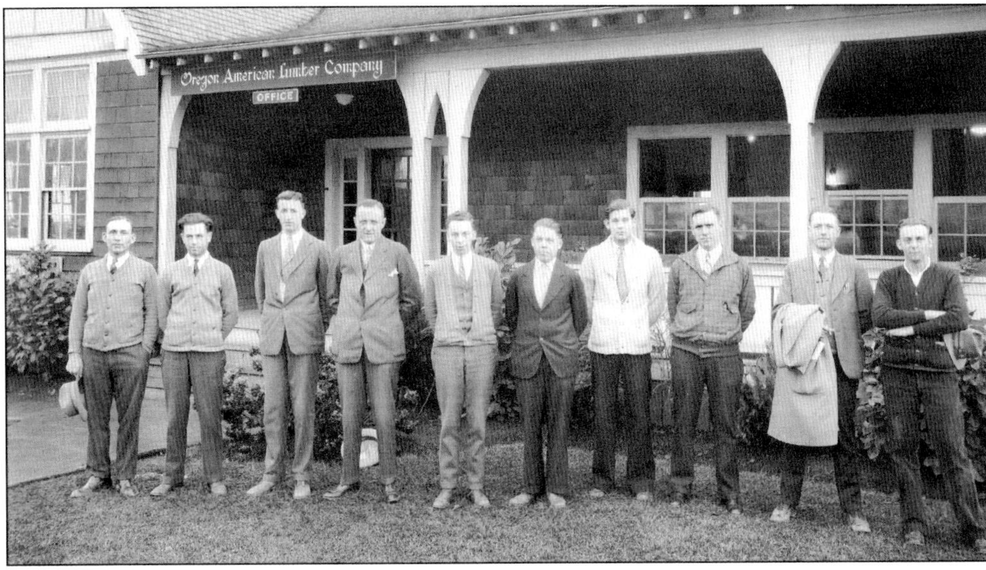

The Oregon-American headquarters staff stands before the administrative headquarters in 1928. From left to right are F. Merle Ruhl, chief clerk; Phil Taylor, tallyman; Charles Richardson, stenographer; Judd Greenman, general manager; J. Vernon McAllister, statistics clerk; Walter Wolff, agent; Herb Hollyfield, bookkeeper; Carl Davidson, logging superintendent; Frank Crosby, paymaster; and Ulas Scott, assistant paymaster. In 1947, Judd Greenman was promoted to president, and Conrad "Connie" Anderson became the general manager. Anderson Park is named for him. In the photograph below, the accounting office staff of the late 1940s is shown inside the mill office building. Pictured from left to right are Lillian Helvie, Isabel Kasper, F. Merle Ruhl, Vera Finnell, Alma Prickett, Marjorie Aldrich, R. B. Fletcher, John Lyon, and Catherine Skuzie. Judd Greenman's longtime secretary, Rose Valpiani, is not pictured, but she was responsible for the preservation of the mill's records, especially Greenman's 30 years of correspondence, when the company closed. (Both, VPMA.)

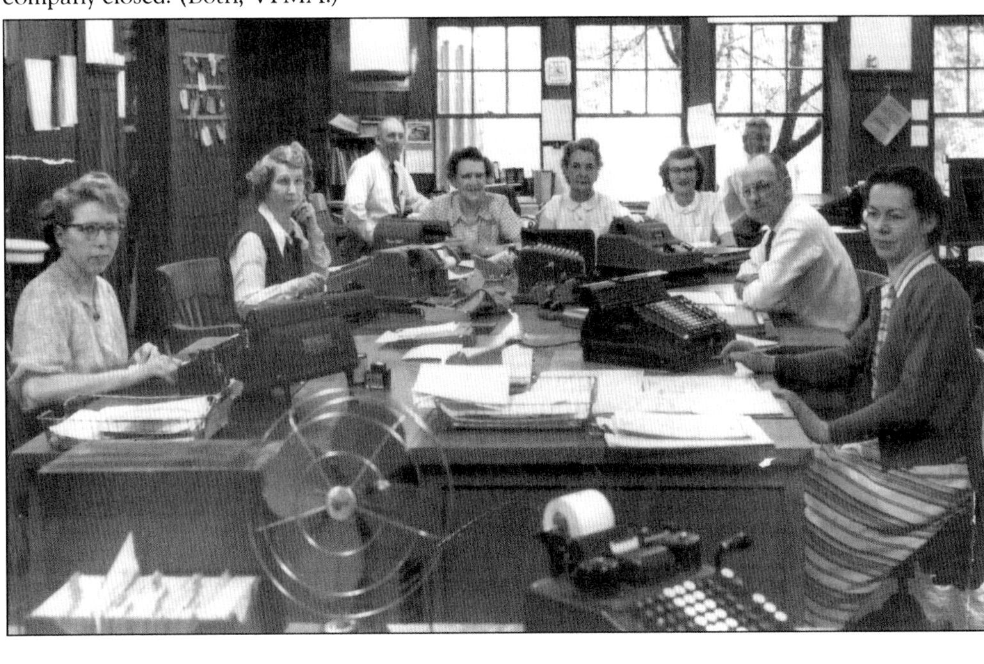

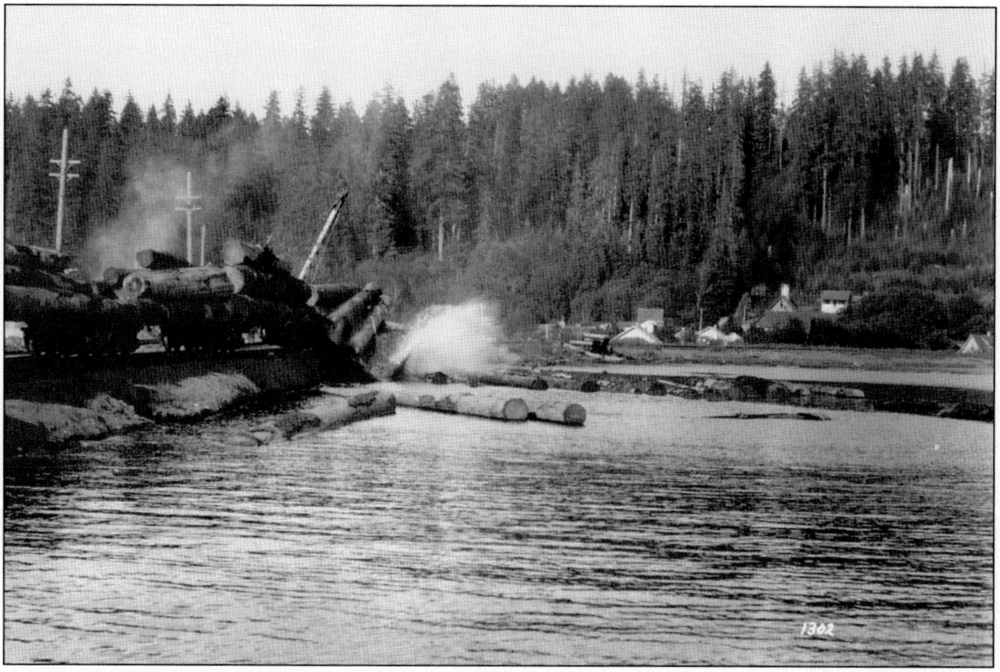

A log train dumps its payload into the millpond at the O-A Lumber Mill. Millponds were used to store the logs to keep them from drying and splitting until they were ready to be processed. Water was diverted into the excavated pond area from the nearby Nehalem River. The railcars came in from the various logging operations to the mill, dumped the logs into the pond, and returned to the woods for more. The other side of the log dumping procedure, using an electric log-unloading engine, can be seen below. On the left, Cecil Johnson watches the O-A men at work. (Above, VPMA; below, New.)

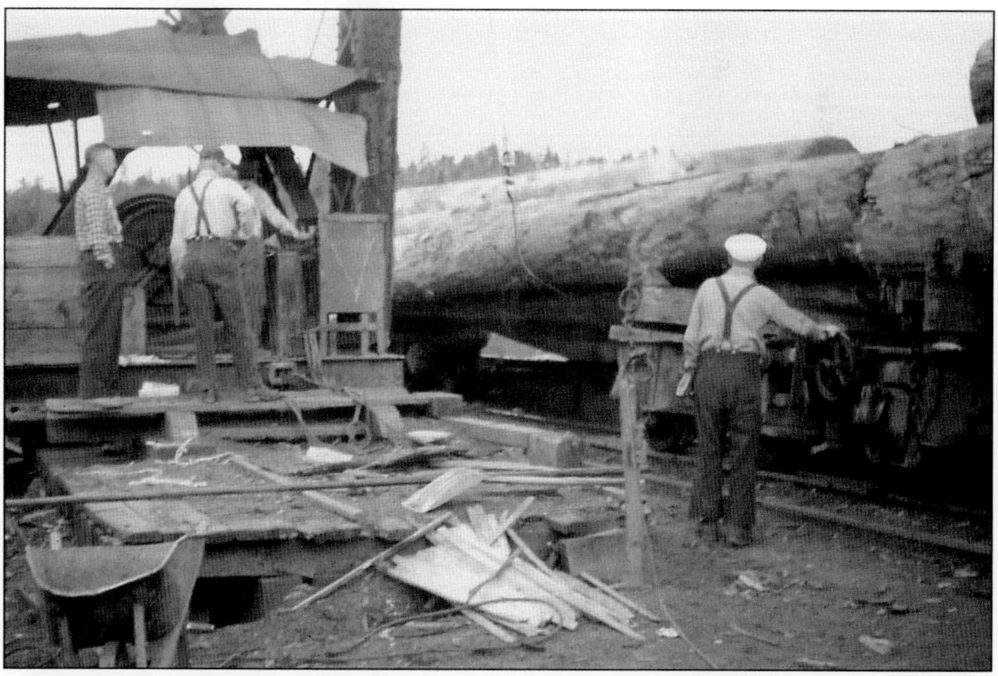

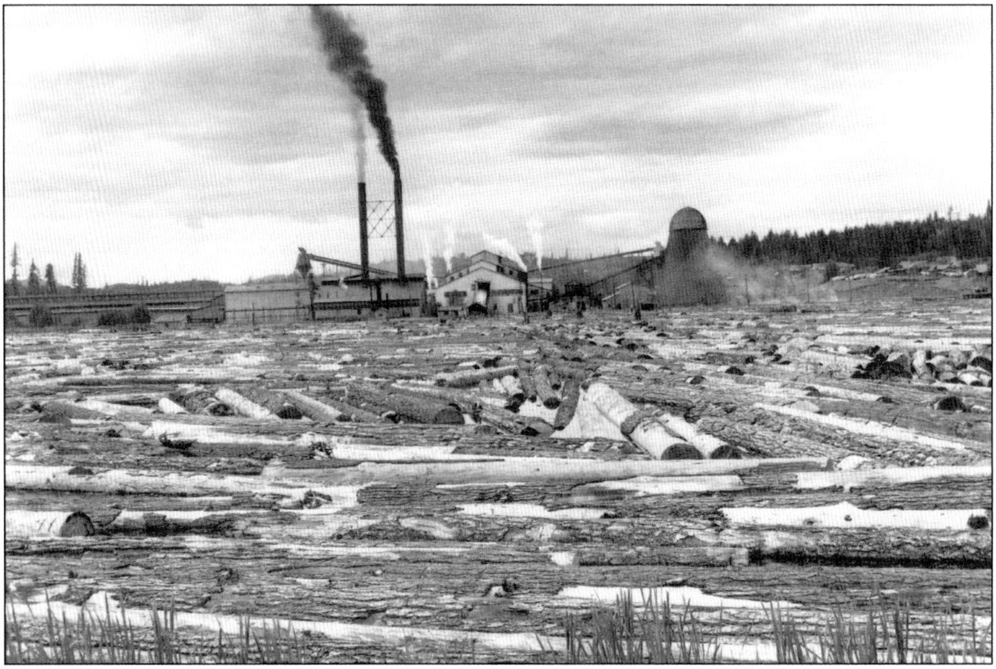

Taken in June 1955, this Jim Blain photograph shows a full millpond from the eastern shore. The light-colored, windowless building to the left of the smokestacks was the fuel bunker that held the scrap wood chips that were burned to fuel the steam-powered electric generator to its right. The bark and discarded cuttings from the large old-growth trees were coarsely ground for fuel. Finer wood waste was conveyed to the wigwam burner to the right of the steam plant. (VPMA.)

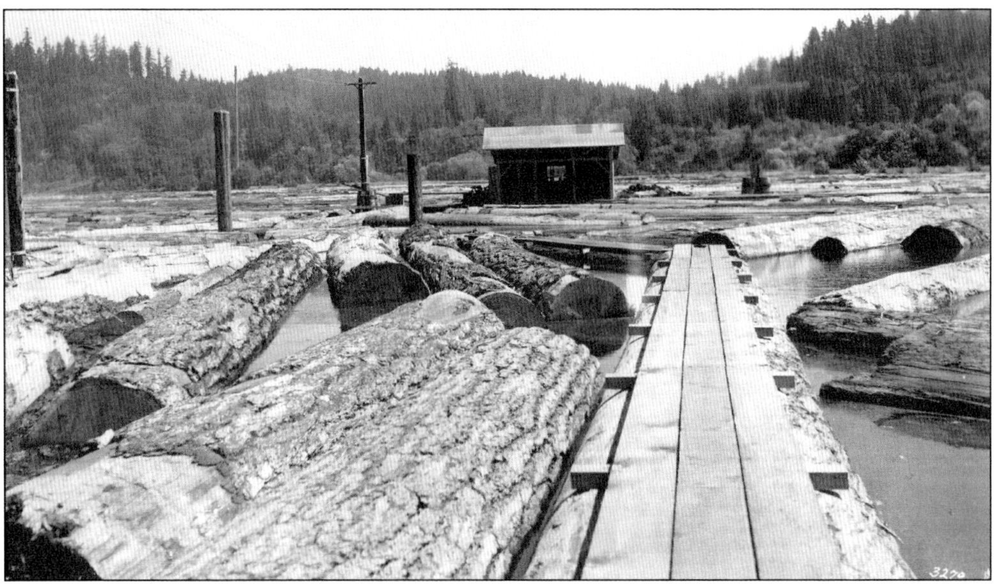

Floating wooden walkways provided access to the logs in the pond. Workers wearing spiked (calk) boots and carrying peaveys moved the floating wood toward the log slip where they were lifted from the water and onto the conveyer that began the milling process. Logs that were not suitable for lumber due to smaller size or imperfections were lifted from the pond and loaded onto railcars by a powered hoist and shipped by rail to plywood mills elsewhere. (East.)

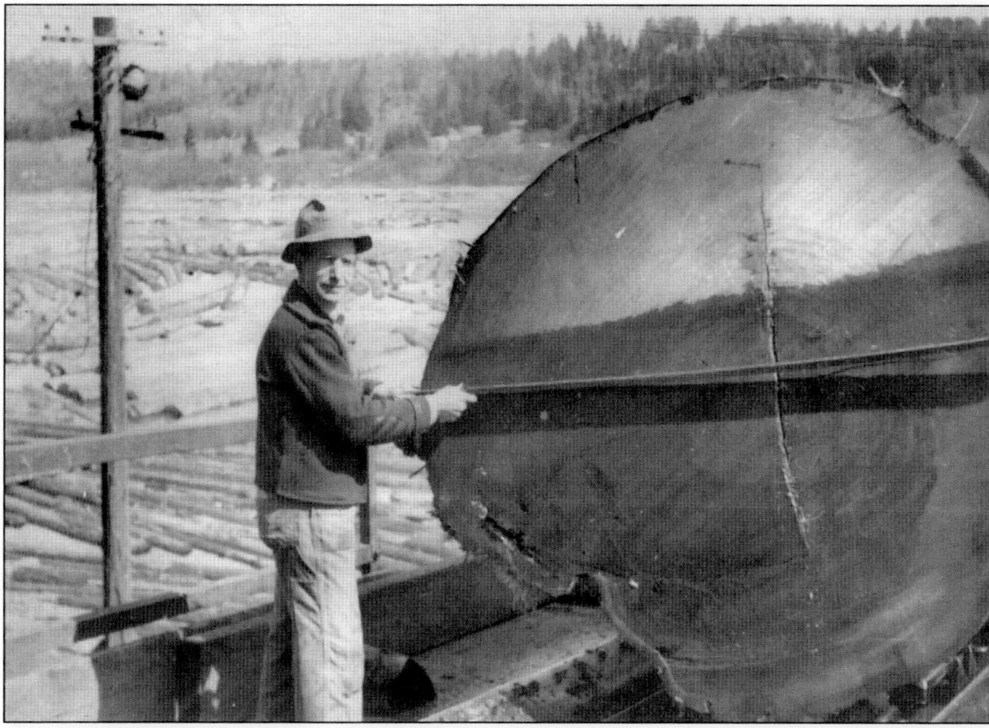

Elton "Pidge" Elliott was a log scaler at the O-A mill for 20 years. Scalers measured the diameter of the logs as they came up the slip toward the mill to estimate the value in board feet of lumber in that log. Scalers also worked at logging sites with the fallers and the buckers whose job it was to cut the fallen logs into mill-specified lengths. In the photograph below, Lynn Michener steers his motorboat on the O-A pond. He used the boat to push logs to various areas of the pond for sorting. (Above, VPMA; below, New.)

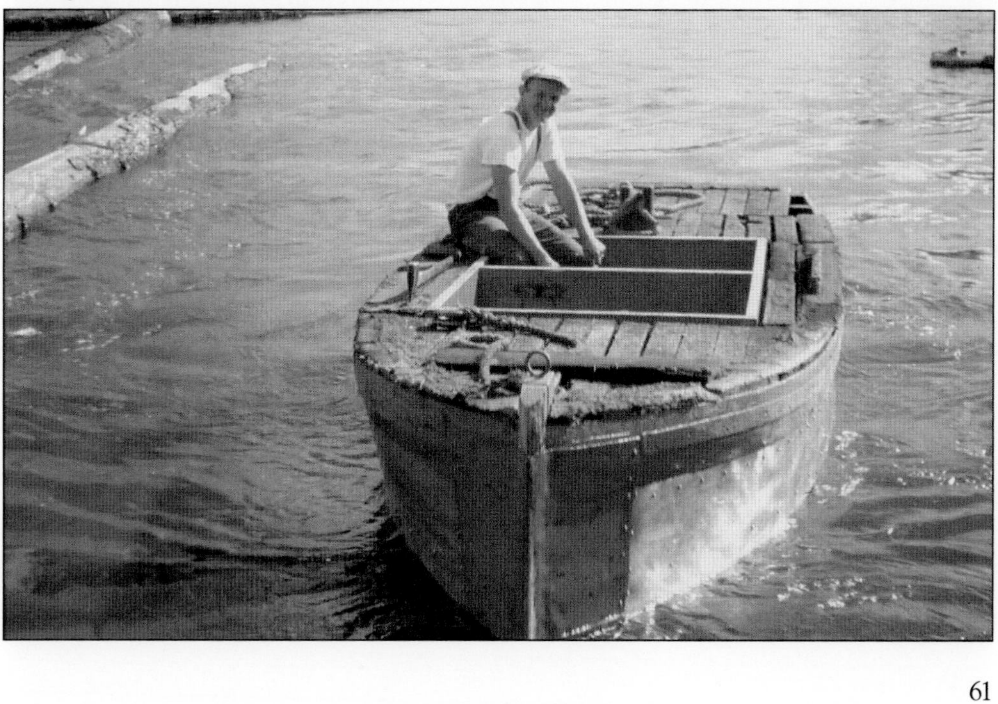

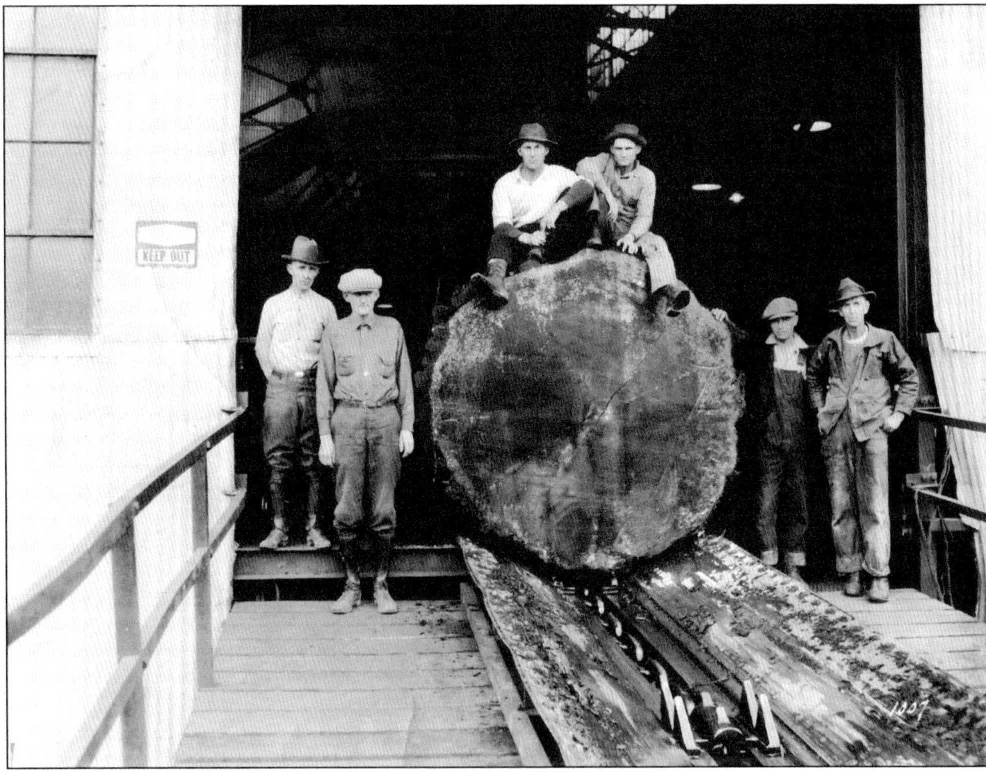

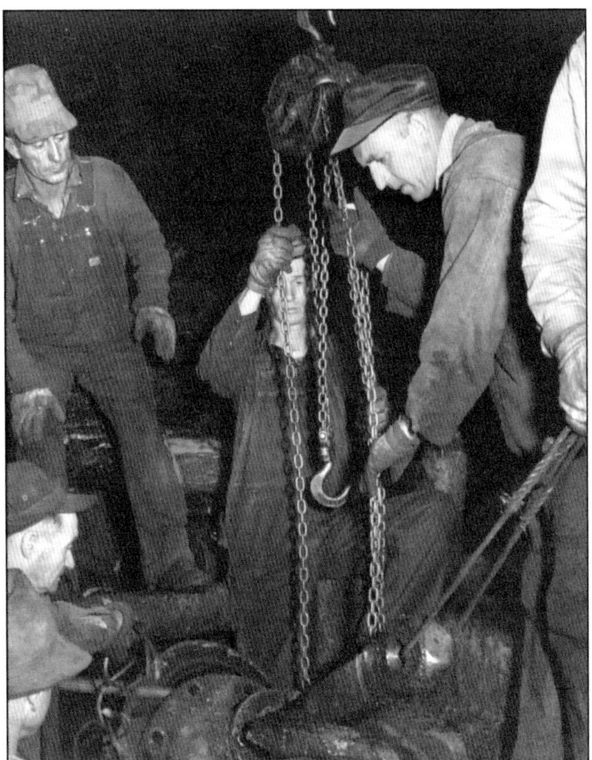

Mill workers surround a big log at the top of the log slip in this late-1920s photograph. From here, logs were conveyed to the big saws that cut them to the required lengths and widths. A gang saw made boards up to 2-inches thick from the large cants, the big blocks of wood cut from the center of the old-growth logs. Glen Gibson operated the gang saw for about 15 years following Frank McCabe, who ran it until 1936. Standing to the left of the log are W. A. McGilvary and Troy Smith. Byron Oveson and Bob Fulton are seated, and an unidentified man and Bill Gibson stand to the right. At left, Claude Gibson works to free some tangled equipment. (Both, East.)

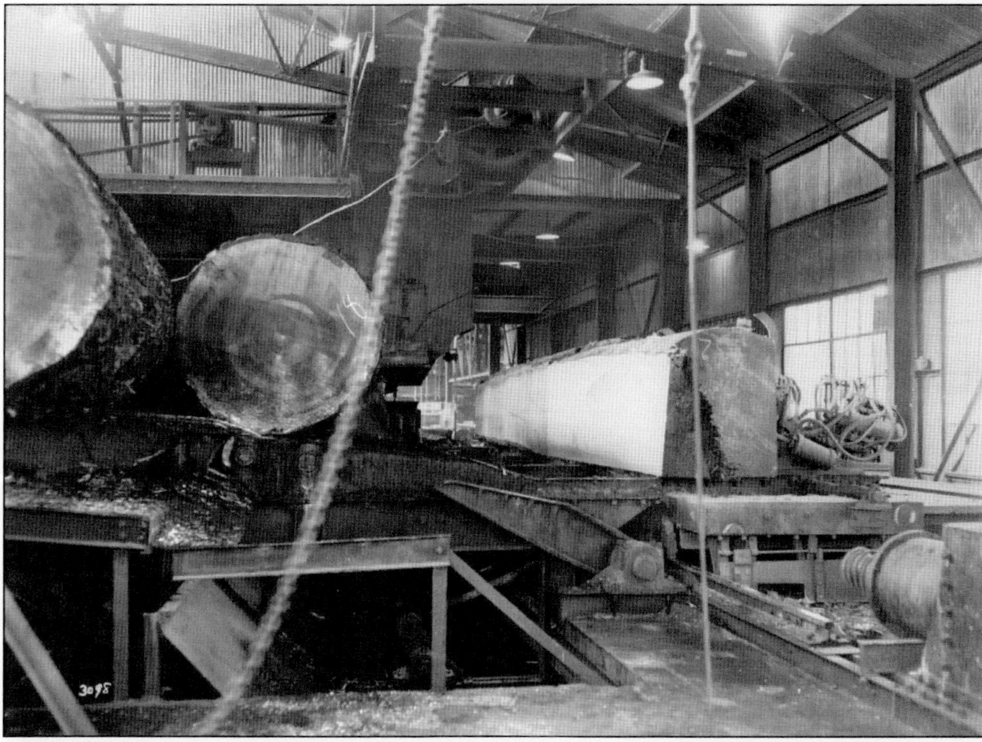

Ernest East was a sawyer at O-A from 1936 until the closure of the mill. His workstation was at the far end of the log being sawed in the photograph above. The block setter is standing on the carriage on the right; only his hat can be seen. Due to the high noise-level, the sawyer used hand signals to tell the block setter how to position the log for the cut in progress. The multiple-bladed trim saw, shown below, cut boards to the desired length. Defective boards were removed at this point for scrap. Bill Lindley operated the trimmer for many years. (Both, East.)

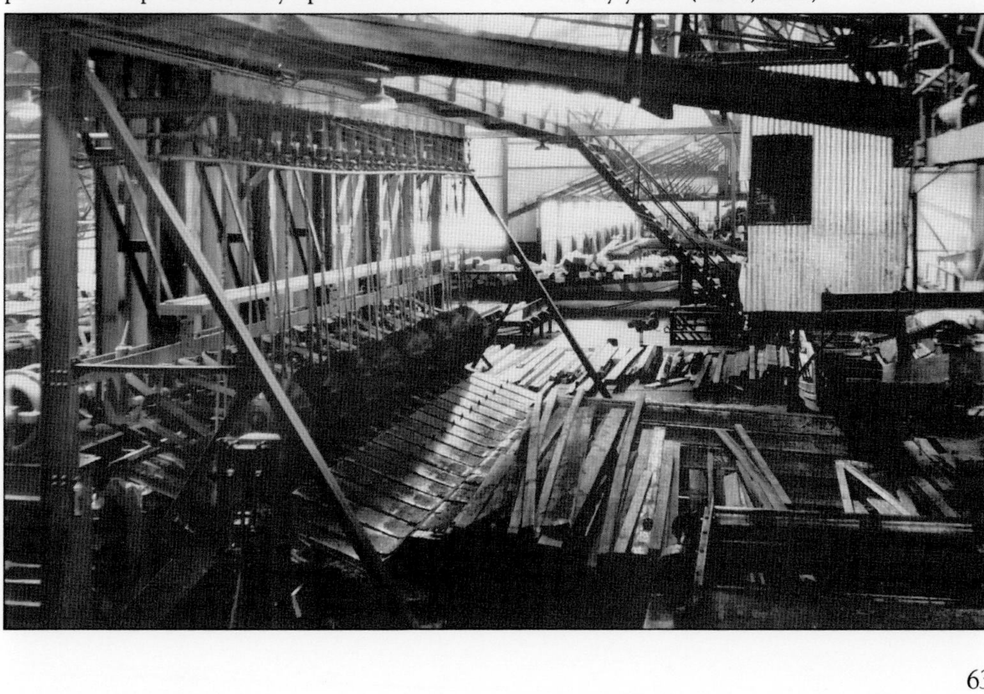

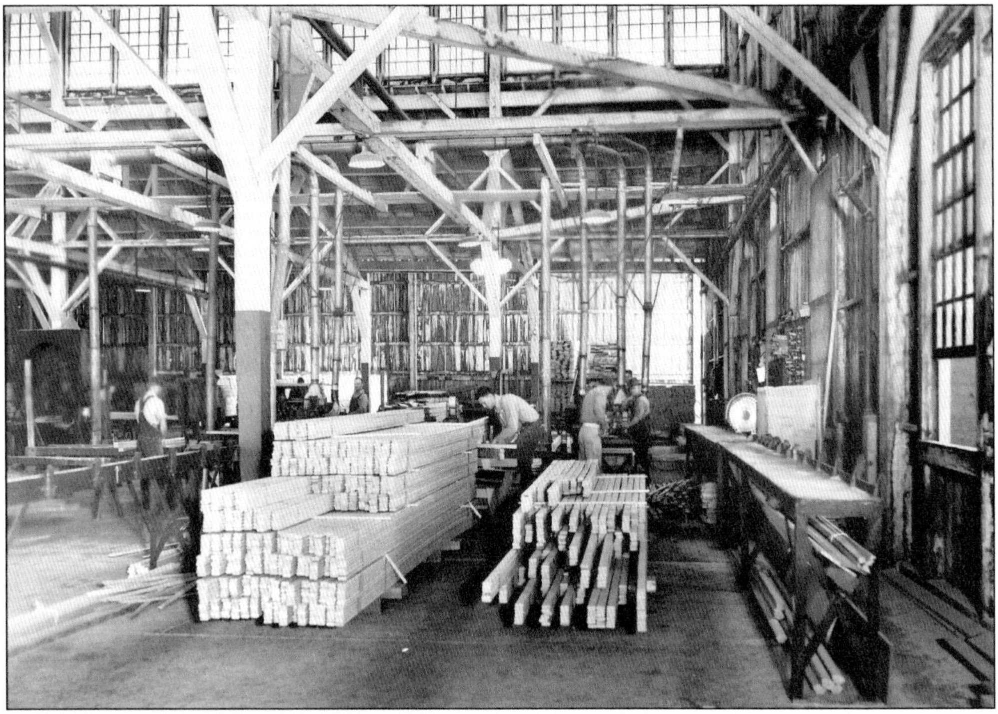

The sawyer had to make split-second decisions to maximize the value of each log. Some parts were finished as large timbers for beams. Other sections were cut into lumber of varying lengths and widths. The molding mill on the right cut smaller pieces into quarter-round sections. After the cut lumber was dried in the steam-powered kiln and finished in the planing mill, it was stacked into the long, dressed lumber sheds until it was ready to ship out. The O-A mill had the capacity of processing a quarter-of-a-million board feet of lumber in an eight-hour shift. (Both, East.)

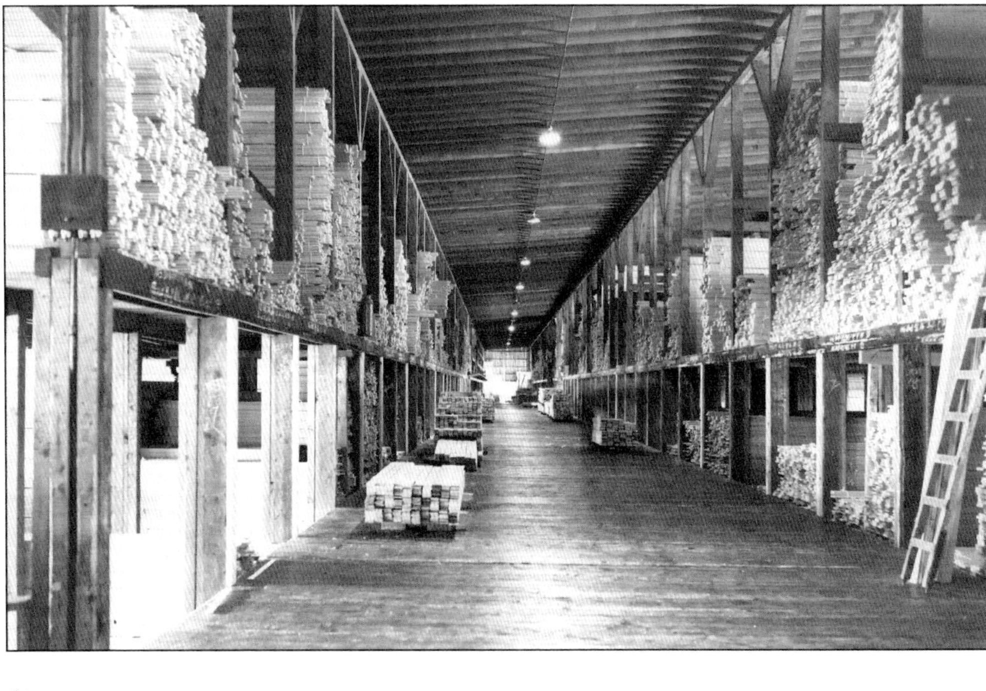

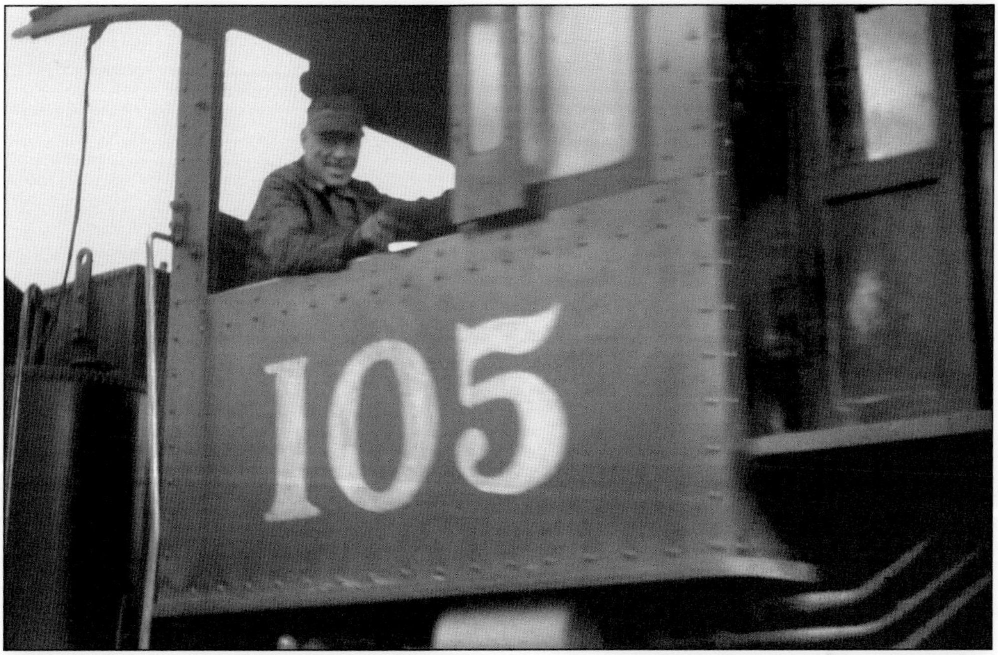

Chester "Chet" Alexander was a locomotive engineer and worked for O-A from 1922 until the mill closed. He is seen in the picture above in the cab of O-A engine No. 105, the engine that brought in the last load of logs to the mill on August 27, 1957. The sawmill cut its last log on September 11, 1957, and the last boxcar of lumber was shipped the following April. In the photograph below, another of the five-man train crew, Vincent "Shorty" Monaco, watches the load of logs about to be dumped into the pond. Like Chet, Monaco worked at the mill for its entire existence. (Both, New.)

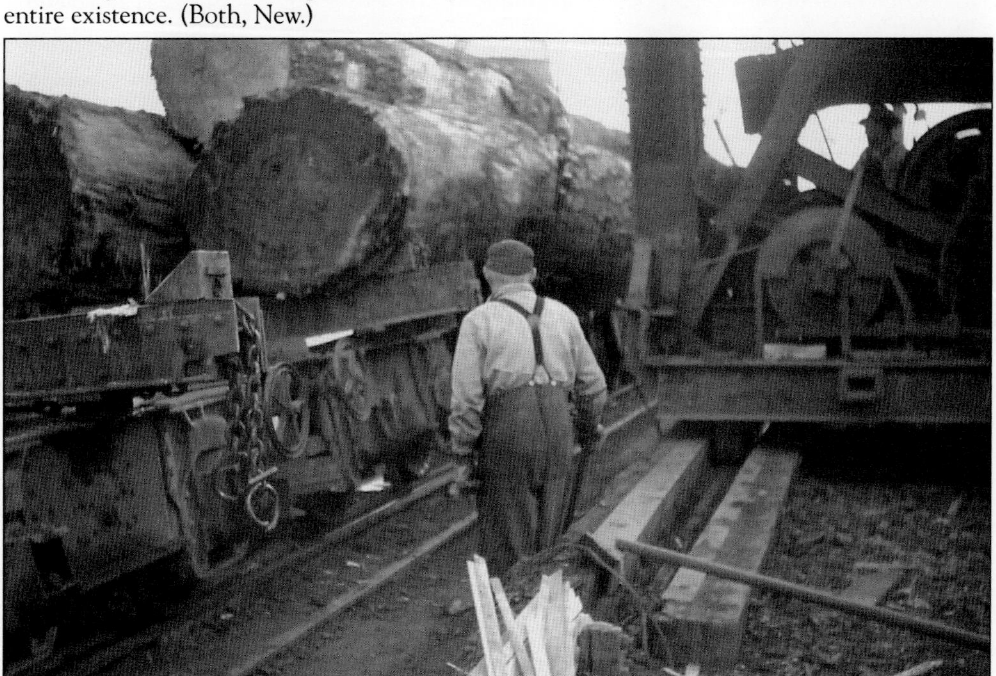

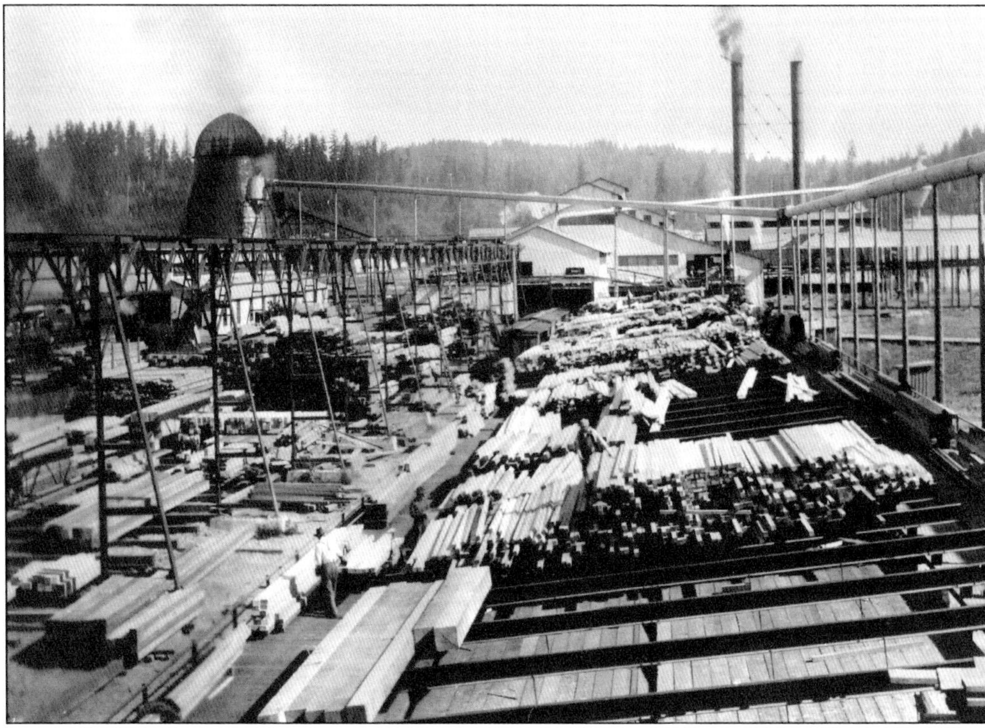

The lumber in this exterior photograph was still rough and on the timber ramps awaiting planing. A big crane brought the larger timbers from the mill. The crane tracks can be seen on the right. The mill had an overhead monorail system that was 5 miles in total length, which transported bundles of sawed lumber to and from the dry kilns, rough sheds, rough lumber dock, and planing mill. (East.)

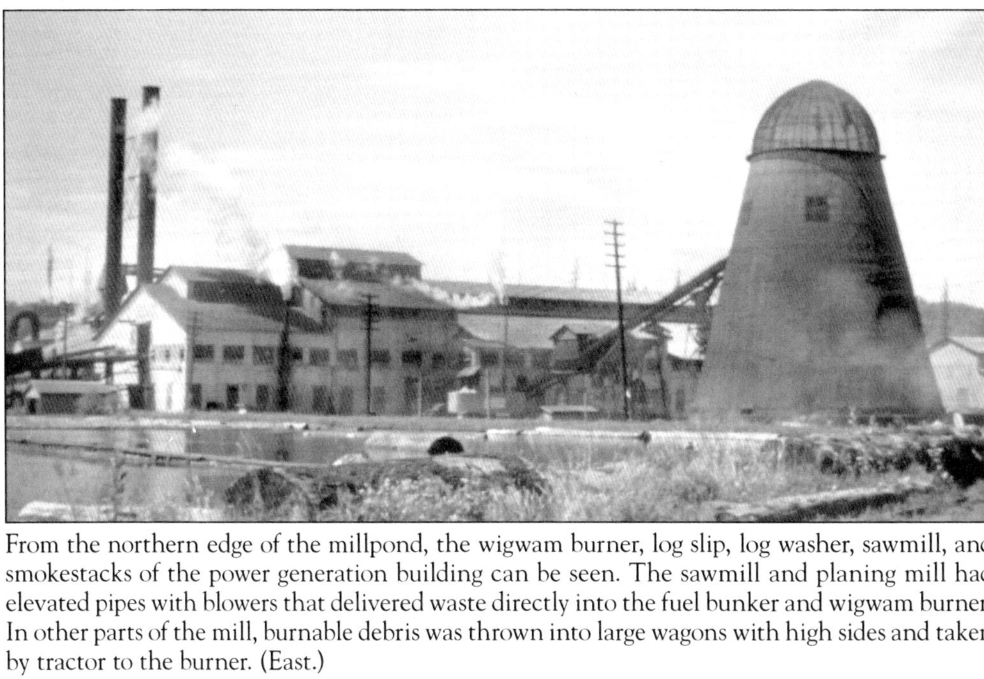

From the northern edge of the millpond, the wigwam burner, log slip, log washer, sawmill, and smokestacks of the power generation building can be seen. The sawmill and planing mill had elevated pipes with blowers that delivered waste directly into the fuel bunker and wigwam burner. In other parts of the mill, burnable debris was thrown into large wagons with high sides and taken by tractor to the burner. (East.)

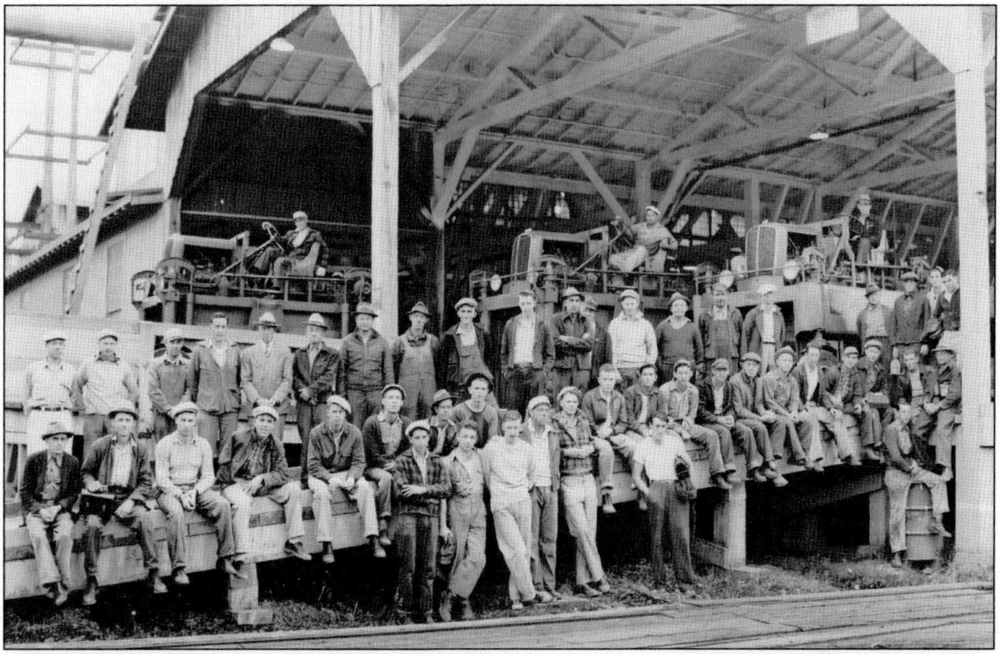

Traveling commercial photographers frequently took photographs like these of logging operations and groups of mill workers nearby. The large group photograph above was taken in the late 1920s. In the back, three men are seated on straddle carriers used to lift and move the loads of cut lumber. The straddle carriers replaced the spoke-wheeled lumber buggies that were used at first. Some of the African American workers brought to Vernonia from the South are seen in the photograph of the sawmill crew below. They were paid the same as the white workers but usually were given the less-skilled jobs. (Above, Minger; below, East.)

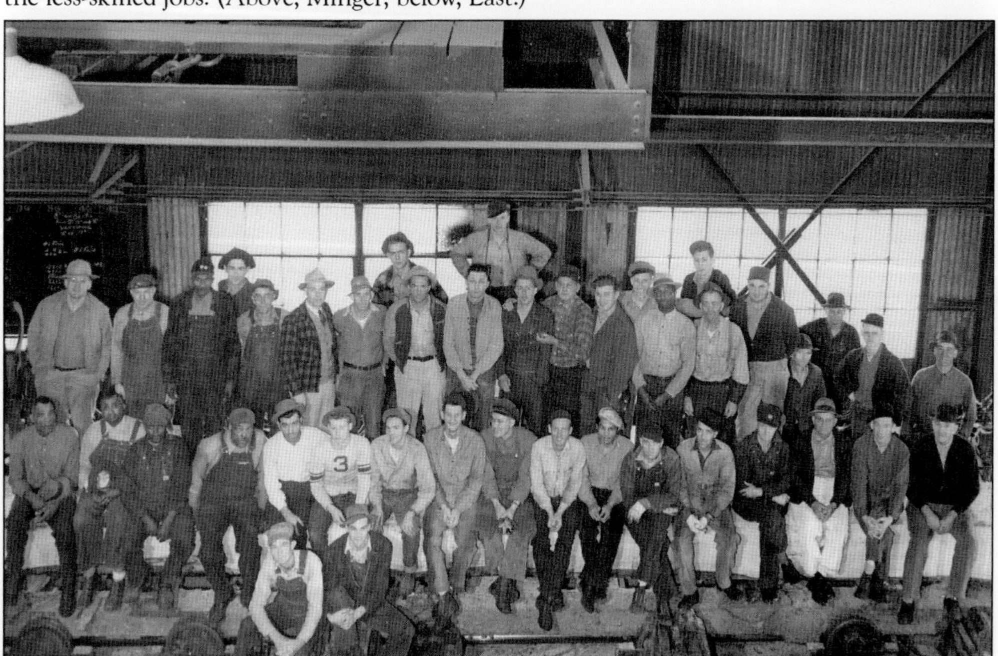

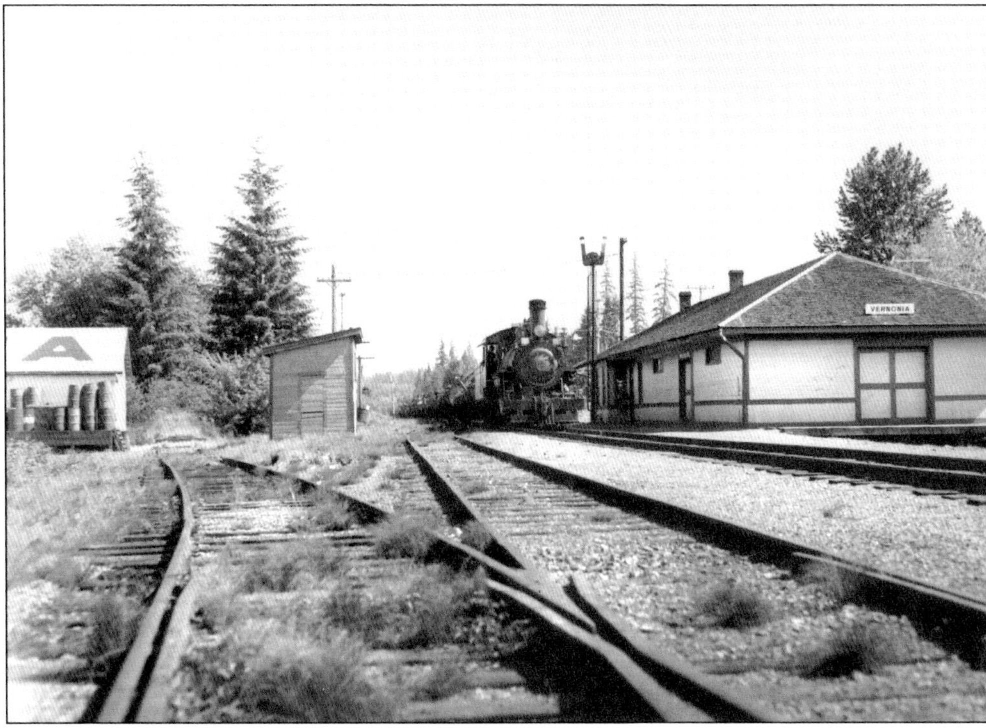

O-A engine No. 105 hauls a trainload of equipment into town as it stops at the Vernonia depot. Shay engine No. 102 would later be placed in Shay Park next to the Rock Creek Bridge. The Shay locomotives were the true workhorses of the woods in the Pacific Northwest. They were specially gear-driven to navigate steeper slopes and tighter turns than rod-driven locomotives like engine No. 105. O-A used 11 locomotives of both types in its operations. (VPMA.)

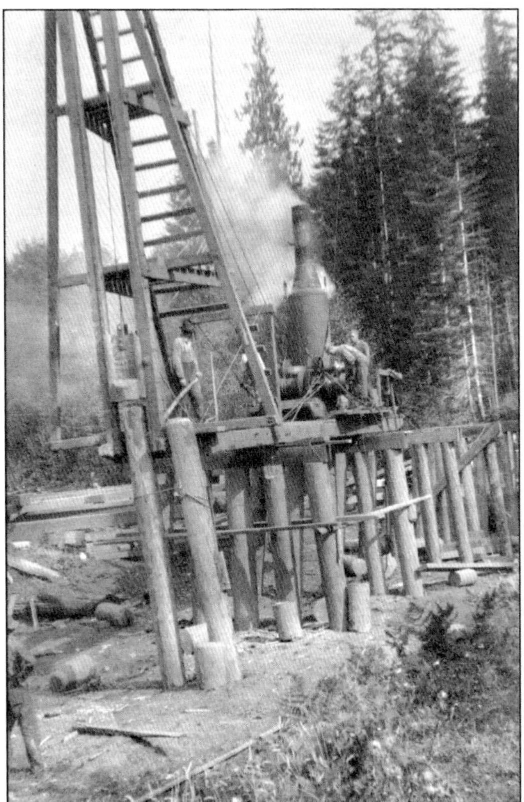

A steam donkey powered the pile driver shown on the left of the engine in the construction of the railroad that ran west from Vernonia up Rock Creek. This equipment was used to build one of the many trestles needed to bridge the rugged terrain with its many tributary creek valleys. The photograph was taken in the early 1920s on what was then the Hess place. (Keasey.)

Log trestles had to be built across the numerous canyons and ravines that characterize the landscape in Oregon's Coast Range. An unidentified crew of timber workers stands on the recently completed trestle. The image below was taken in June 1955 when a Spokane, Portland, and Seattle (SP&S) diesel freighter crossed a trestle over State Highway 47. Following the mill closure, the rail lines from Vernonia to the Clatsop/Columbia County line were removed. SP&S abandoned the Vernonia passenger train and depot in 1960, and the building was razed the following winter. Excursion trains from Banks to Vernonia—known as the Vernonia, South Park, and Sunset Steam Railroad—operated from 1964 through 1969. Shortly thereafter, freight traffic had so diminished that SP&S abandoned the line, and the rails were lifted in 1973. (Right, Queen; below, VPMA.)

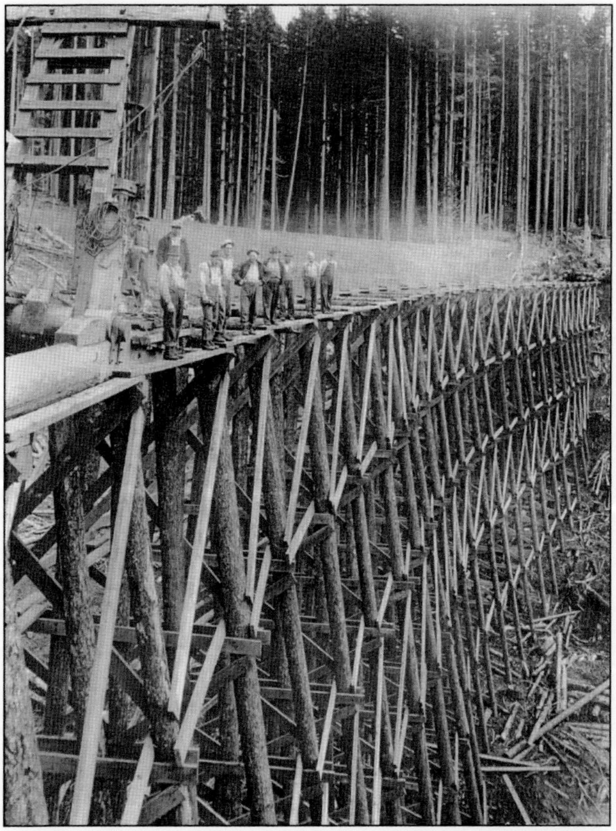

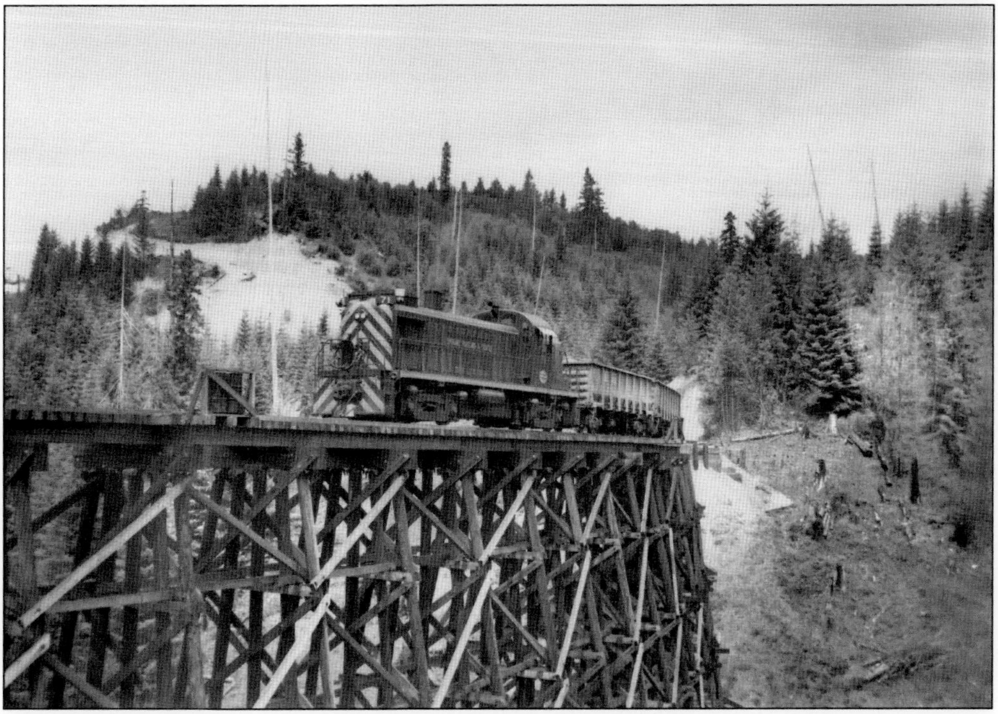

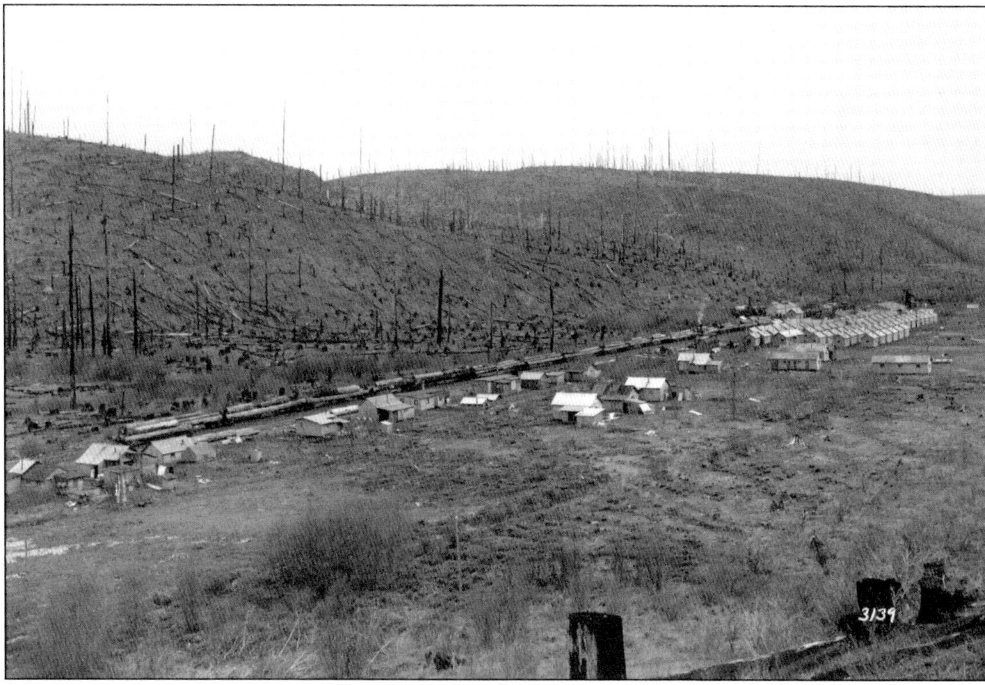

Camp McGregor, the first of the O-A logging camps, was destroyed by the 1933 Wolf Creek fire. New cabins were assembled at the O-A mill, loaded onto flatcars, and delivered to the camp. The charred remains of thousands of trees can be seen on the hills in the background. The rows of the new cabins are in the right center portion of the photograph. Below, a train takes the first group of new cabins to Camp McGregor after they were assembled at the O-A mill in 1936. The mill and its logging camps resumed operations that year after a three-year closure due to the Depression. (Both, VPMA.)

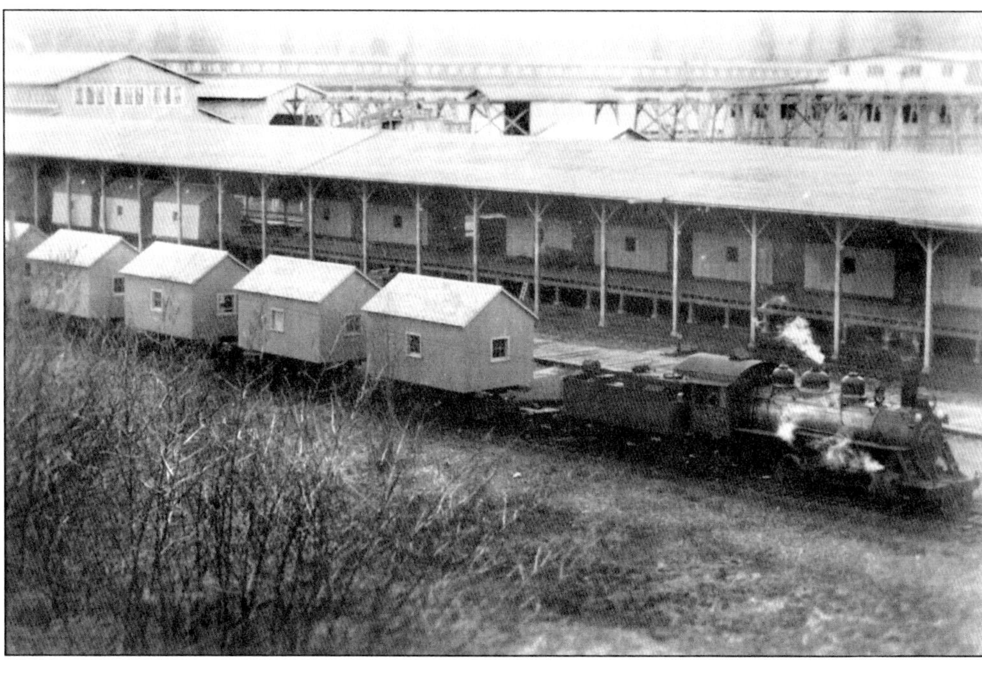

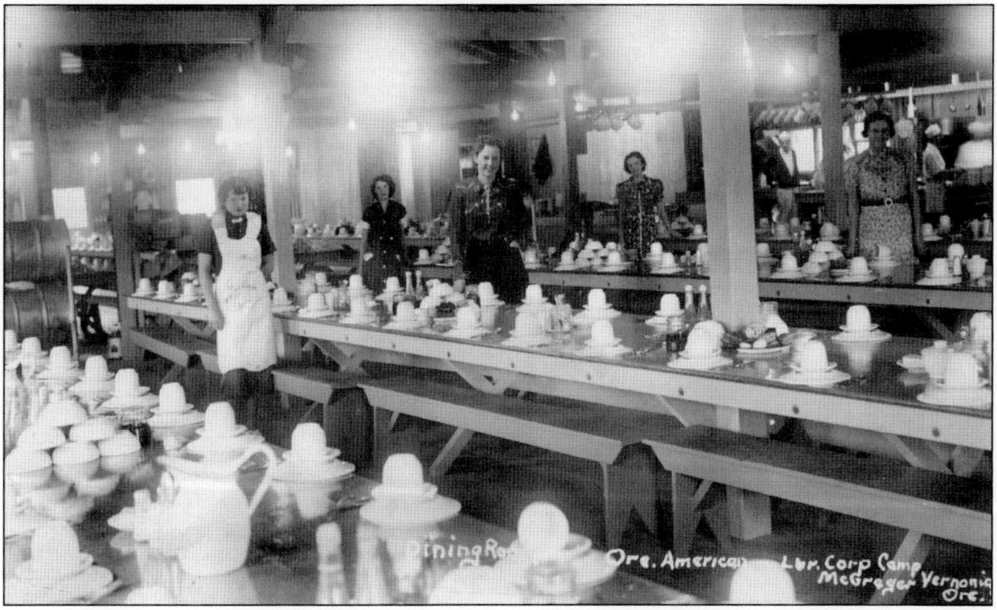

Camp McGregor's main dining hall is ready for another meal. The heavy white crockery plates and mugs and trestle tables and benches were typical of logging camps throughout the Pacific Northwest. In the photograph below, a group of Camp McGregor's dining hall staff members pose outside of Diner No. 3. Providing three hearty meals per day (with a packed lunch for the working day) was a more than full-time job. Loggers could burn up to 7,000 calories a day working in the woods. Camp cooks who could keep the men well fed were prized. (Both, VPMA.)

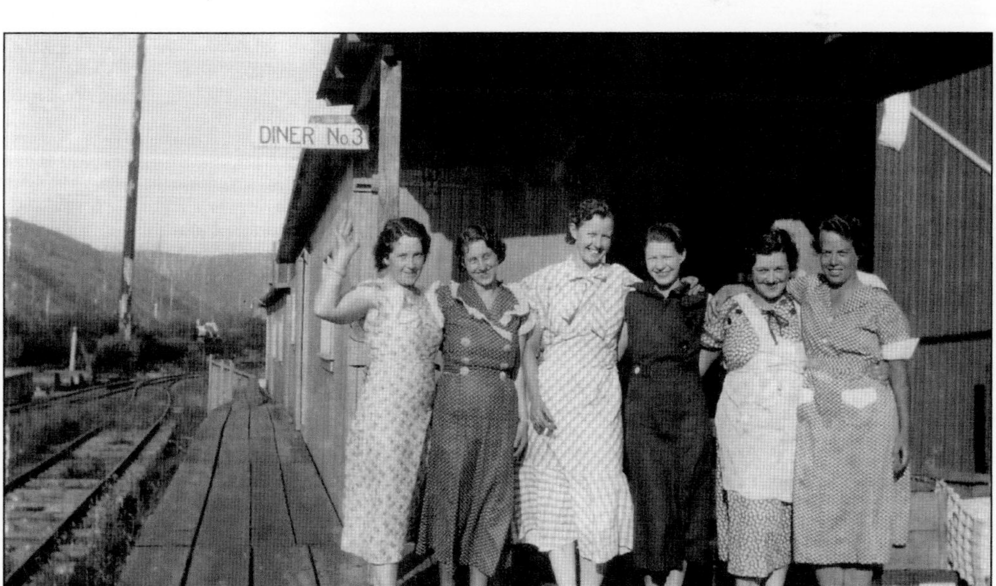

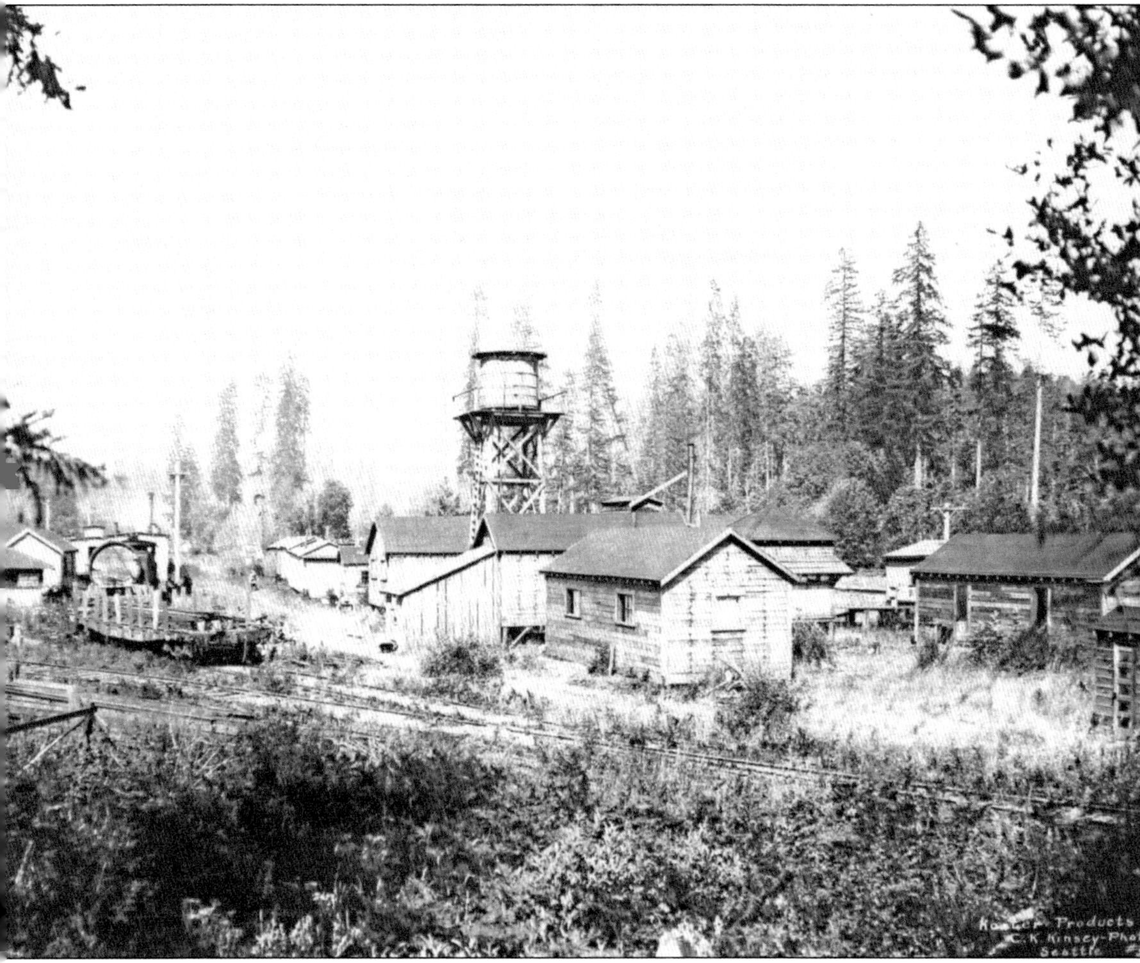

Logging camps were built close to the sites of forest operations. Intended for use for a few years at most, the structures were built as quickly and inexpensively as possible. The larger camps had cabins for families and schools for the children. In one, a railcar was converted to a classroom. Camp buildings were sometimes moved to new locations when the timber was exhausted at the current location. Camp Koster was located 6 miles south of Vernonia along the SP&S railroad tracks. The photograph was taken the in the mid-1920s and shows the typical features of a logging camp of those days. The water tower that supplied the steam locomotives stands above the homes of the workers next to the main rail line behind the cabins. A rail siding is in the foreground. Mary Ann Johns lived in this camp as a child. She later married fellow Vernonia High School graduate Gordon Cline. (Cline.)

Four

Growing, Going But Not Gone

By the time the mill was in full operation, the population increased tenfold from 150 to 1,500. Additional stores, restaurants, hotels, and theaters provided services for the rapidly growing population. Six automobile dealerships were established, as were multiple automobile repair and service stations. The *Vernonia Eagle* newspaper was started in 1922 in anticipation of Vernonia becoming a "big payroll" town. The new dam on Rock Creek provided electric power for the downtown area, which was supplemented by a power feed from the O-A mill.

During this time, a number of service and fraternal organizations were established, including the American Legion, which replaced the Grand Army of the Republic, Masons, Odd Fellows, Eastern Star, Rebekahs, and others. Where there was once a single church that served the early settlers, new churches were established, and the first church constructed a new building for its expanding congregation. There were dances at the Grange Hall, the American Legion Hall, and at other venues. Restaurants and taverns extended their hours to accommodate the shift workers.

After the mill ceased operations, the town's population decreased rapidly as people left to find work elsewhere. Many businesses closed, resulting in a number of empty commercial buildings. The railroads that carried passengers and millions of board feet of lumber were abandoned. Although some of the former vitality brought by a big payroll company was lost, Vernonia continued. New businesses gradually filled the abandoned storefronts, and new residents, many commuting to jobs in the nearby Portland area, moved in to enjoy small-town life.

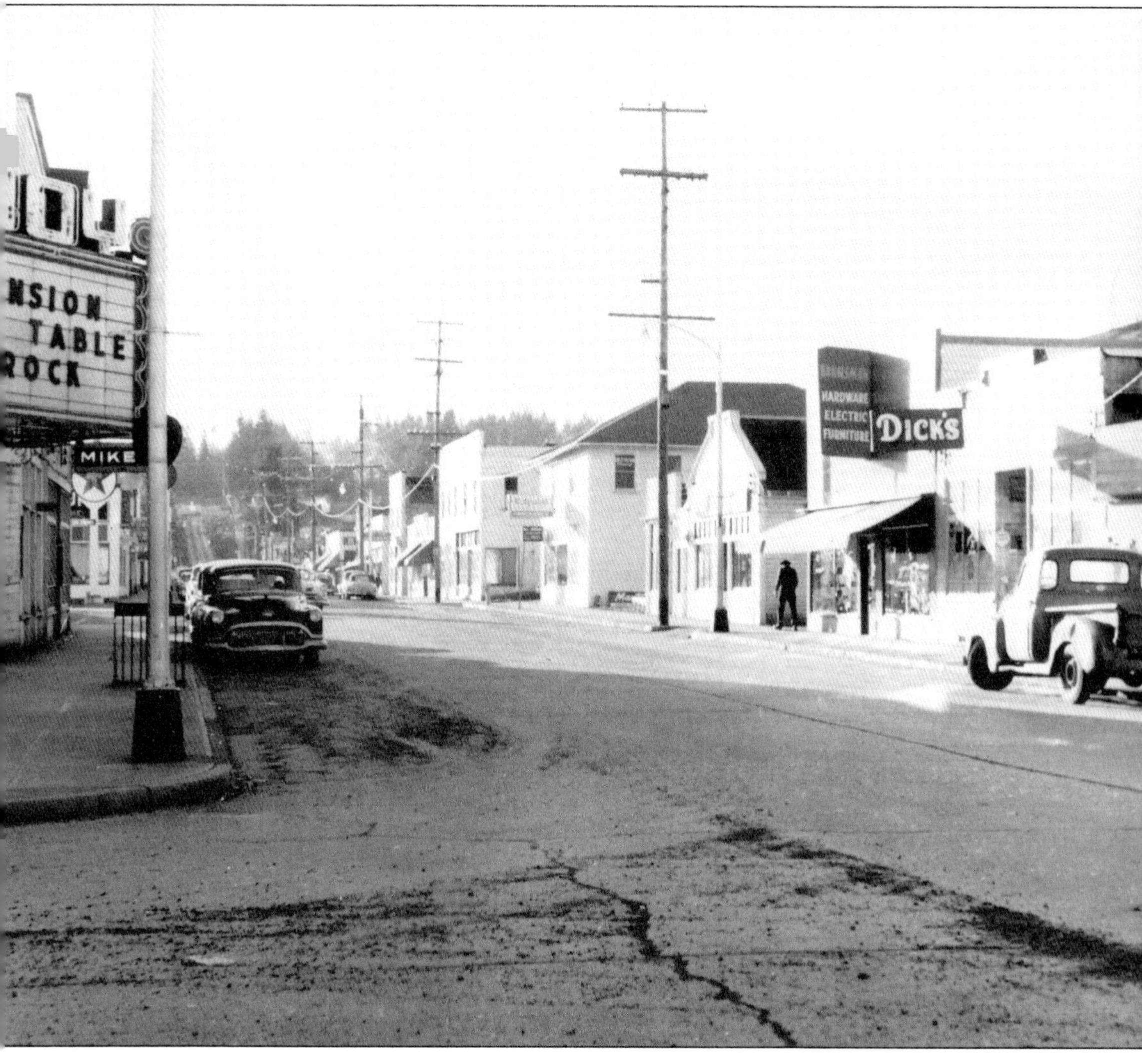

Taken in the 1950s, this Bridge Street scene shows many of the businesses of the time. The Joy Theater faces Brunsman's Hardware Store. The Joy Theater was built in 1926 by J. H. Bush after the Majestic Theater burned. J. C. Penney's later built its store on the former theater site. The Joy Theater building was the most elegant in town and was also home to Kullander's Jewelry on the corner and other businesses, including a barbershop, beauty shop, and café. There were professional offices upstairs. The building that held Brunsman's Hardware was built in 1915 and had been a tavern, a candy store, and a clothing store. As is true with most of the commercial buildings along Bridge Street, the structures seen in this photograph still stand but are now occupied with other ventures. *Pride's Historic Walking Tour,* a book complied by the Vernonia Pride civic organization, describes the uses of the downtown buildings over the years. (VPMA.)

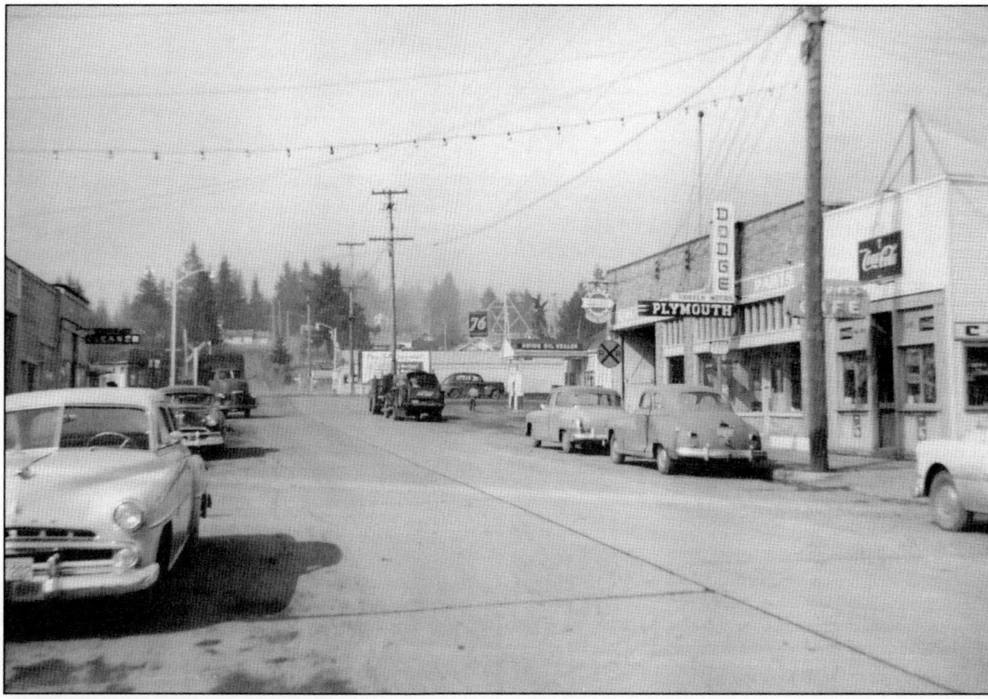

This view of Bridge Street shows several businesses that were active in the early 1950s. The Union 76 gasoline station, a restaurant, the local Dodge and Plymouth dealers, and Ma Vike's Café line the north side of Bridge Street just east of the railroad tracks. Bridge Street ascends Corey Hill in the background. (Thompson.)

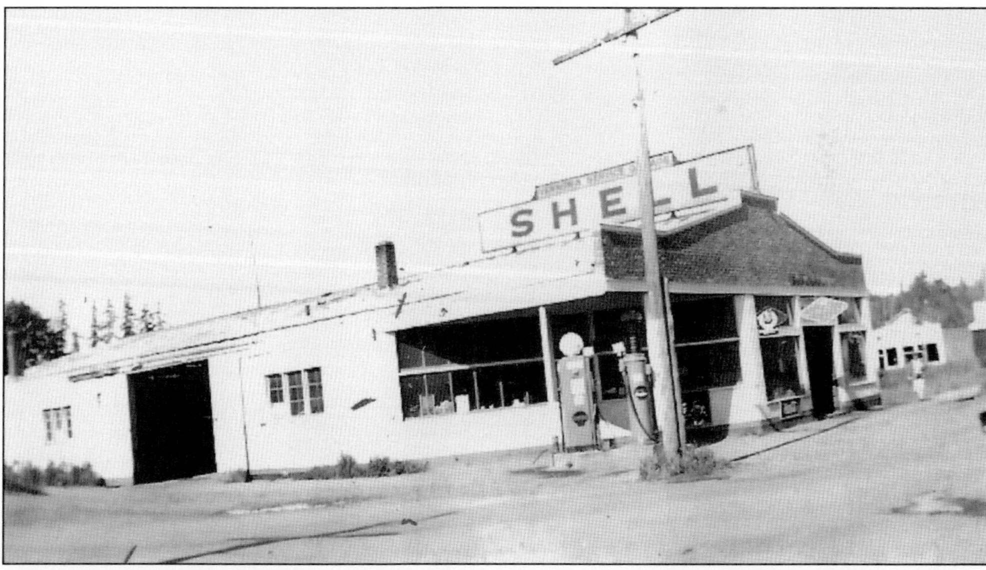

George Johnson's Shell service station stood at the corner of Bridge Street and Rose Avenue. Ralph's Chevron was two blocks south, and the Mobil station was three blocks east. At one time, there were a total of seven gasoline stations in town. In 1942, when this photograph was taken, gas rationing for World War II had just begun. The building has been extensively remodeled and today houses Vernonia Hardware. (Queen.)

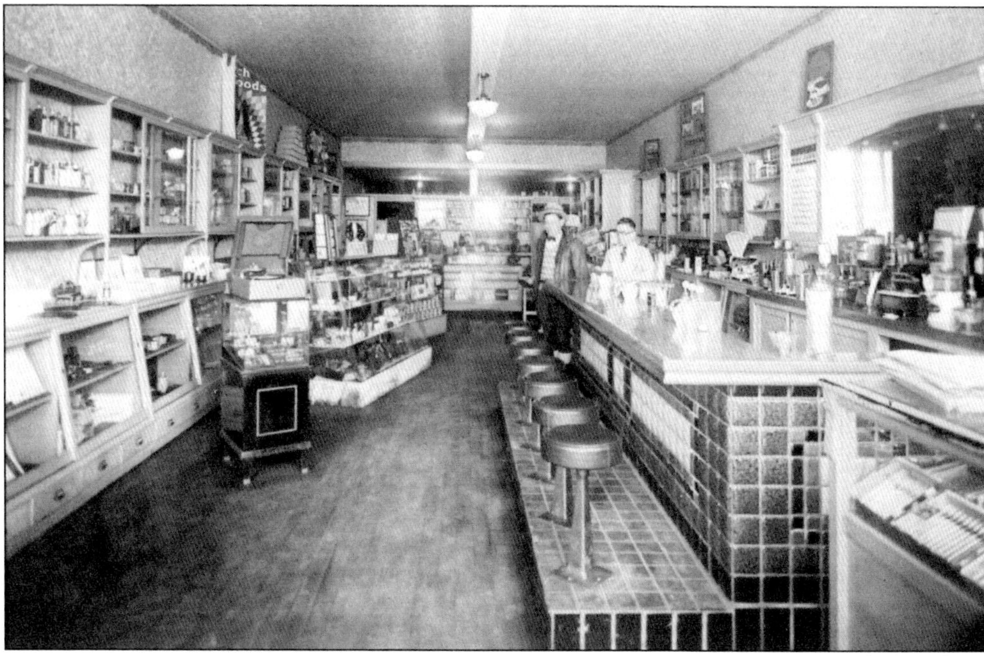

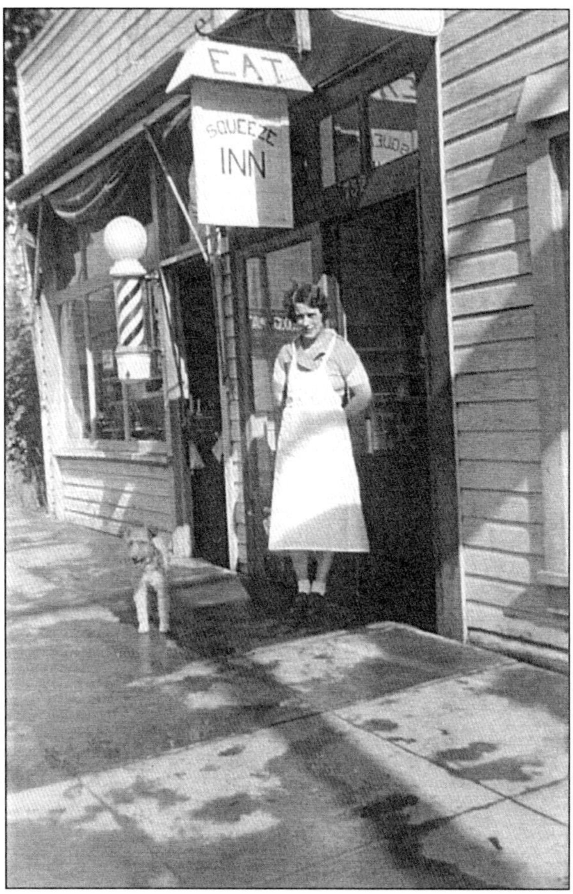

Mac's Pharmacy, owned by Kenneth McNeill, operated on Bridge Street from 1923 to 1937. Mac was active with the chamber of commerce and chaired the airport committee when the Vernonia Airport was established. Mac (left) and another employee stand at the far end of the soda fountain counter, a common feature in pharmacies well into the 1960s. (VPMA.)

Gladys Dial and her dog, Whizzer, stand outside the Squeeze Inn. The restaurant had a counter and nine stools with a sign, "We can feed 1,000 people a day—nine at a time." The inn was open nearly 24 hours a day most days during the late 1930s to accommodate the loggers and mill shift workers. Whizzer sat outside while Gladys was working. Loggers would buy him ice cream cones and put them in a nearby dog-height flag stand. (King.)

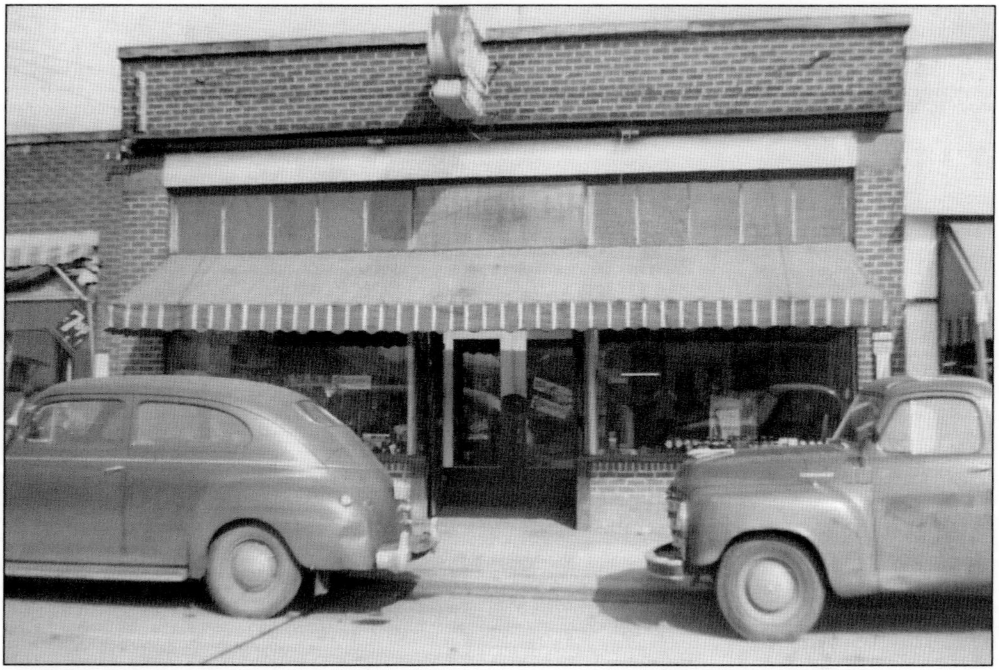

Jack Thompson ran the Vernonia Rexall (pictured above). Below, an unnamed employee stands in front of the store. Ma Vike's Café sign can be seen in the background. It was later converted into a small bowling alley. In the years following the mill closure, chain stores such as Safeway and Rexall closed. Although it was part of a chain, the Safeway was small compared to today's standards. Until the 1960s, small, neighborhood groceries were found distributed throughout town within walking distance of the nearby homes. As more families had second cars, larger supermarkets with a wider variety of goods became the place most homemakers shopped. Vernonia now has just one supermarket and a convenience store. (Both, Thompson.)

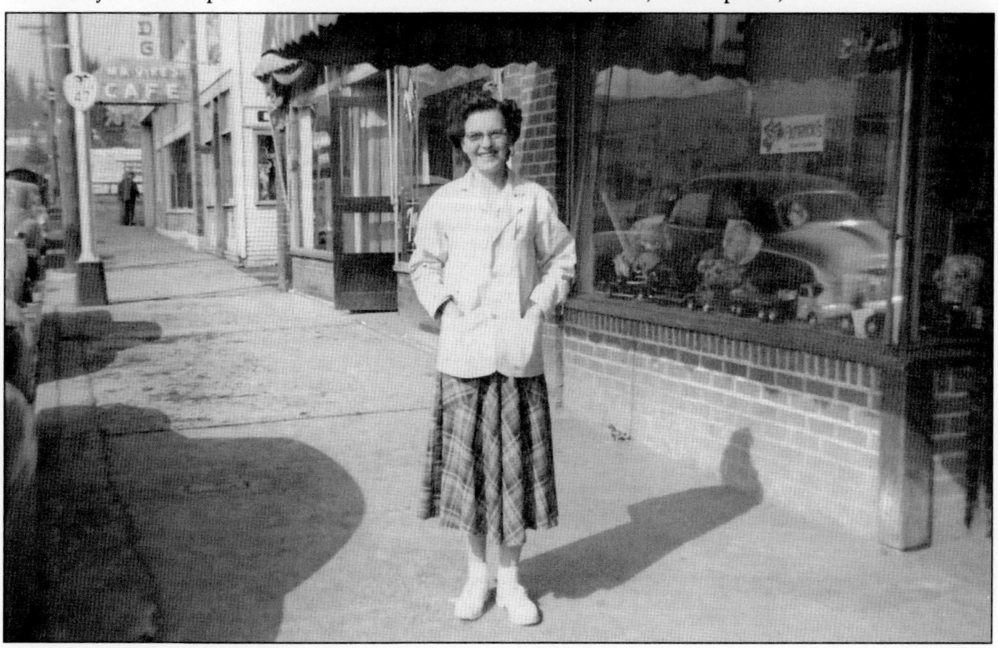

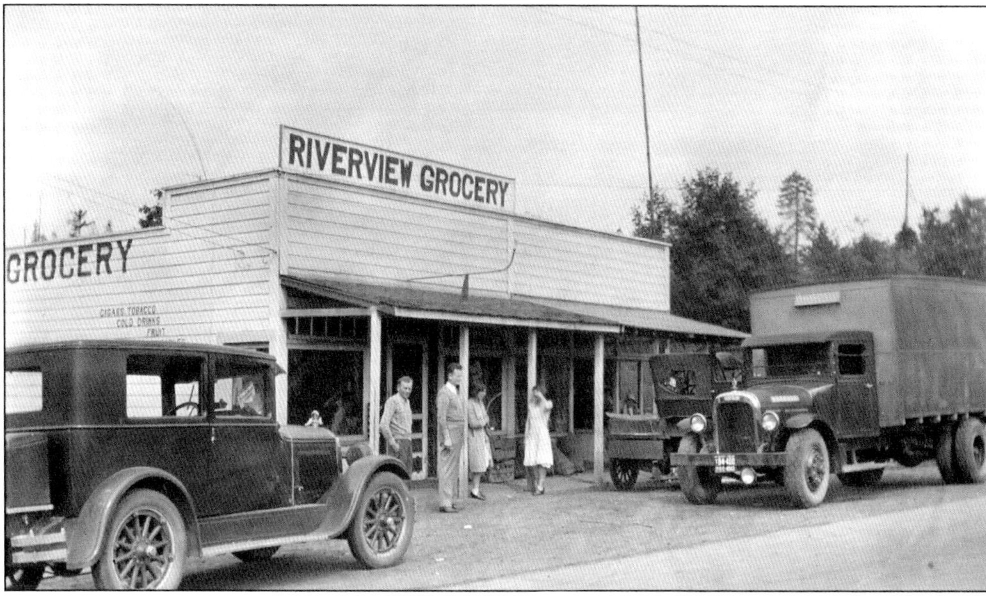

The Riverview Grocery, owned by brothers Milo and Harry King, was located on the west side of Mist Drive along the Nehalem River until the flood of 1935. The photograph below shows the store surrounded by floodwaters. The store was moved across the street in 1936 and renamed King's Grocery. Harry later bought out Milo. His children Bob, Earl, and Marjorie also worked in the family business. Pauline Dial married Earl King and worked at the grocery until her first child was born. Bob King married Vesta Christensen, who worked at the Commercial Bank, which later became a branch of U.S. Bank in 1954. She worked at the bank for 34 years. Vesta's twin sister, Lesta, married and left Vernonia. She died from lymphoma at the age of 30, leaving a husband and two children. (Both, King.)

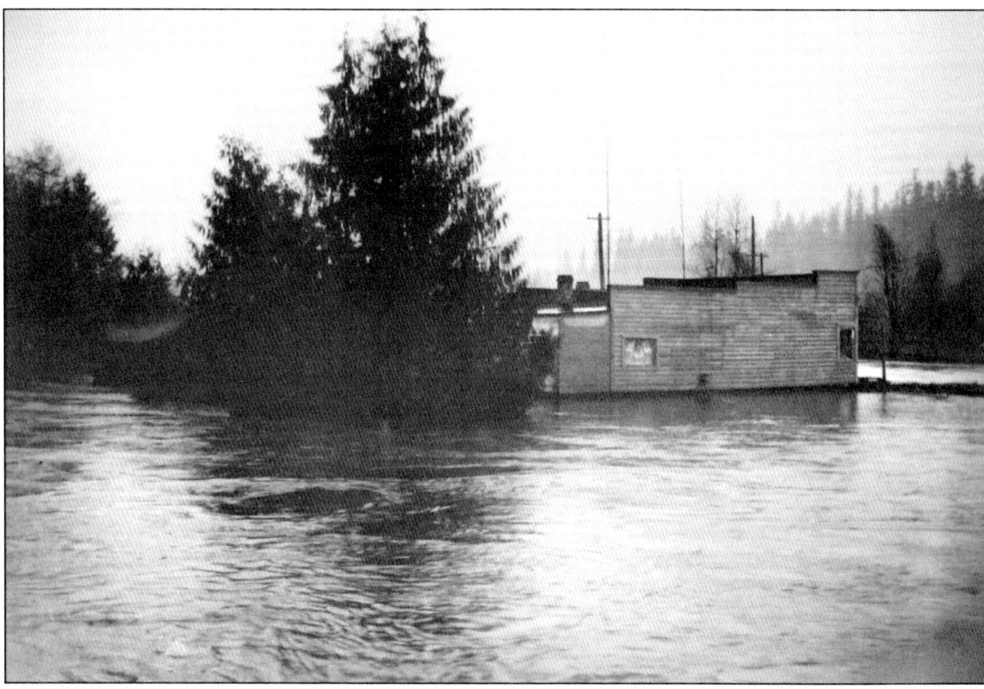

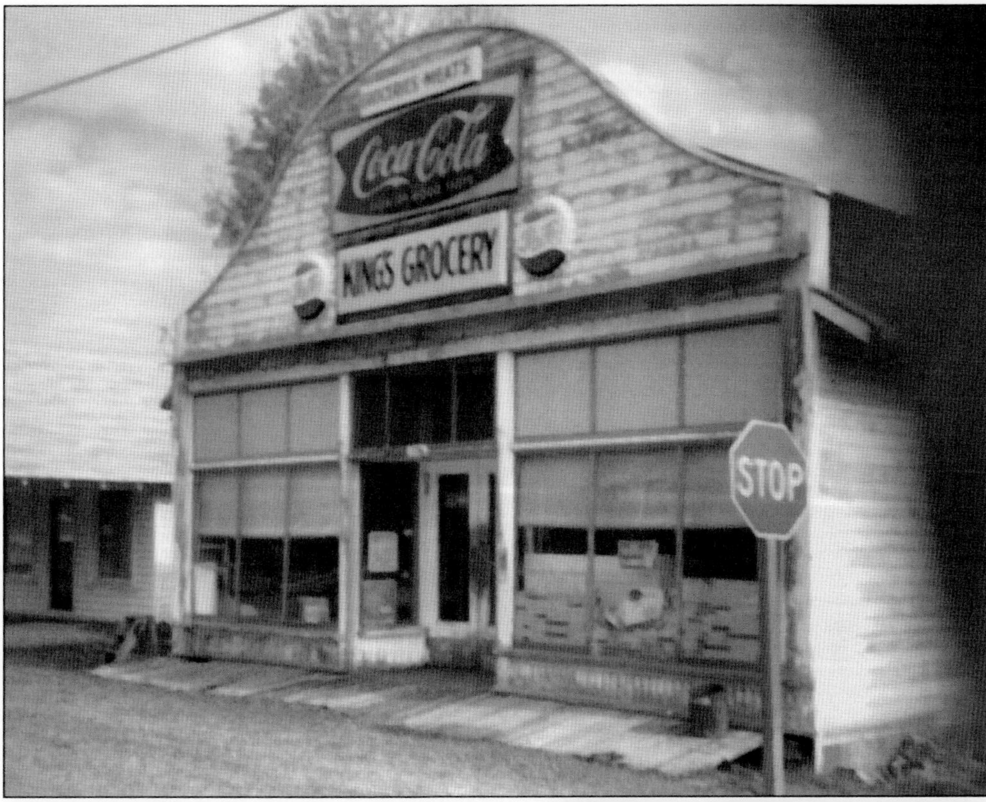

Harry King and his wife, Emily, ran the business until Harry's death in 1950. The store had a fresh meat counter, and all meat was cut to order. Although a majority of the store's customers lived on O-A Hill and in Riverview, Camp McGregor residents telephoned in their orders, which were packed and put onto logging trains headed for the camp. Bob's brother, Earl, later bought the meat market part of the grocery. Bob and Emily ran the grocery until it closed in the early 1950s. Emily lived in the attached house at the back of the store until her death in 1981. The photograph above was taken several years after the store closed. Harry King is pictured at right inside the grocery in the 1940s. (Above, Queen; right, King.)

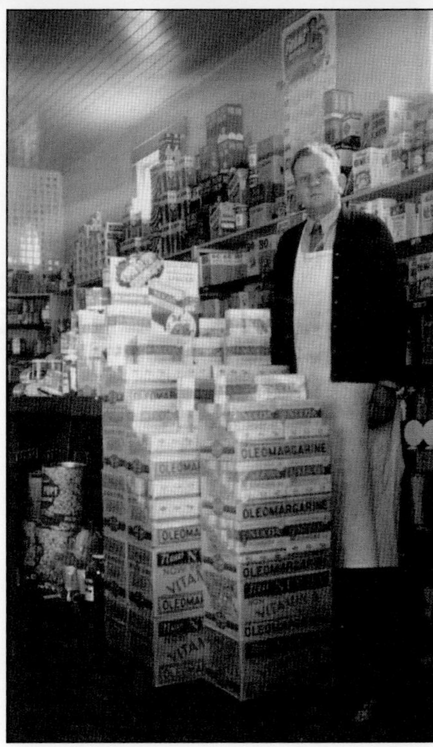

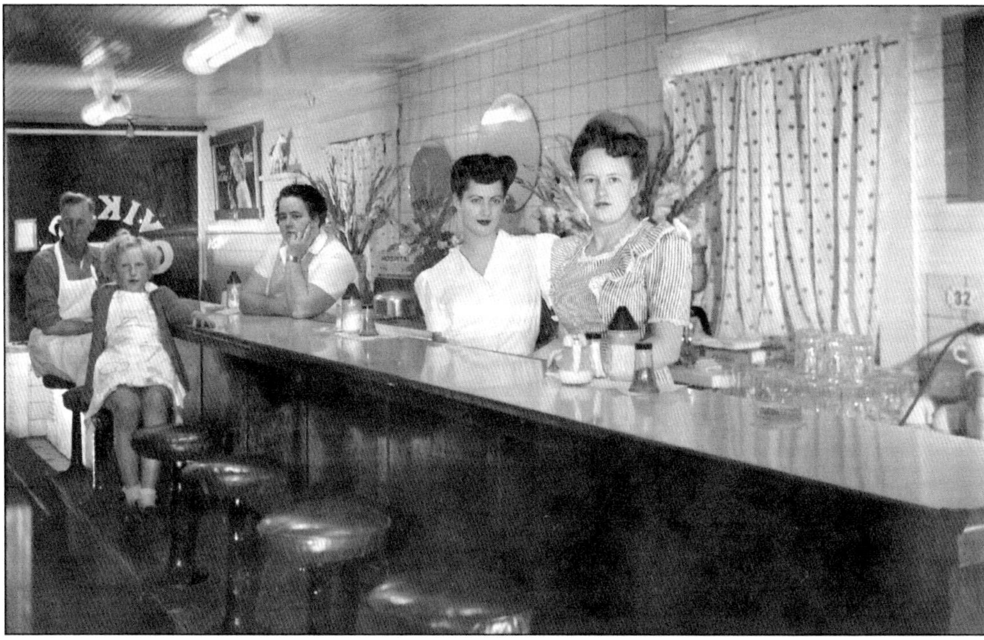

Ragena "Ma" and Oscar Vike owned Ma Vike's Café, a popular Vernonia restaurant in the 1940s and one of four run by Ma Vike. Pictured above at the counter are, from left to right, Oscar Vike, Shirlee Vike Daughtry, Ragena Vike, Marianne Tomlin Poole, and Nora Vike Redmond. The menu cover noted that they purchased their meats and groceries locally, including milk from the Nehalem Dairy, which was owned by the Bush family on Rose Avenue. Oscar Vike worked as a logger and spent most of his time running Lidgerwood steam skidders. The photograph below was taken in the early 1940s. The Vernonia Hotel was built at the top of Madison Street in the 1920s. At one time it was known as the Hy-Van because it was built in 1925 by Hiram VanBlaricom on his homestead. It has been remodeled and is now the Vernonia Inn Bed and Breakfast. (Above, King; below, Malmsten.)

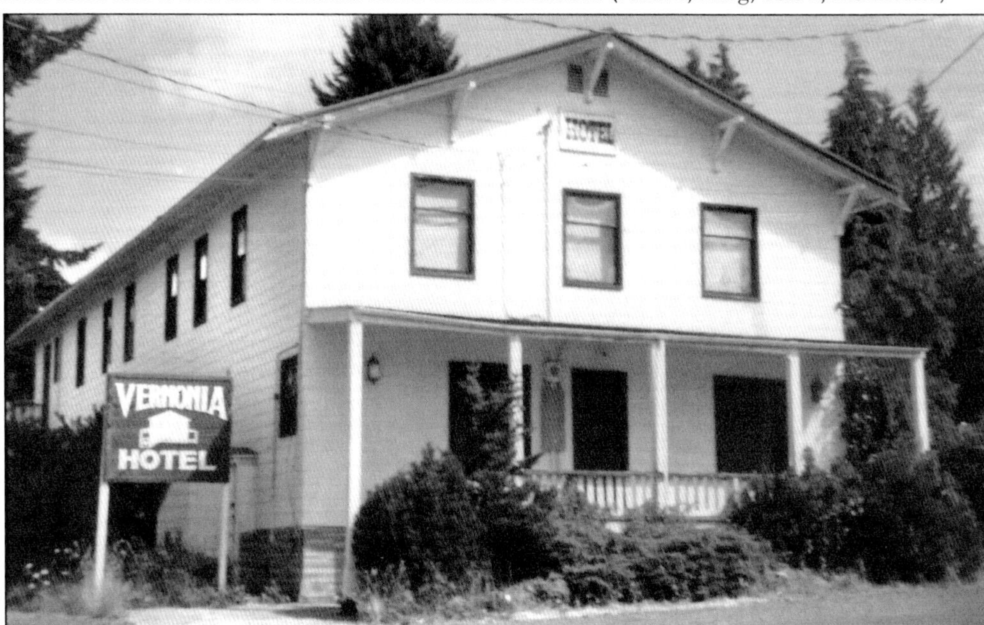

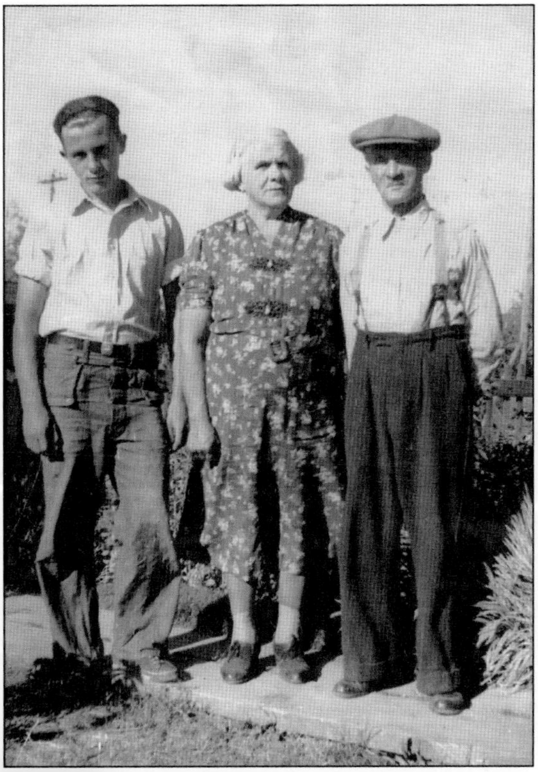

From left to right, Charles, Rose, and Emil Minger were photographed in 1937 on the Minger place in what is now Anderson Park. Charles was born in Biel, Switzerland, to Emil and Rosa Minger in 1922. A year later, they came to America, first to Scofield and then Vernonia. He married Dessie Irene May and worked in the woods on a rigging crew before getting a job at the O-A mill, where he worked until its closure in 1957. Irene May and Charles Minger are seen in the picture below in 1942 on the wood walkway to his parents home. Rose Minger stands in the doorway. (Both, Minger.)

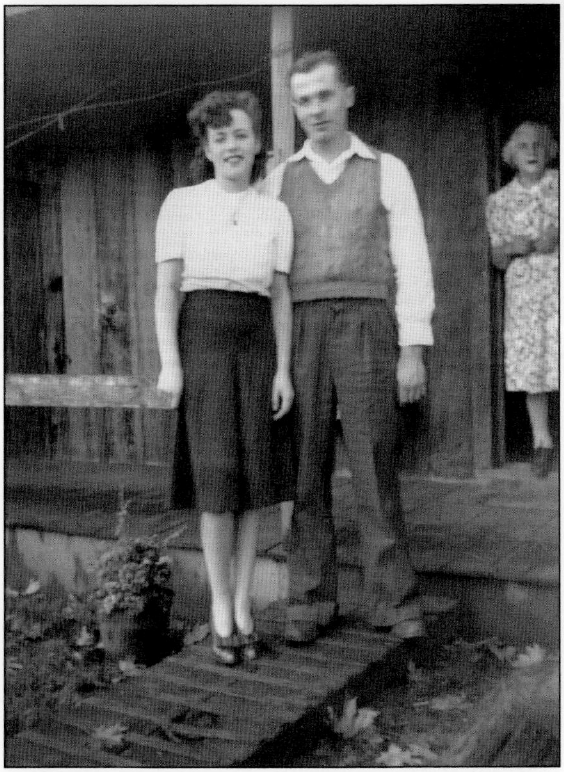

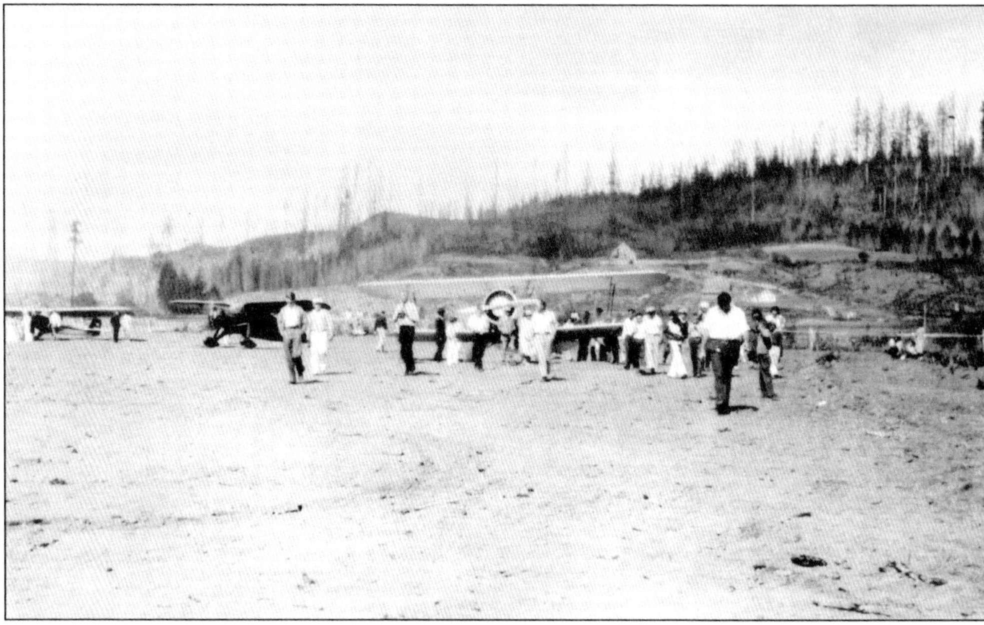

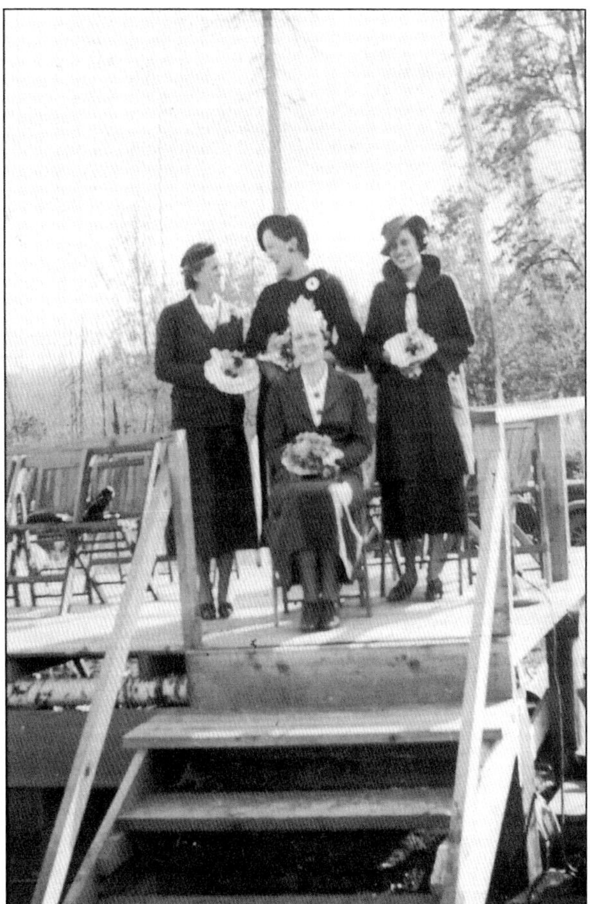

In March 1934, Kenneth McNeill, a local businessman and chairman of the aviation committee of the Vernonia Chamber of Commerce, sent a $100 money order to the McPherson Corporation as down payment on the land that would become the Vernonia Airport. Begun on forested land as a Depression-era Civil Works Administration project, the grass-strip airport opened for business on Saturday, September 20, 1935, with a big two-day celebration. Pilots from all over Oregon were invited to fly in for the festivities. Vernonia mayor Ben Owens officially dedicated the airport, assisted by city and county officials. This was followed by the coronation of the Airport Dedication Queen. Four young women competed for the title; Dorothy Gwin won. She is pictured seated at left with the other contestants (from left to right) Julia Wangler, Helen Messing, and Edna Owens—the mayor's daughter. (Above, VPMA; left, Gwin.)

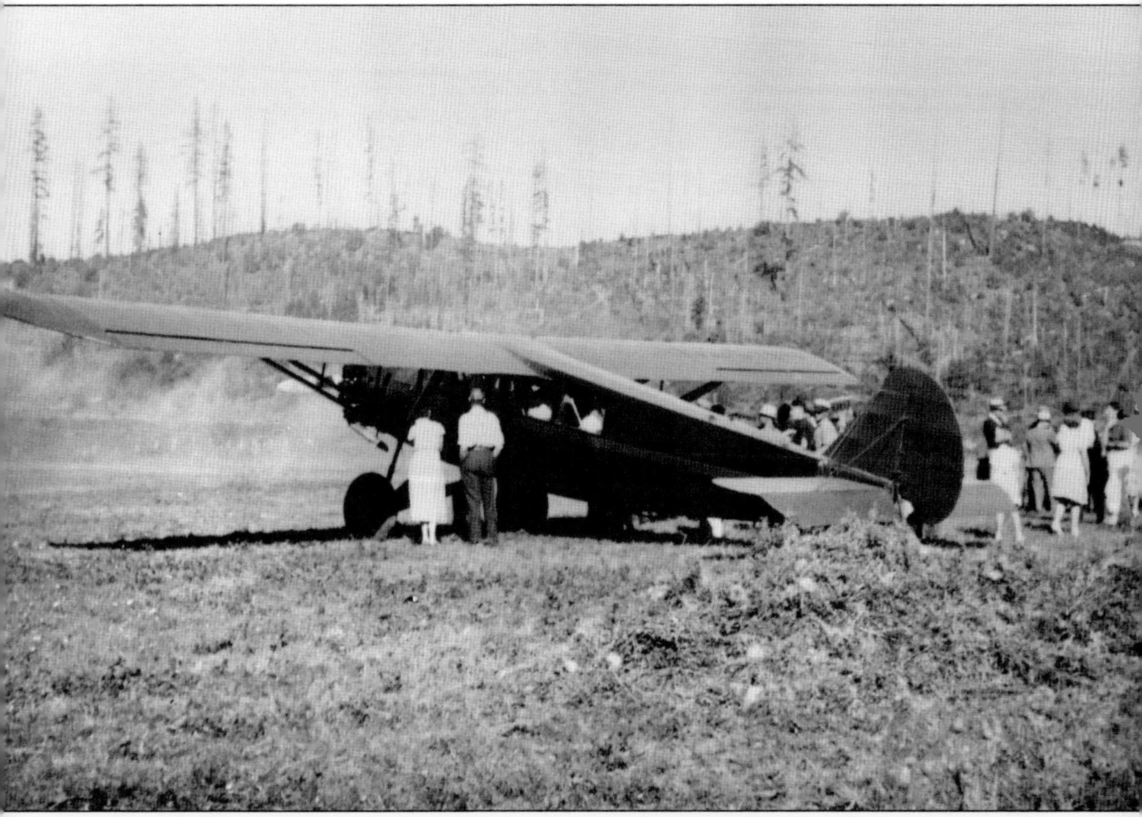

A variety of private airplanes flew in for the airport dedication celebration. A banquet and dance was held Saturday evening at nearby Arcadia Park, a dance hall and picnic ground that was a popular place in the 1930s. On Sunday at noon, the visiting airplanes made a mass flight over Vernonia, and the afternoon was filled with various flying contests and exhibitions. For a time, commercial flights between Portland and Astoria would make a stop in Vernonia if notified in advance. The airport was designed as an emergency landing site in the hilly terrain between Portland and Astoria. It has been in continuous use for general aviation since its dedication. (VPMA.)

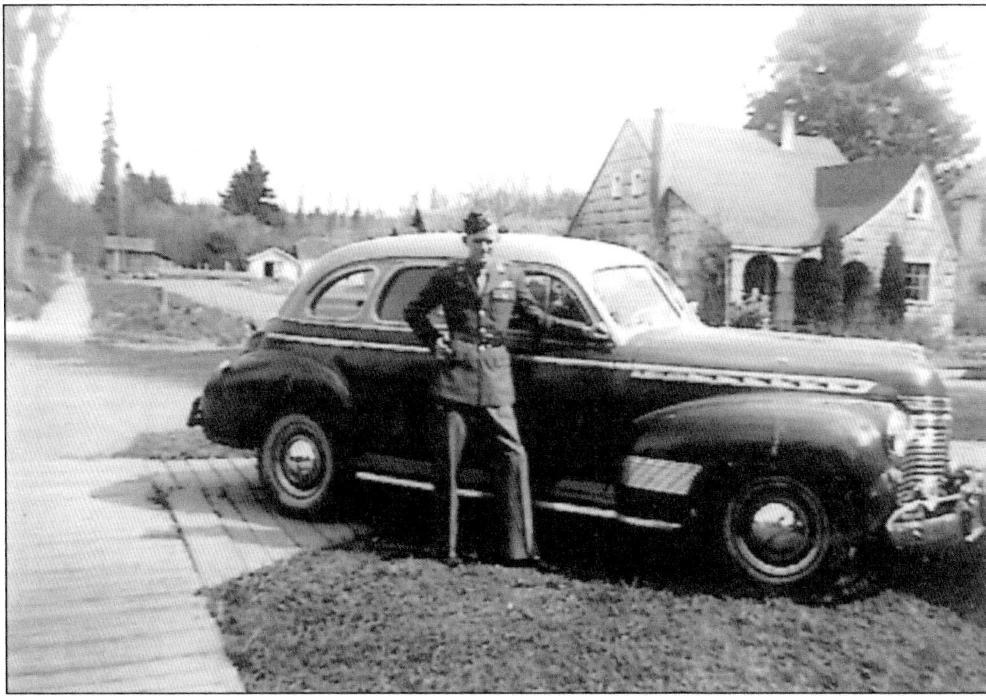

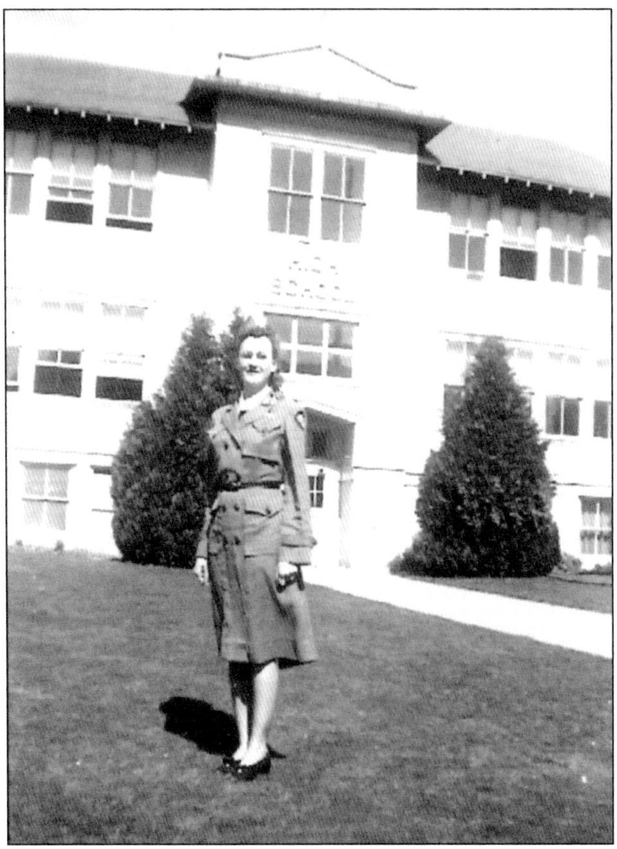

During World War II, many of Vernonia's young men enlisted in the armed forces. Elliott Vernon "Lige" Robertson was in his early 20s when the above photograph was taken near the corner of Grant and North Streets. The home in the background still stands. Some young women joined the services while others volunteered for organizations such as the Red Cross. Orene Nance, shown at left in her Red Cross Motor Corps uniform, stands in front of Vernonia High School. Nance later married Cleve Robertson, and together they ran the Cozy, a restaurant on Bridge Street. Many high school students worked at the Cozy, including Arvela Christensen Robertson and Willie Floeter Chandler. Robertson also worked at the mill during the war years, as did other women to help replace the young men who joined the armed services. (Both, Queen.)

In a patriotic gesture, twins Vesta Christensen (left) and Lesta Christensen (right), age 17, stand on either side of their sister Arvela, age 19, in 1942. Shorter skirts were in vogue during World War II as a wartime textile conservation measure. As was true across the United States, Vernonians were issued ration cards for commodities such as gasoline and certain food items that were in short supply due to the war. (Queen.)

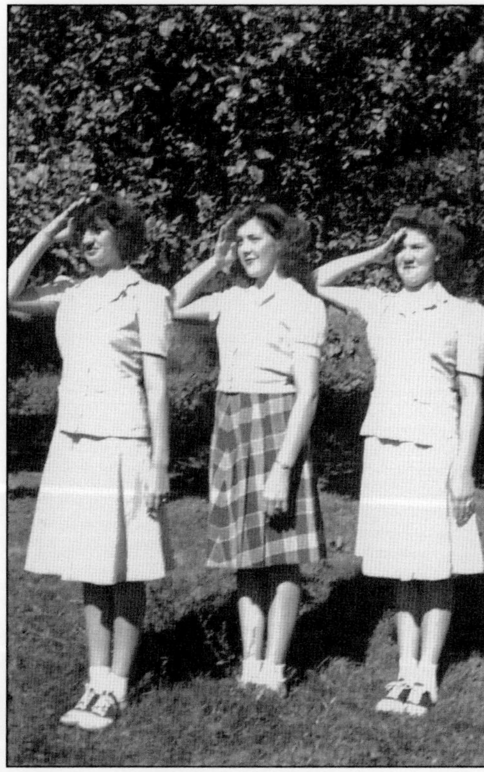

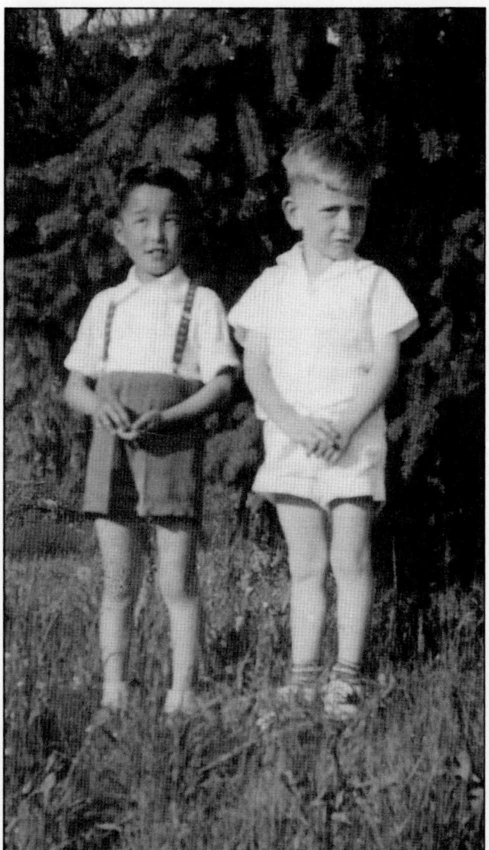

Before the war, Japanese Americans worked at area logging camps, including Clark and Wilson Camps No. 2 and No. 8, and owned small businesses such as laundries and restaurants. Mike Grady (right) and Johnny ? were friends and played together often until one night in May 1942, when Johnny and the rest of the local Japanese population were taken to relocation camps. Japanese Americans such as Ben Soejima occasionally return for the annual picnic for former graduates of Vernonia High School. (VPMA.)

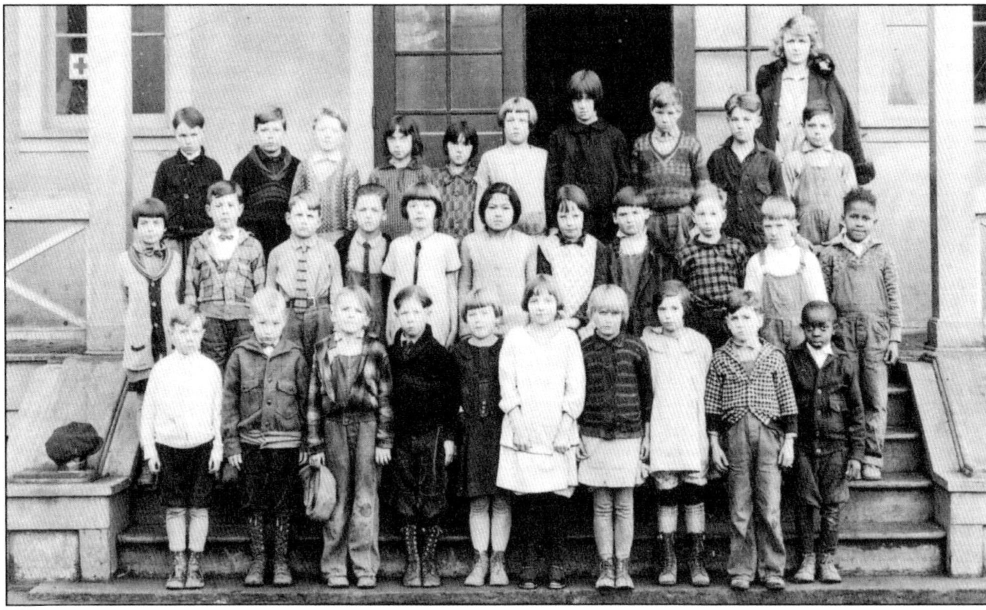

The Washington School third grade picture was taken in January 1928 on the school's front steps. At first, African Americans were prohibited from attending Vernonia's schools. But under pressure from the NAACP, the schools admitted African American students in 1926. Children from all ethnic groups were included in regular school life, including sports and student government. (Condit.)

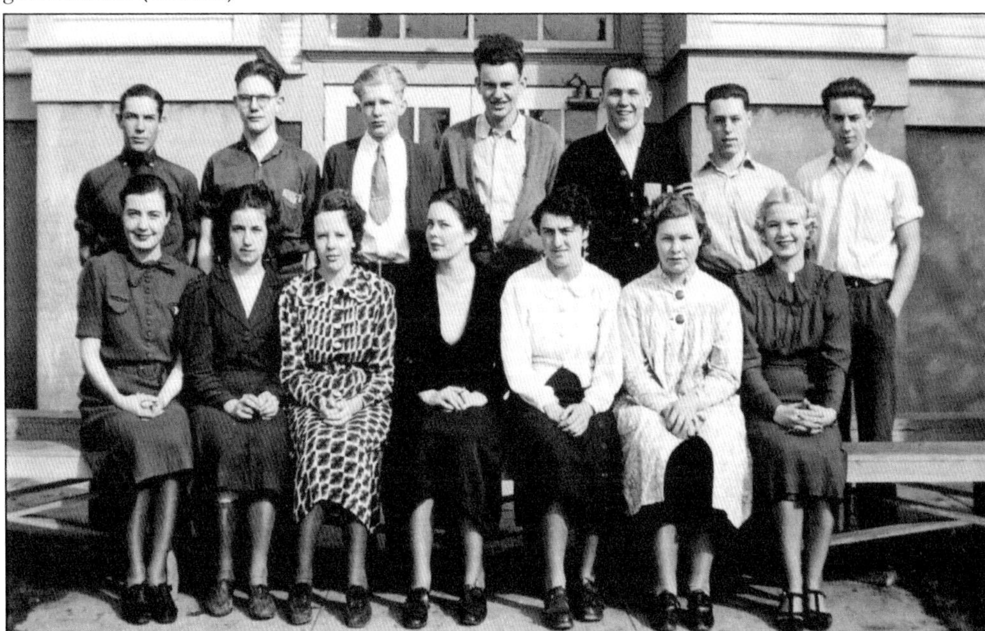

The cast of the three-act junior class play *Arizona Dude Ranch* poses for this 1937 Memolog picture. The play was held on the Washington Grade School stage. The cast included Elizabeth Wall, Harold Davis, Aubrey Fitzgerald, Fred Ervin, Bill Thompson, Louise French, Norman Crowder, Ruby Condit, Bertha Thompson, LaVerne Thompson, Kathryn McKenzie, Sonny Schalock, and Clarence Lamping. (Condit.)

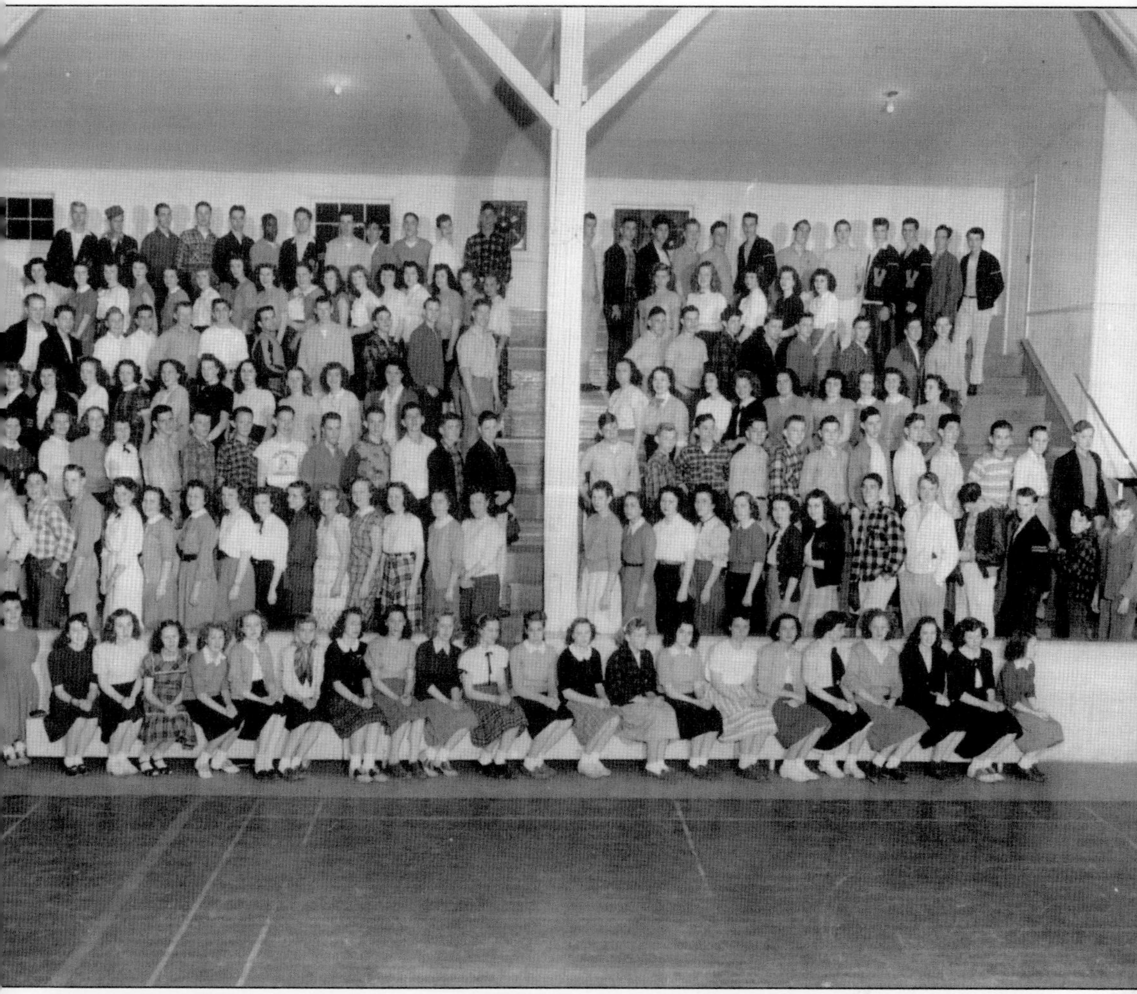

The entire student body of the first Vernonia High School (VHS) poses for this 1948 photograph in the high school gymnasium. Among the students pictured are current VPMA members Shirley Harpersberg (first row, far left), Genny Schwab Fisher (second row, second to right of column), Bill Sword (third row, first to right of column), Dolores Johnson New (sixth row, second from left), Derl Roberts (seventh row, second from left), and Lee Enneberg (seventh row, fifth from left). VHS was a two-story wooden structure built in 1923 on A Street near State Avenue. The last class to graduate from this school was the class of 1952. The new high school on Bridge Street opened in 1953. (Sword.)

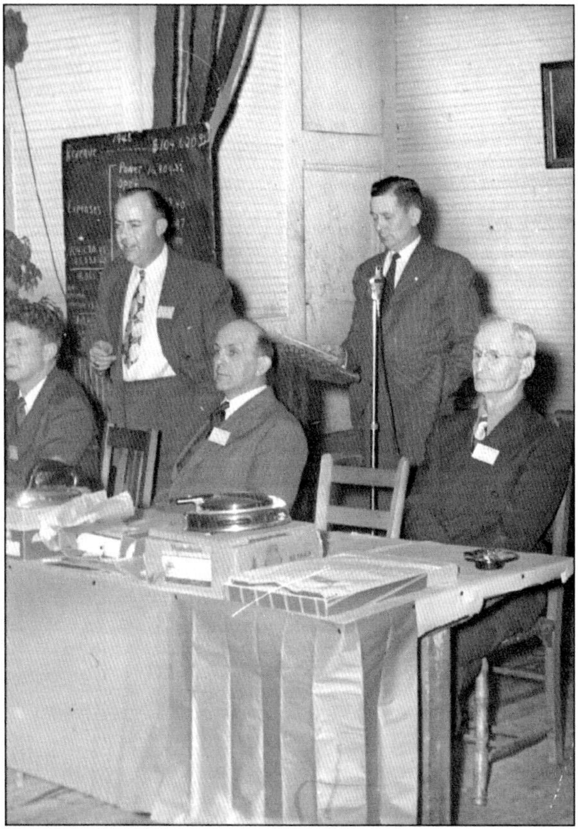

The West Oregon Electric Cooperative (WOEC) annual meeting in 1950 was held at the American Legion Hall on Adams Street. Pictured from left to right are (seated) board members Paul Gordon, Fred Know, and Lee Wooden; (standing) general manager Guy Thomas and WOEC attorney Neal Bush. WOEC was established in 1945 and remains the electric power utility for Vernonia and more than 1,200 square miles of the surrounding territory. WOEC's annual meeting always includes door prizes for its members. Below, an unidentified woman was happy to win an electric toaster at this late-1950s meeting. Pictured with her is Guy Thomas, WOEC general manager. (Both, Thomas.)

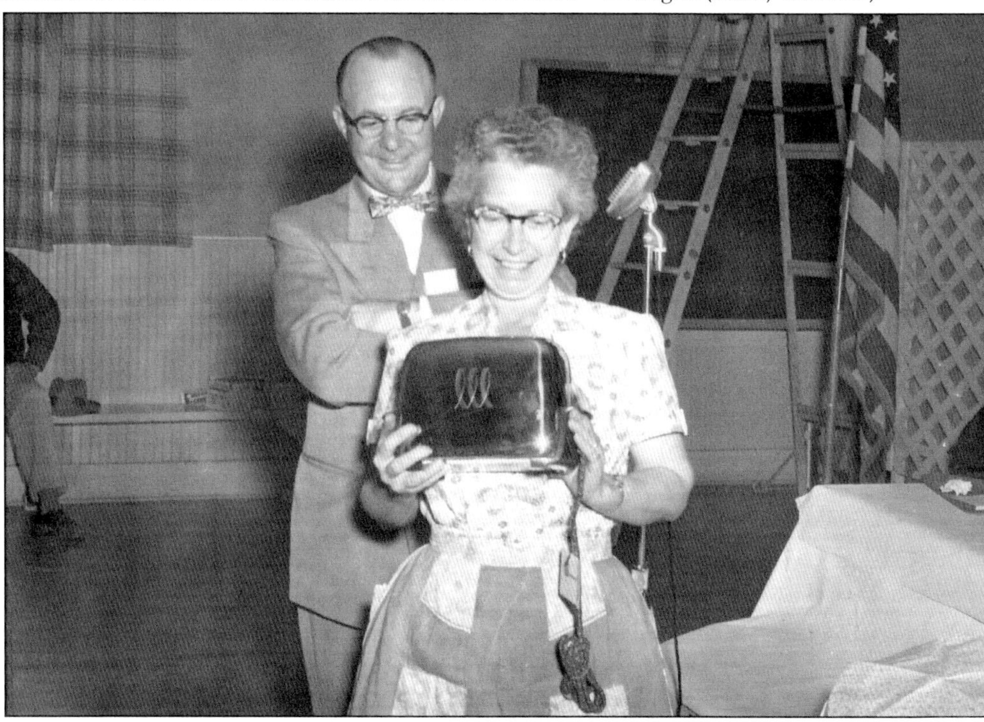

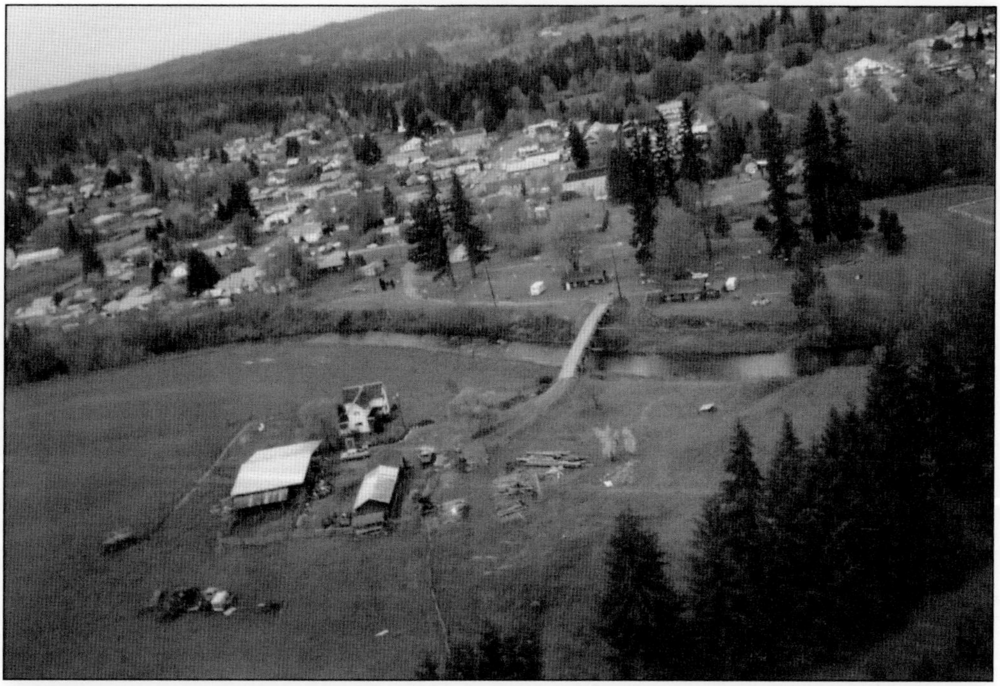

By 1968, when this aerial photograph of Vernonia was taken over the Sword homestead, the O-A mill had been closed for more than 10 years. Many of the once-thriving businesses had closed, leaving behind many empty storefronts. Fortunately, Vernonia had not been exclusively a company town, so many residents, including both the descendants of the early settlers and those who came to work at the mill, found new jobs locally or by commuting to the Portland area. (Sword.)

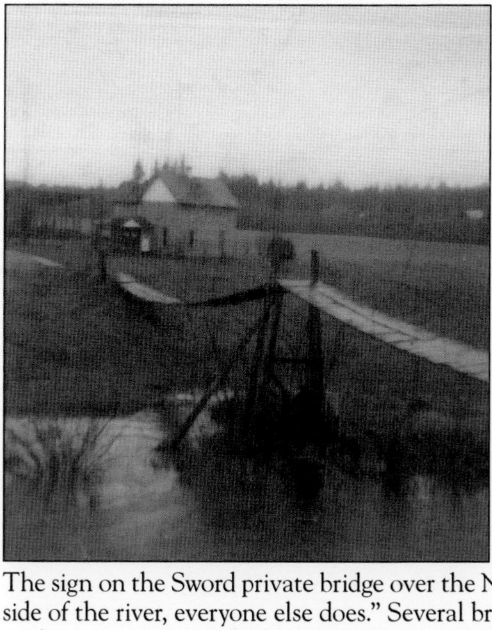

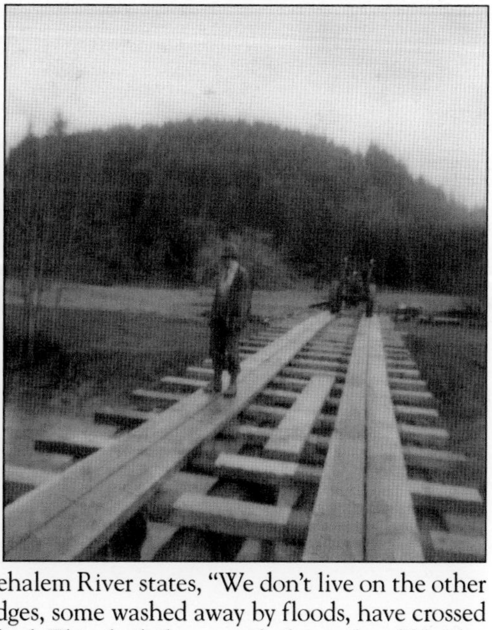

The sign on the Sword private bridge over the Nehalem River states, "We don't live on the other side of the river, everyone else does." Several bridges, some washed away by floods, have crossed to the property since the homestead was established. This dual photograph shows the old bridge leading toward the house and the bridge constructed in 1965, which has since been replaced. Bill Sword, then aged 34, stands on the new bridge. (Sword.)

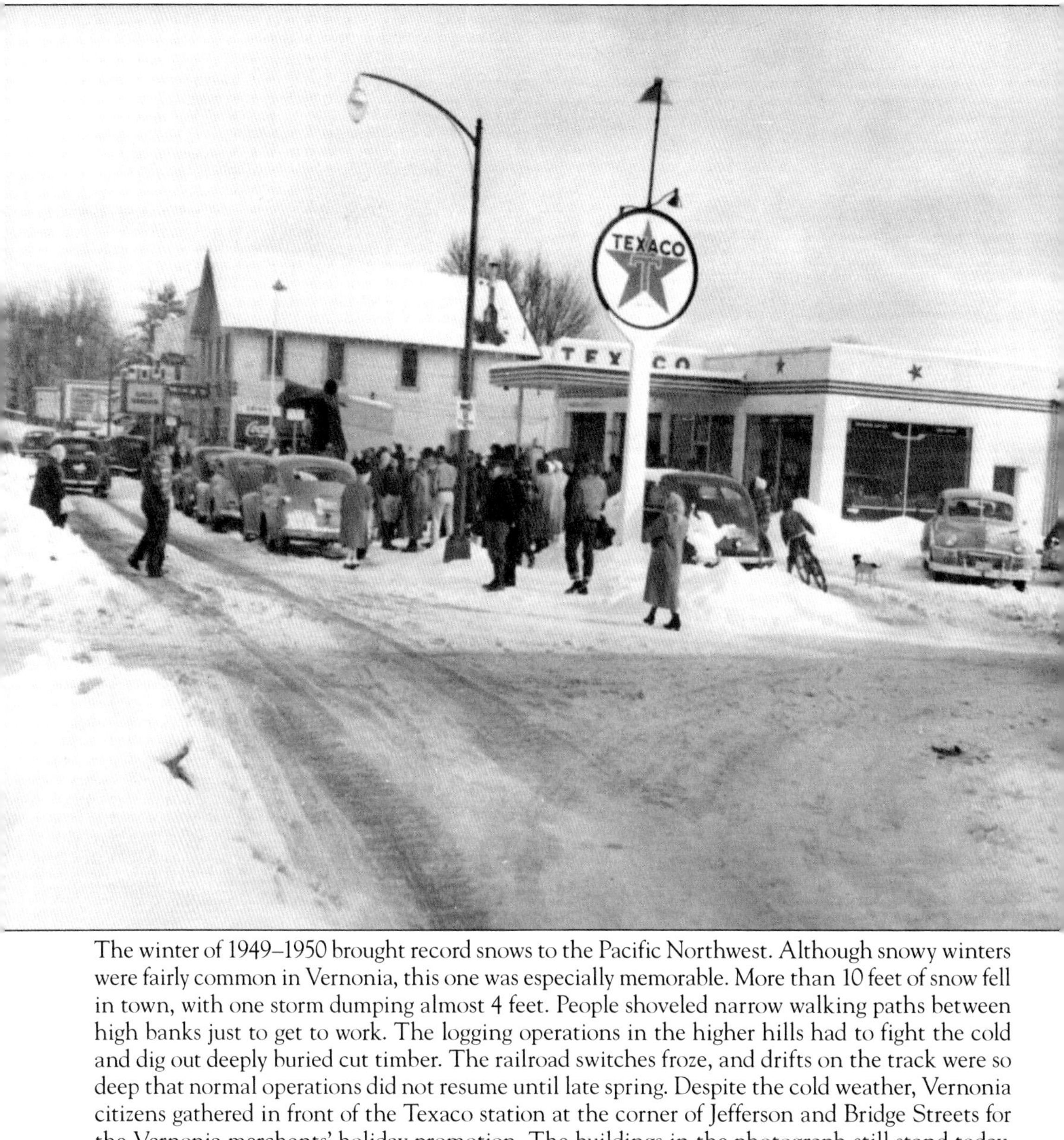

The winter of 1949–1950 brought record snows to the Pacific Northwest. Although snowy winters were fairly common in Vernonia, this one was especially memorable. More than 10 feet of snow fell in town, with one storm dumping almost 4 feet. People shoveled narrow walking paths between high banks just to get to work. The logging operations in the higher hills had to fight the cold and dig out deeply buried cut timber. The railroad switches froze, and drifts on the track were so deep that normal operations did not resume until late spring. Despite the cold weather, Vernonia citizens gathered in front of the Texaco station at the corner of Jefferson and Bridge Streets for the Vernonia merchants' holiday promotion. The buildings in the photograph still stand today, although the Joy Theater has been vacant for decades. (VPMA.)

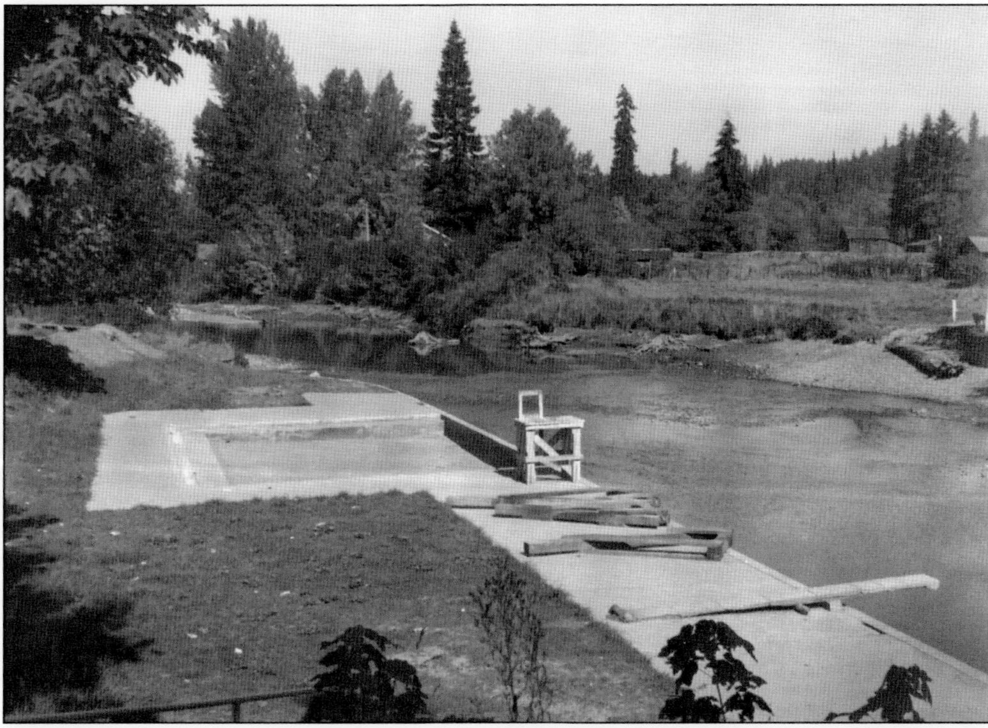

During the summer months, Rock Creek is blocked with a temporary wooden dam to create a swimming hole known as the Dewey Pool. It was named for Les Dewey, manager of Miller Mercantile, who championed the effort. The new pool was opened after the last day of school in 1938. A concrete wading pool for small children was filled from the nearby stream. Note the size of the creek and the lifeguard tower. Look at the photograph below to see this same location and the stranded lifeguard chair during the Flood of 1955. Waters from the floods of 1996 and 2007 rose much higher. (Both, Thomas.)

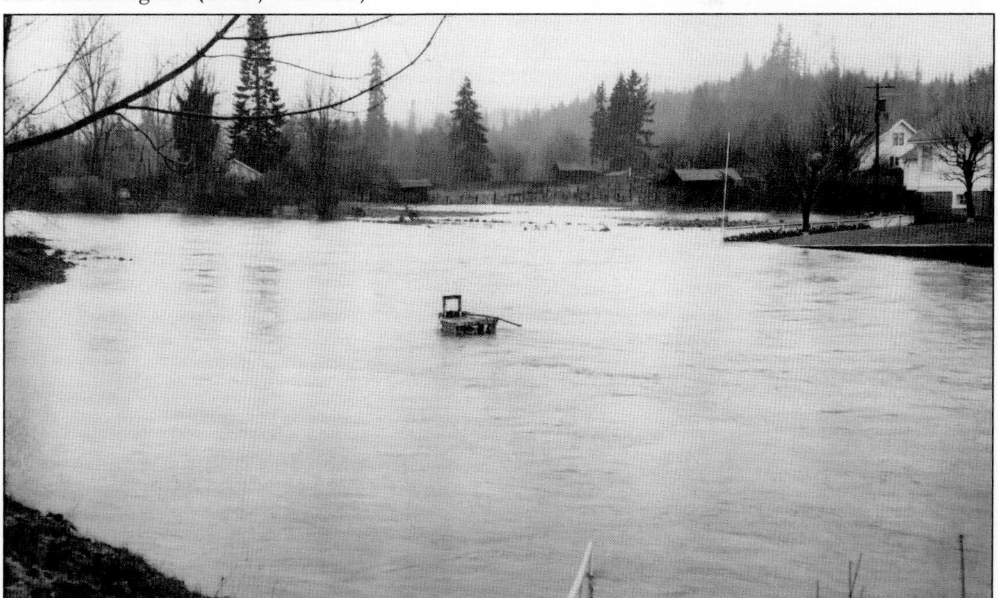

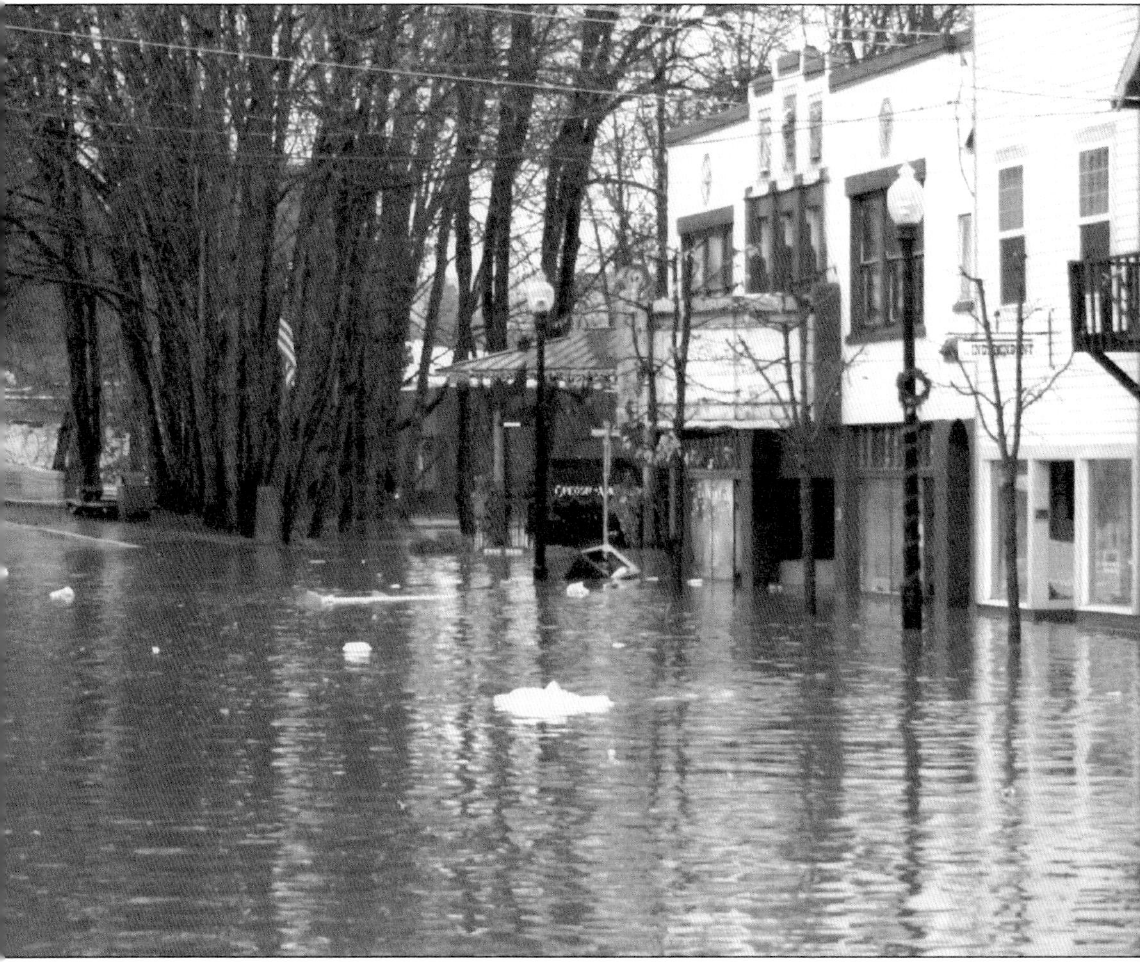

The Nehalem River crested on the night of Monday, December 3, 2007, at a height of 18.59 feet, 7 feet above flood stage. The prior Flood of 1996 was caused by heavy, warm rain on a deep snow pack that caused the river to rise somewhat more slowly. This time, a tropical storm of hurricane strength stalled over the Coast Range, dumping nearly 12 inches of rain on Sunday. The water rushed down the slopes and into all the tributaries of the Nehalem Riber, reaching Vernonia the following day. This photograph was taken on Bridge Street near the Rock Creek Bridge in the heart of town. The marquee of the long-abandoned Joy Theater and the *Independent* newspaper office are seen after the waters had receded a few feet. The old Oregon-American Locomotive No. 102 sat up to its cab in water at Shay Park. As of 2009, the town is still recovering, with many houses being raised onto 8-foot foundations, and other plans are in progress to move vital services and the schools to higher ground. (Courtesy of the *Independent*.)

Five

Recreation and Celebrations

Hunting, fishing, picnicking, and school sporting events have been perennial favorite pastimes in Vernonia. In the early days, hunting and fishing provided a substantial portion of the protein in the local diet. Elk, deer, bear, game birds, salmon, and steelhead were welcome additions to the table. Crawdad feeds and community picnics by the river provided family outings. The Dewey Pool dam creates a swimming pool from the end of the school year through Labor Day. It is then removed to allow the annual return of salmon to their Rock Creek spawning grounds.

Holidays were celebrated in grand style, as were events of local significance, such as the arrival of the first passenger train to Vernonia in 1922 and the placement of the cornerstone for the new Evangelical church in 1924. The Memorial Day service and the Fourth of July parade and fireworks are enduring celebrations.

After the mill closed, people leaving Vernonia looked for a way to stay in touch with their friends and former coworkers. The Vernonia Friendship Jamboree was established in 1957 to meet this need. Now, every summer, on the first full weekend in August, the town hosts a weekend festival that includes a parade, a loggers competition, horse gaming, arts-and-crafts sales, a car show, and other activities. Newer events include the St. Mary's Quilt Fair in September and the Salmon Festival in October, which celebrates the return of spawning salmon to the Nehalem River and Rock Creek.

In 1959, the planned burning of the former O-A planing mill became the focal point of the movie *Ring of Fire*, starring David Janssen. Almost 60 Vernonians were hired as extras for the crowd scenes, and the West Oregon Electric Cooperative's headquarters became the sheriff's office. A number of movies, none of which has achieved wide distribution, have been filmed in the area. In 2008, the film *Twilight* turned Vernonia into Forks, Washington, and, as in 1959, Vernonians were employed as extras.

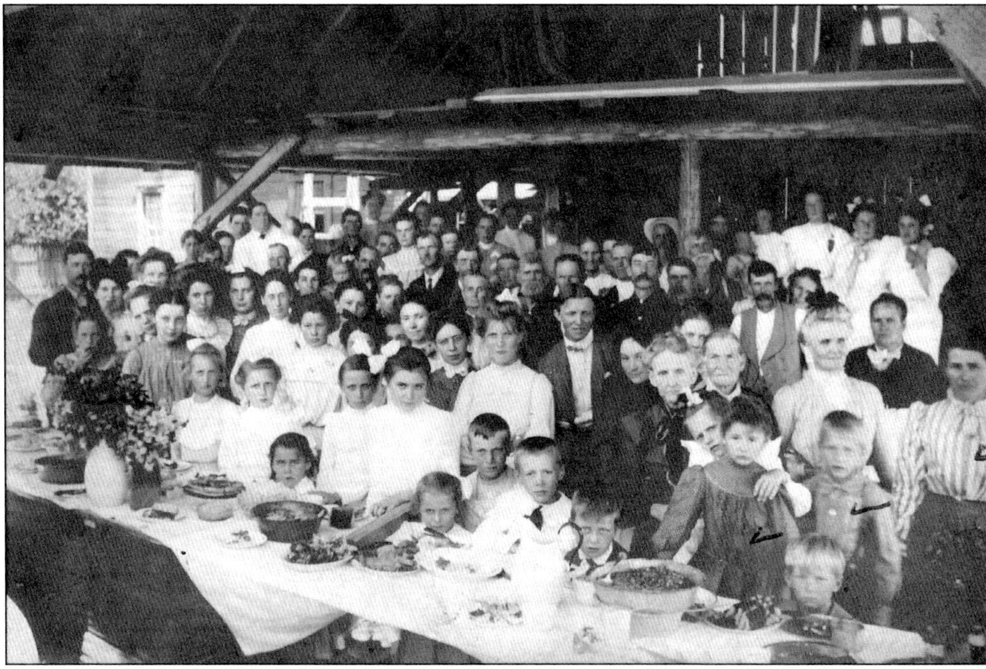

Community picnics and potluck suppers were a popular way to bring townspeople together to celebrate holidays and special events. This photograph of Vernonia's annual Fourth of July picnic was taken in 1907 in Schmidlin's barn. Minnie Sword is standing in the striped shirtwaist in the extreme lower right corner of the picture. Her son, Bob, and daughter, Chris, stand nearby. (Sword.)

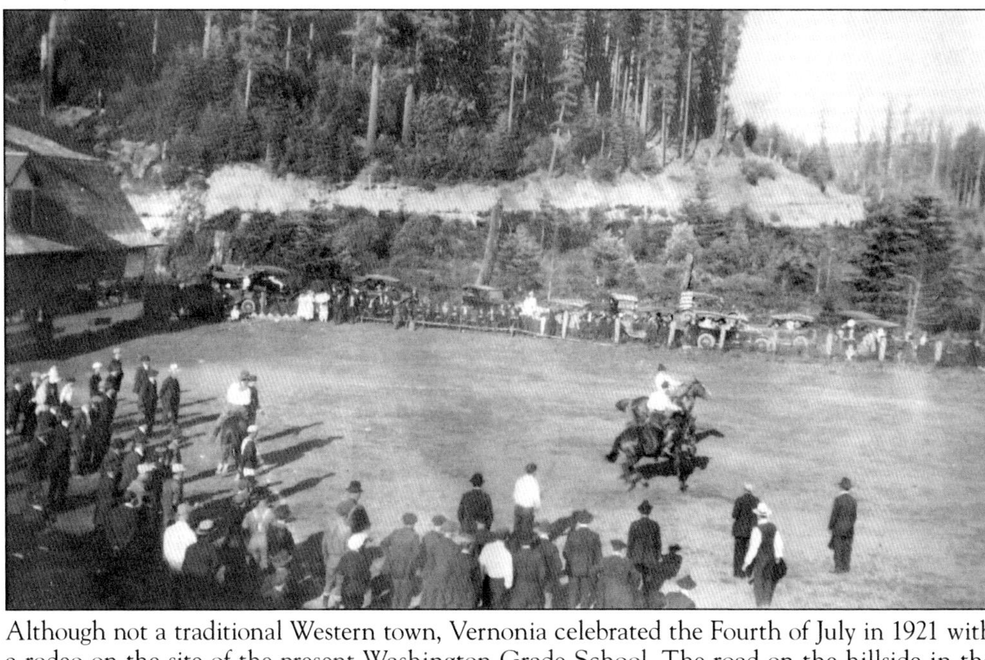

Although not a traditional Western town, Vernonia celebrated the Fourth of July in 1921 with a rodeo on the site of the present Washington Grade School. The road on the hillside in the background was the main route between Vernonia and Pittsburg, and this hill on Israel Spencer's homestead would soon be known as O-A Hill. (Keasey.)

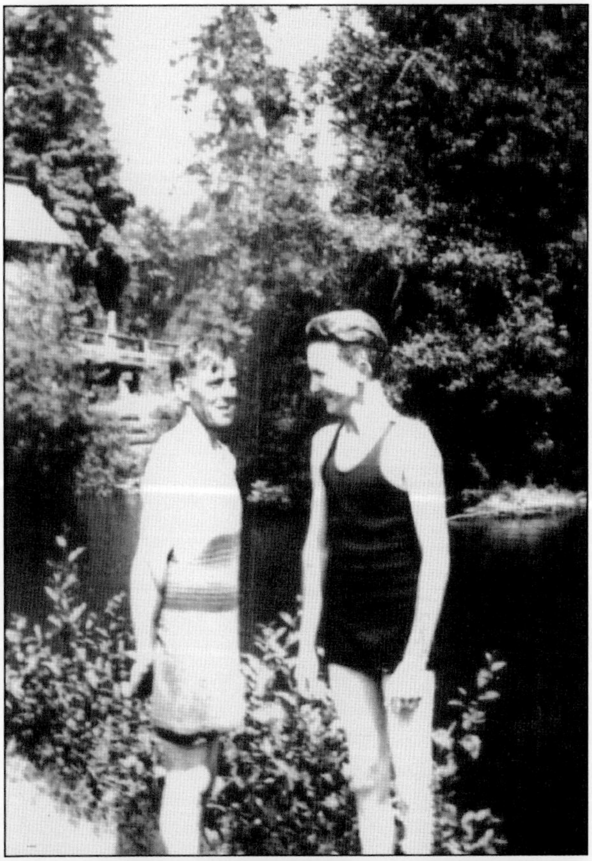

Although the Nehalem River and Rock Creek are less than knee-deep in most places in the summertime, there are a few natural swimming holes that provide places to cool off. Vester Christensen (left) and an unidentified friend are seen getting ready to enjoy a summer day's dip in the Nehalem River in the photograph at right. The quiet summer ripples of Rock Creek can be seen in the photograph below. Hilda Keasey (center) and her friends appear to be ready to enjoy a string of frankfurters in this mid-1920s scene on the Keasey homestead. (Right, Queen; below, Keasey.)

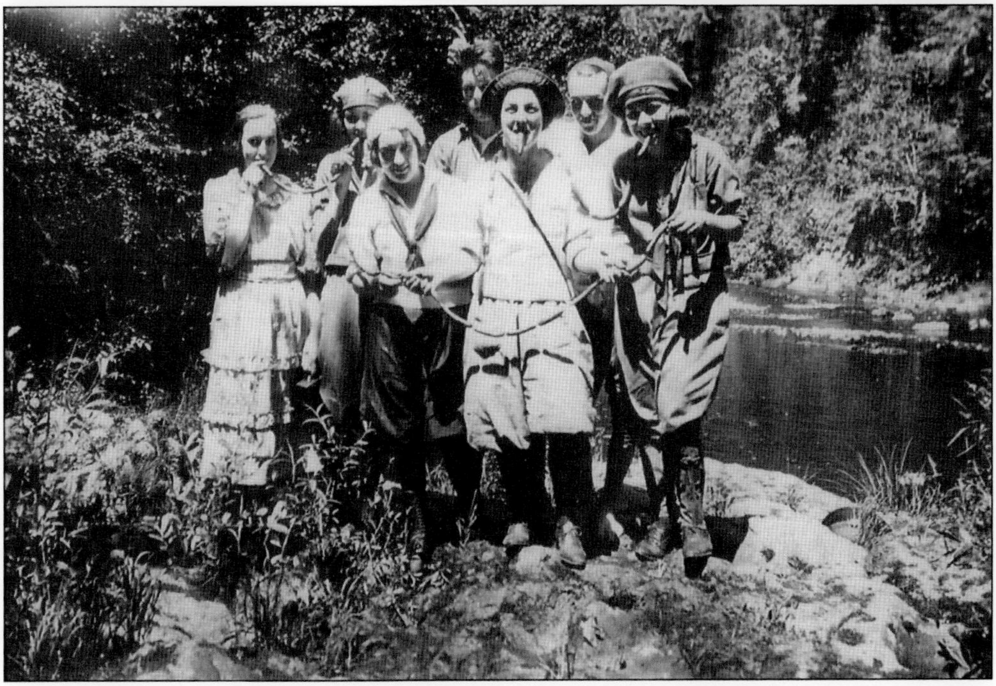

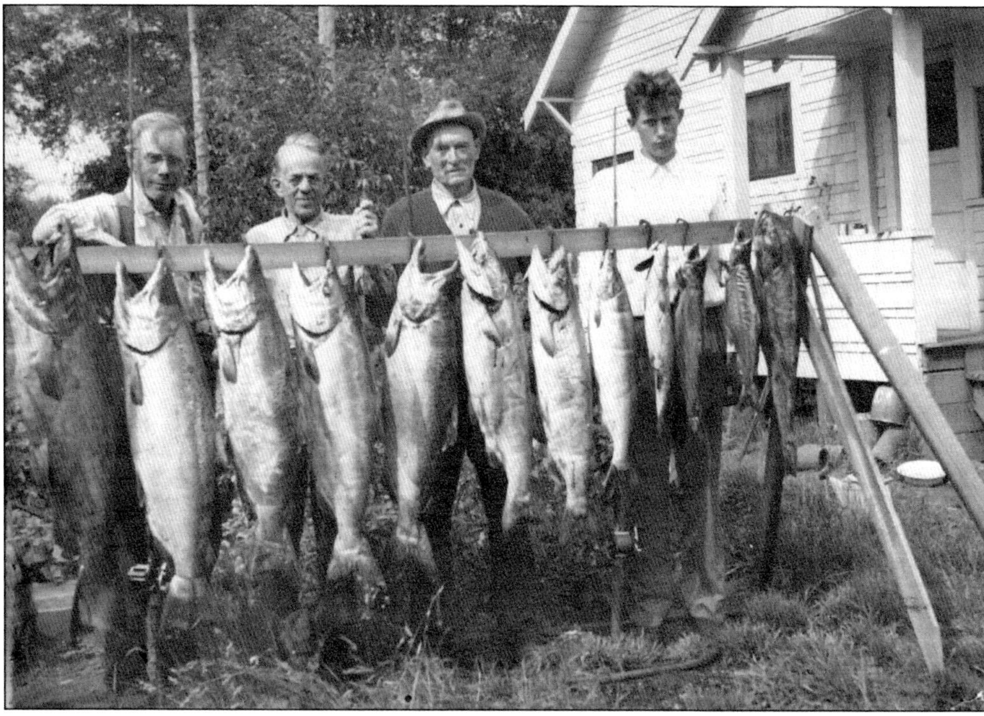

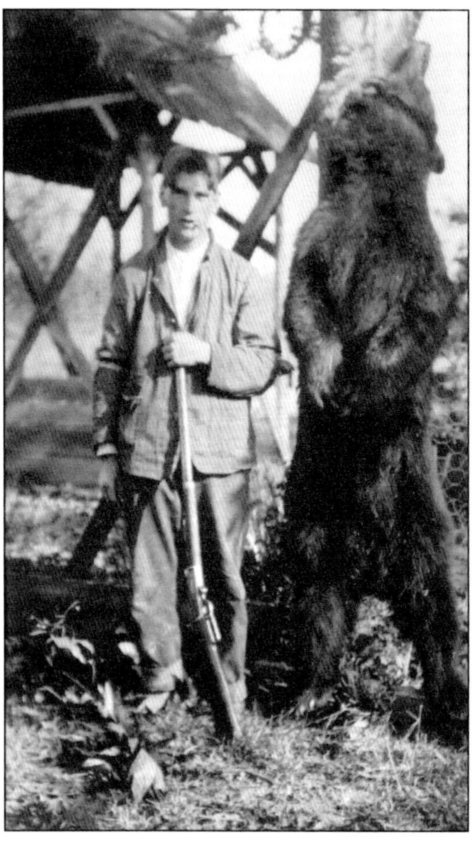

Fishing was both a sport and a means of subsistence for the early settlers. The abundant salmon in the Nehalem River's tributaries provided an important source of food. Newt Parker stands third from the left with the bounty of caught fish along with two unidentified men. Newt's son, Walter, is on the far right. (Gwin.)

In the early 1910s, Walter Parker posed with the bear he shot on Rock Creek. The bear had killed his dog. Bear and human encounters, sometimes fatal, were regular occurrences as the forestlands were turned into homesteads. Bear hunting as a sport and for subsistence has been done in the forestlands around Rock Creek since the early days. (Gwin.)

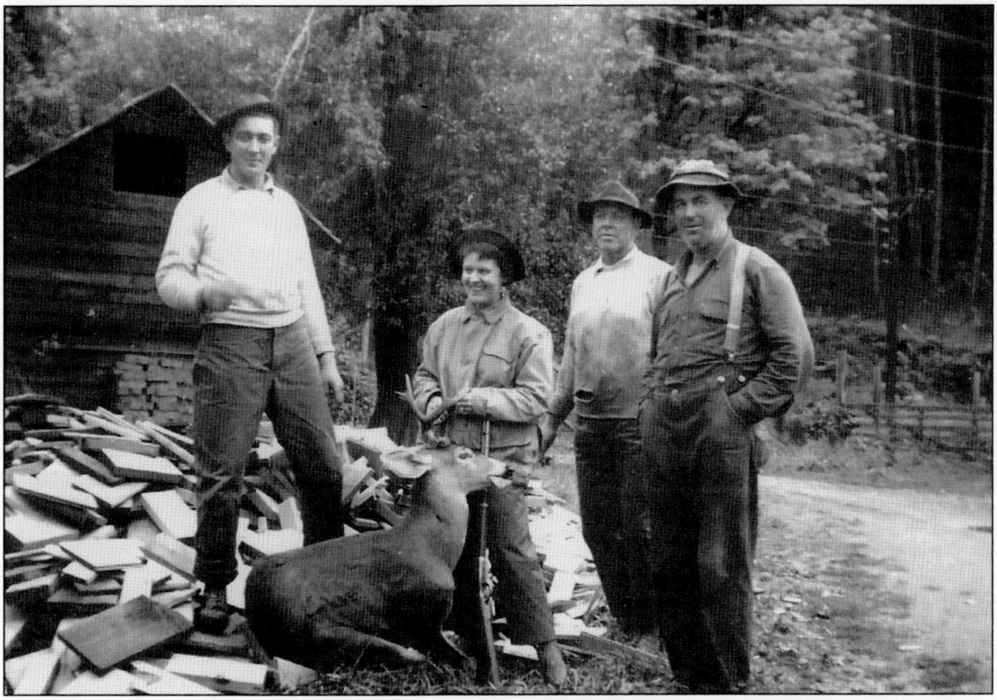

There is a long-standing tradition of deer and elk hunting in Vernonia that continues to the present day. Venison was an important part of the pioneer diet, but it continues to be an autumn ritual in many families. From left to right, Ernie and Velva Christensen, Vester Christensen, and Willie Anderson stand by a four-point buck on the Christensen property. (Queen.)

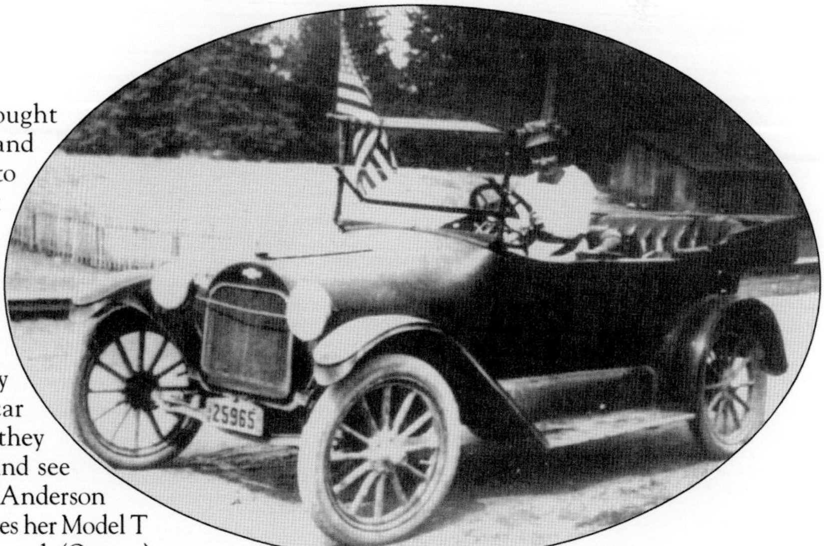

The 1920s brought silent movies and telephone lines to Vernonia, but cars were still a novelty. People watched every passing car and then telephoned ahead to notify others that a car was coming so they could run out and see it go by. Helen Anderson Christensen drives her Model T on the unpaved road. (Queen.)

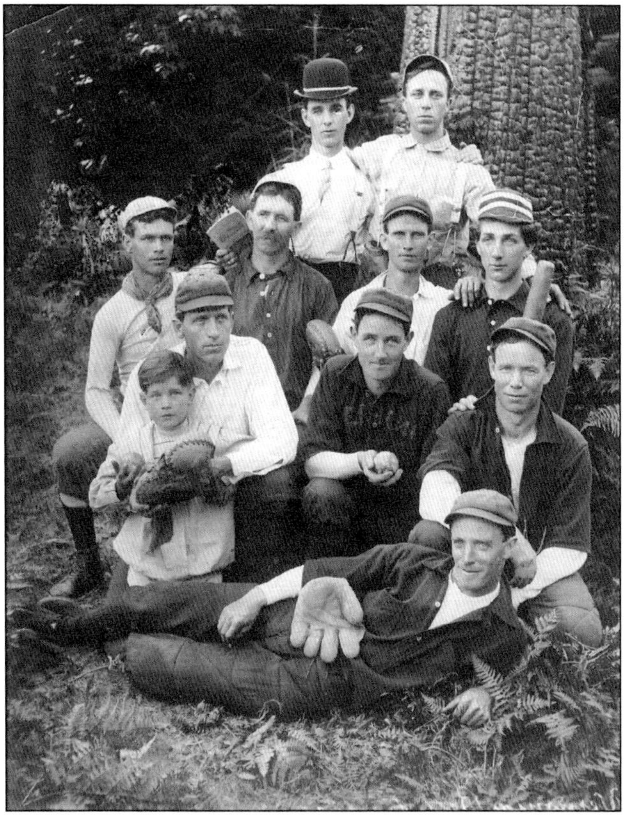

Organized sports have been a popular pastime in Vernonia since the early 1900s. In this c. 1910 photograph, the Vernonia baseball team poses after a game. Pictured from left to right are (first row) Clive "Tex" Mills; (second row) Dow Keasey holding his son Harry; Ed Sessman, pitcher; and Guy Mills. Among the other players pictured are Jim Emmons and Bob Lindsay. In the picture below, a game from this same time period is in progress at an unidentified location in Vernonia. This may have been what is now Spencer Park, a sports field on land donated by Israel Spencer in 1923. (Both, Keasey.)

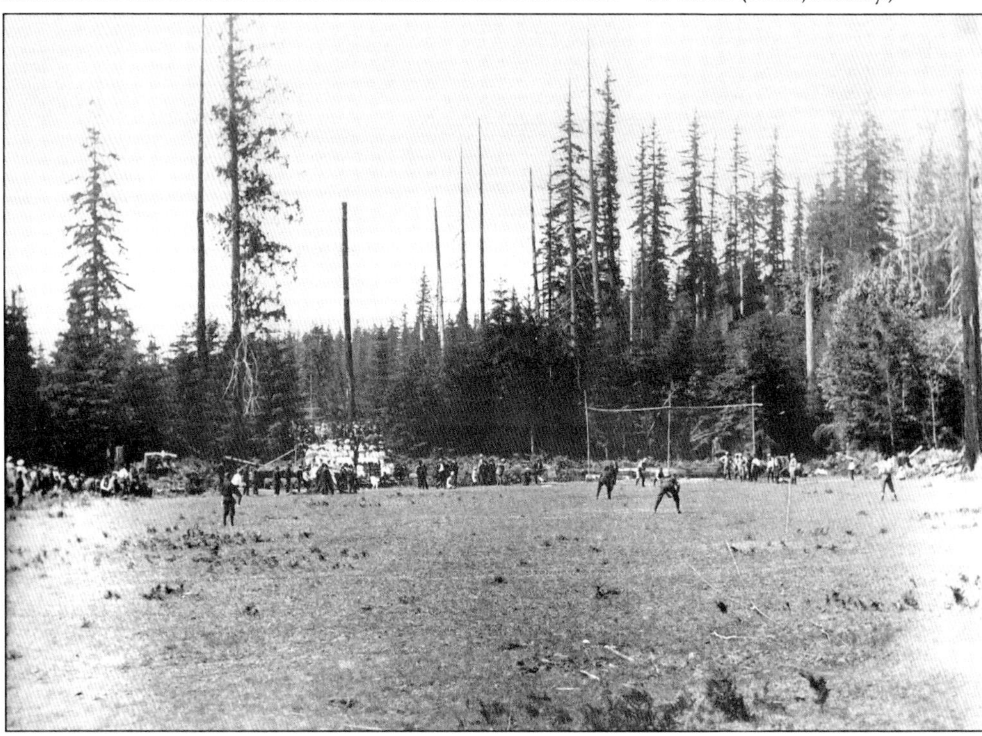

The Pleasant Hill School was located on Timber Route southwest of Vernonia. In 1915, the basketball team members were, from left to right, (first row) Glenn Sheeley; (second row) Jess Armstrong and Ben Smith; (third row) Russell Stanton, Vester Chistensen, and Omar Sheeley. The Sheeleys were cousins to the Christensens on the VanBlaricom side. (Queen.)

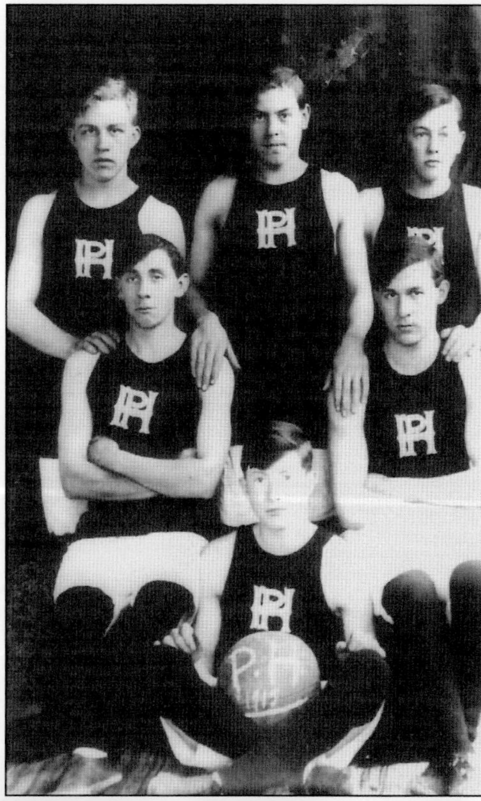

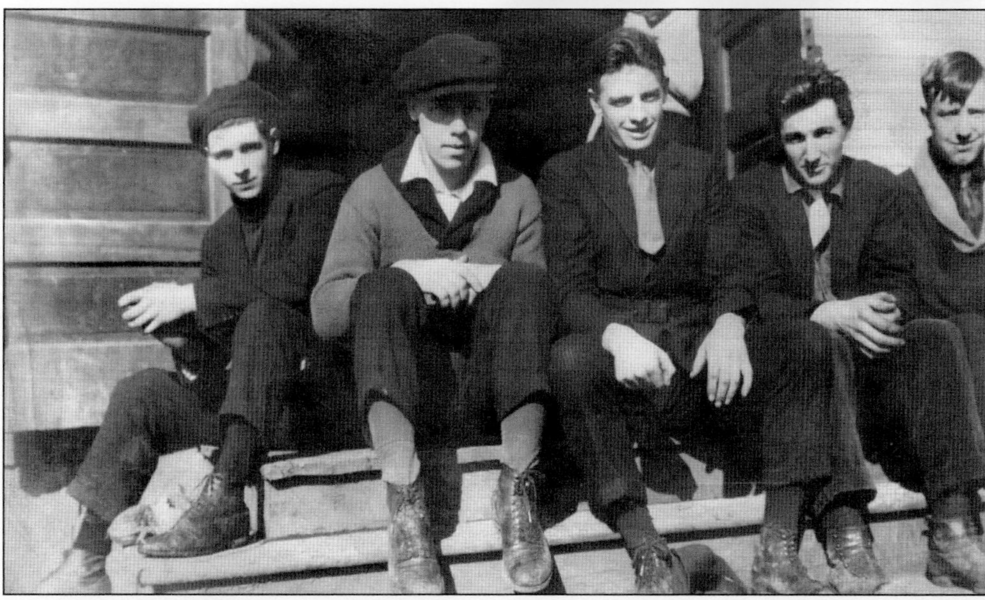

The first Vernonia High School (VHS) basketball team for boys was organized in 1920–1921, the same year that VHS first entered in the State Athletic Association. From left to right are Harry Keasey, Gale Stanton, Earl Condit, Alvin Parker, and Eddy Condit. The prior year, VHS had its first debate team, which consisted of Lola Brown and Hazel Malmsten. They were victorious in competition that year and the next. (Keasey.)

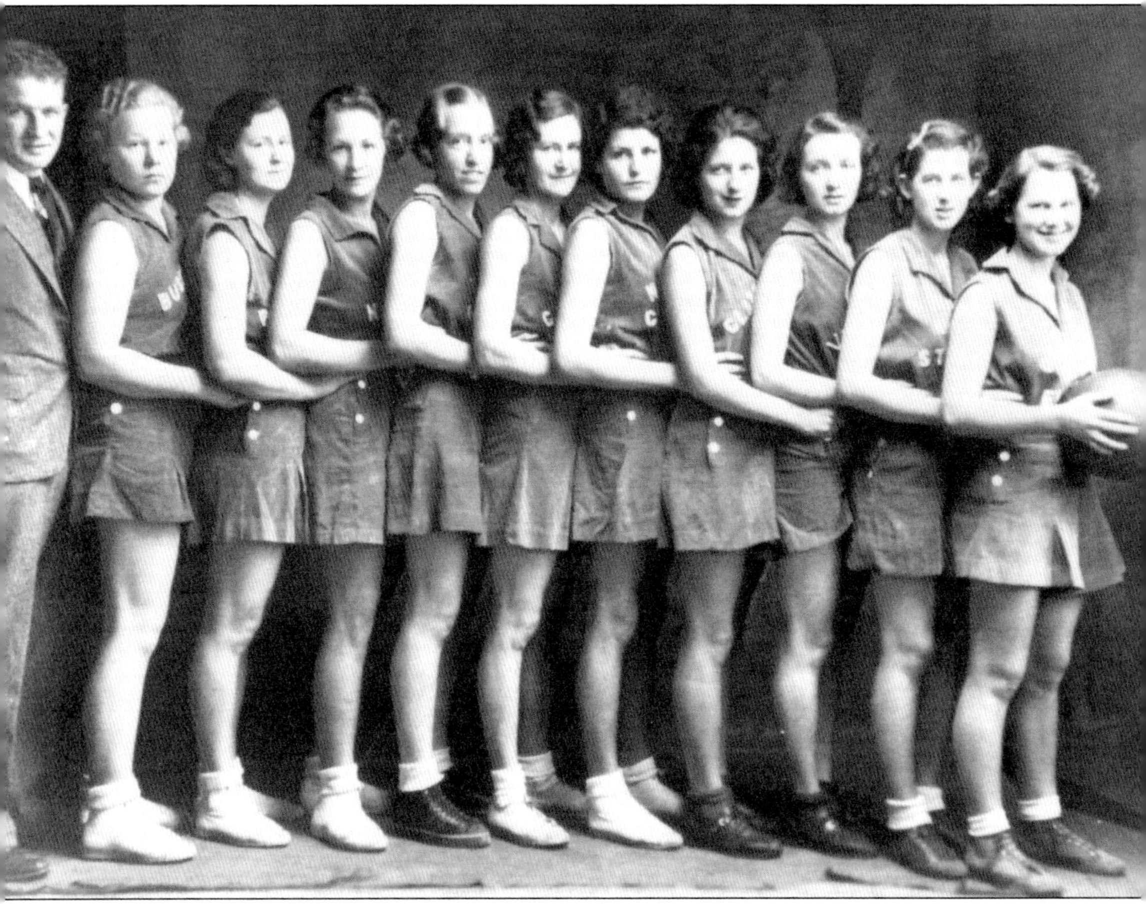

High school girls also played basketball. The girls' team was first organized in 1923–1924 and was the Columbia County champion that year. In the late 1930s, the Blue Jays competed against a championship team from Ogden, Utah, but lost 35–23. Pictured from left to right are coach Paul Gordon, Billie Bergerson, Theresa Goertzen, Mildred Brady, Mildred Hawkins, Doris Vasnick, Josie Hall, Bertha Thompson, Erma Thompson, Neva Christenson, and Montana French. (VPMA)

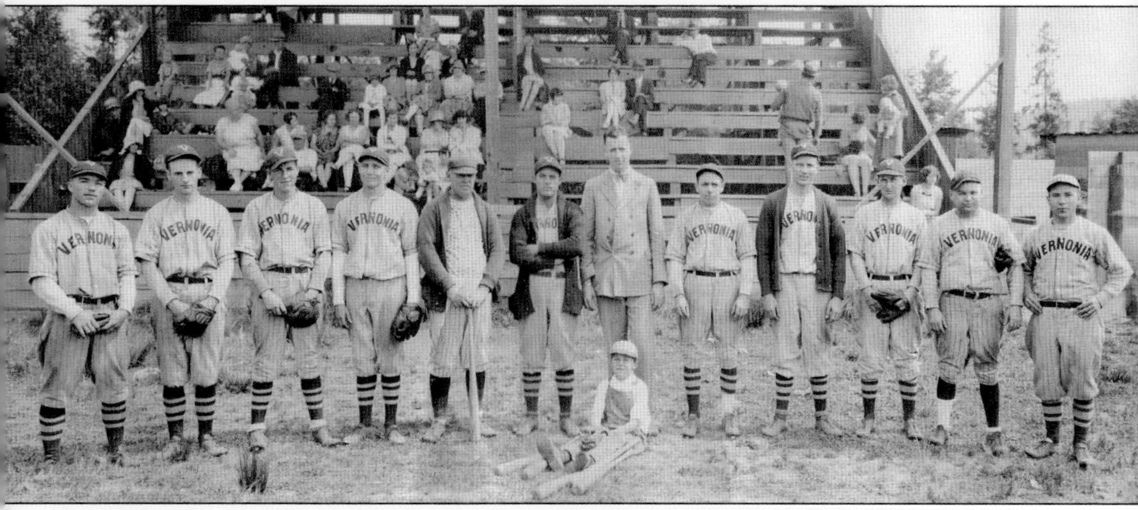

Like many other big companies, Oregon-American (O-A) had its own baseball team. The O-A team members, complete with batboy, pose in their uniforms in the mid-1920s. Having a winning team was so important that it was said, "If you could play ball, you had a job at Oregon-American." Charlie Richardson (wearing the double-breasted suit) was the manager of the team. He worked in the O-A office from 1923 to 1929. Walter Linn and his twin brother stand at opposite ends of the team. Judd Greenman himself—president and general manager of O-A from 1925 to 1955—had been recruited to work at a Colorado lumber company because of his reputation as a pitcher at Kansas City High School. He never lost his interest in sports as he rose to become a nationally recognized leader in the lumber industry. Vernonia High's Greenman Field was named in his honor. Judd Greenman left the company in 1955. He died August 28, 1957, the day after the last log on O-A land was cut. (VPMA.)

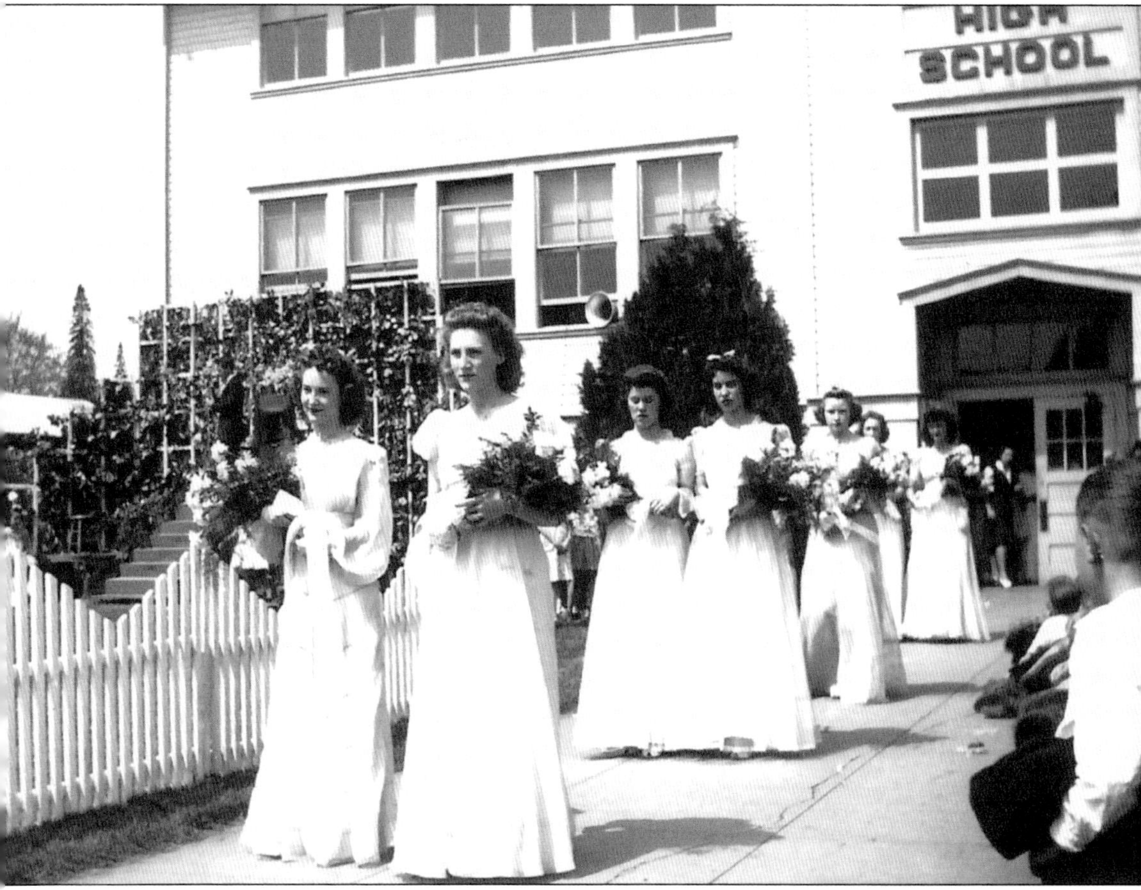

The May Day Festival was the high point of the spring at Vernonia High School through the mid-1950s. High school girls competed to become a May Princess or May Queen. Young women practiced the intricate maneuvers of the May Pole Dance, which was performed on the school lawn. In this 1942 photograph, twins Lesta Christensen (left) and Vesta Christensen appear in the second row of the traditional May Procession. (Queen.)

The tributary streams and the Nehalem River itself are home to crayfish, better known in the West as crawdads. Crawdad feeds are still a popular summer treat, although the crustaceans are not as abundant as in the past. Gathered by the boiling pot on the Christensen family's Timber Route property in 1967 are (from left to right) Jodi Robertson, Cheryl and Randy Peppard, and Vesta Christensen King. Pictured below is a group of Sunday picnickers in September 1952 near the town of Keasey line up at the outhouse they affectionately dubbed the "Kum Squat Inn." (Right, Queen; below, VPMA.)

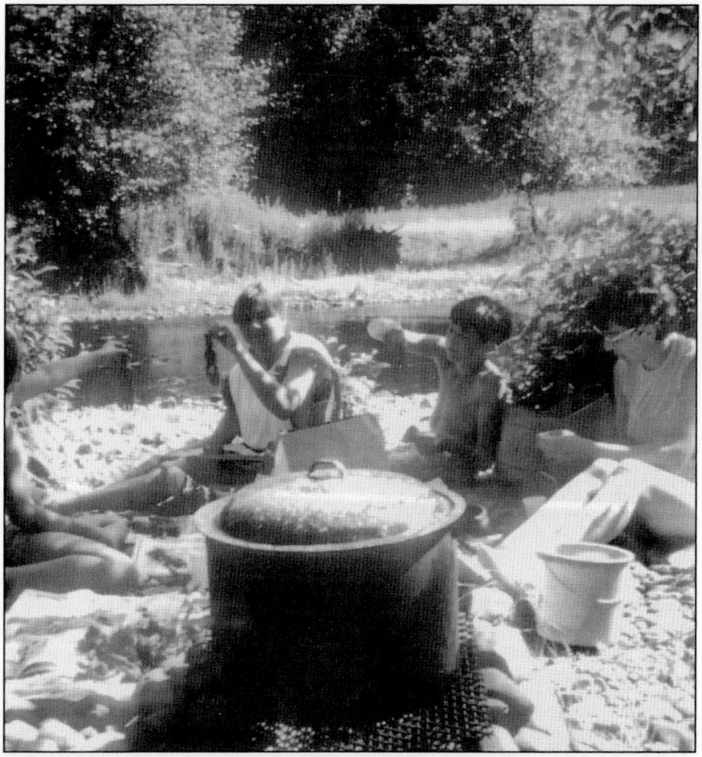

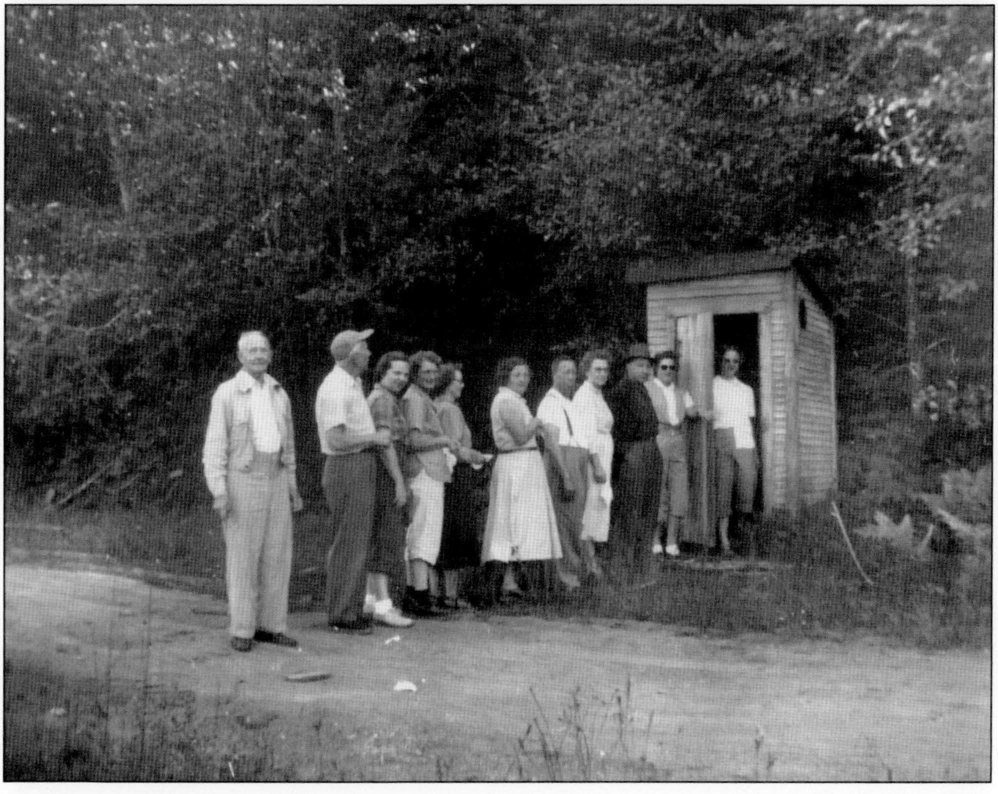

Vernonia Centennial Friendship Jamboree

JULY 17

9:00 P.M. Queen's Cornation Ball. Don Hite's Orchestra. Legion hall.

JULY 18

8:00 A.M. "Million Dollar Golf Tournament. Vernonia Golf Club.

9:00 A.M. Pacific Northwest Horseshoe Tournament, qualifying. City Park.

10:00 A.M. Parade judging starts. Railroad Station.

10:30 A.M. Beard Judging contest. Front of City Hall.

11:00 A.M. Parade.

12:00 Noon, Water Fight ---- Banks Fire Dept. vs. Vernonia Fire Dept.

1:30 P.M. Award prizes --- Parade and and Beard Judging Contest. City Park.

1:30 P.M. Pacific Northwest Horseshoe finals. City Park.

1:40 P.M. Logging Events. City Park.
Falling — Bucking — Log Chopping — Birling — Truck Backing — Ax Throwing — Pole Walking — Shake Splitting & Packing — Tractor Driving — Splicing

2:00-4:00 P.M. High School Alumni Reunion. Legion Hall.

7:30 P.M. Horse Show. City Park.

8:00 P.M. Columbia Co. Horseshoe finals. (Col. Co. Residents) City Park.

9:00 P.M. Street Square Dance.

JULY 19

7:00-11:00 A.M. Cowboy Breakfast. City Park.

8:00 A.M. "Million Dollar Golf Tournament." Vernonia Golf Club.

9:00 A.M. to 1:00 P.M. Trail ride, leaving from City Park.

10:00 A.M. to 3 P.M. Rockhound Tours.

2:00 P.M. Junior Legion ball -- Vernonia vs. Tillamook. High School field. Double Header.

Cedarwood Shingle Mill Open House
July 16 and 17 from 11:00 A.M. to 2:00 P.M.
July 18 from 12:00 noon to 1:00 P.M.

Caylite Candle Company Open House
July 18 from 10:00 A.M. to 1:00 P.M.

Browning Brothers Carnival
JULY 15 - 16 - 17 - 18

Country Store Open July 17, 18 and 19.

Window Displays

CENTENNIAL SPECIALS AT VERNONIA'S LEADING MERCHANTS

FLY-IN GOLFERS — FREE TRANSPORTATION TO GOLFERS

February 14, 1959, was Oregon's 100th birthday, and celebrations throughout the year took place across the state. Vernonia's Friendship Jamboree theme that year focused on the Oregon centennial. Men grew beards and wore Western-style bolo ties, and women and children dressed in pioneer attire. The 1959 jamboree featured a beard-growing contest. The 2009 jamboree held a similar contest in recognition of the Oregon sesquicentennial, the state's 150th birthday. (VPMA.)

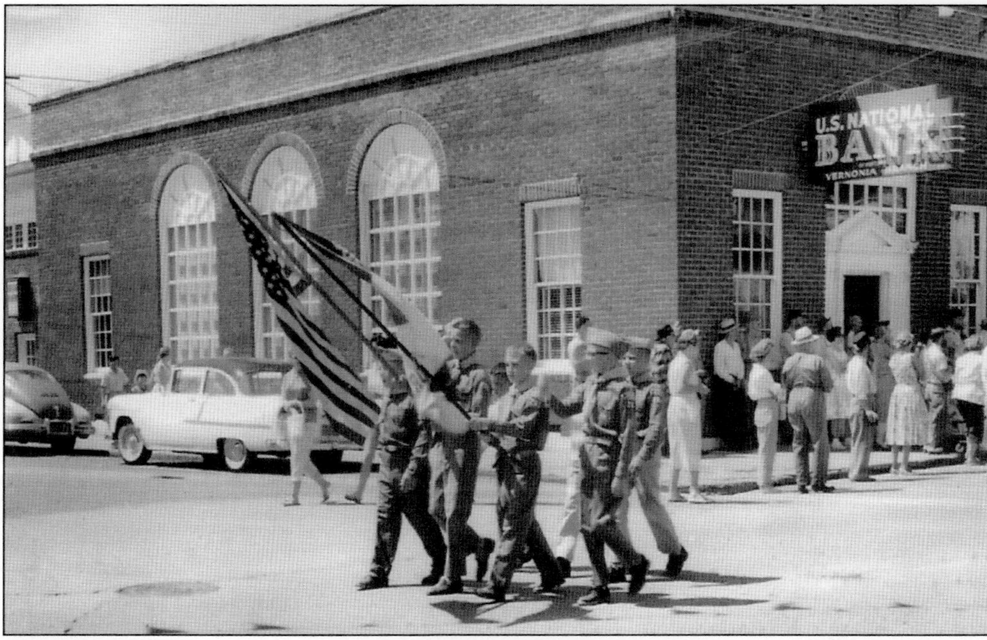

The Vernonia Friendship Jamboree and Logging Show Parade begins each year with an honor guard bearing the U.S. flag. In 1959, the Cub Scouts with Gary Robertson on the right (wearing glasses) lead the parade. The U.S. Bank office in the background was originally built in 1924 for the Bank of Vernonia, which failed during the Depression. In later years, it was the Commercial Bank before its 1954 acquisition by U.S. Bank of Oregon. (Queen.)

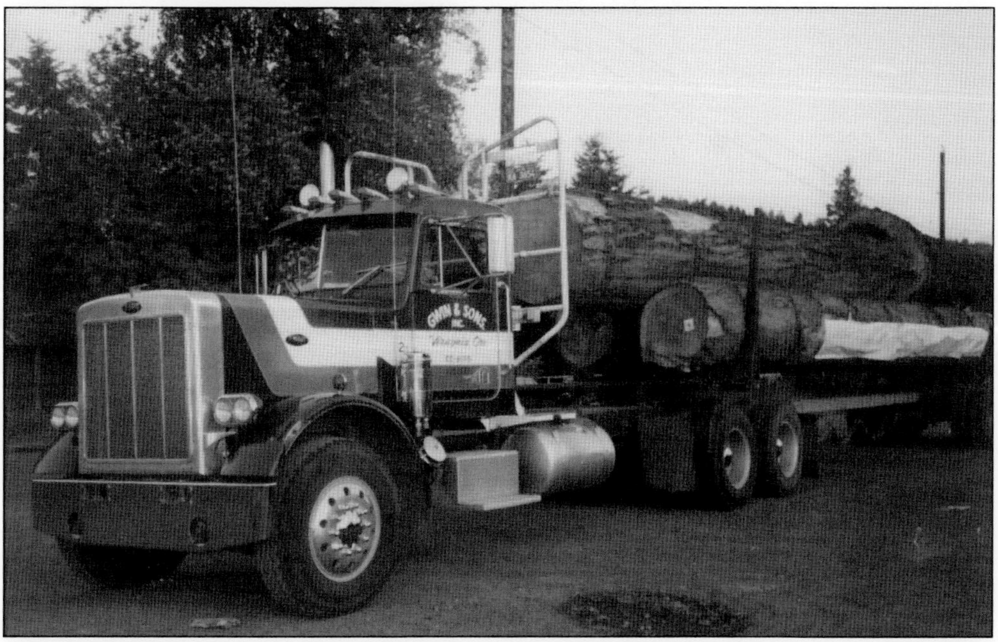

Each year, the Vernonia Friendship Jamboree and Logging Show Parade has a variety of entries from local businesses and community groups. Vernonia logging companies are always a popular feature. Gwin and Sons Logging participated in the 1984 parade with this truck and its full load of logs. (Gwin.)

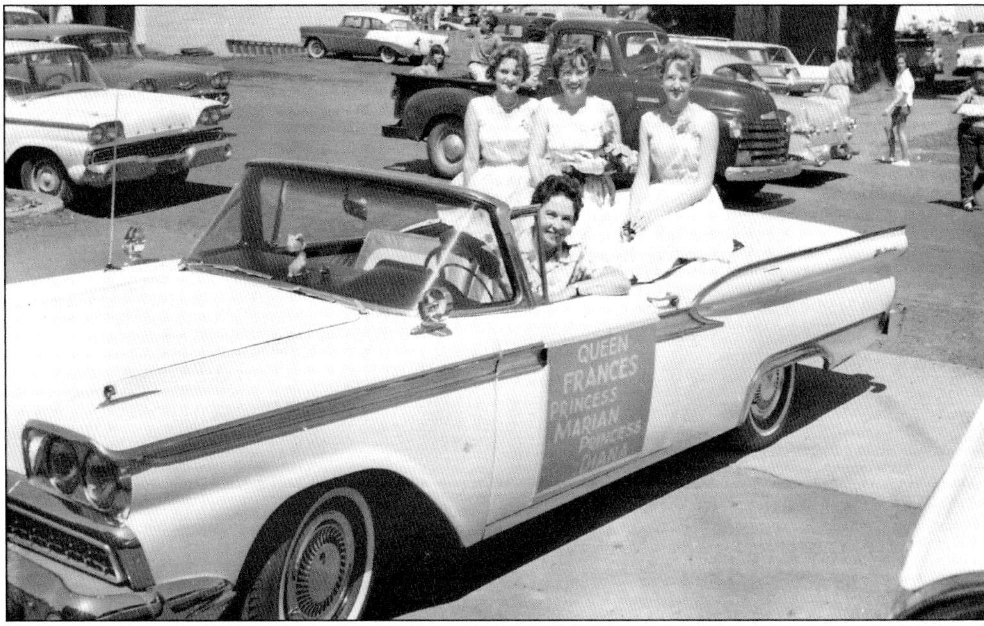

Mrs. Guy (Nell) Thomas was the chaperone and driver for the jamboree queen and princesses in the early 1960s. Ready for the jamboree parade, the court is seated on top of the convertible's back seat; from left to right are Princess Marian Matthews, Queen Fran Dinger, and Princess Diana Minger. (Thomas.)

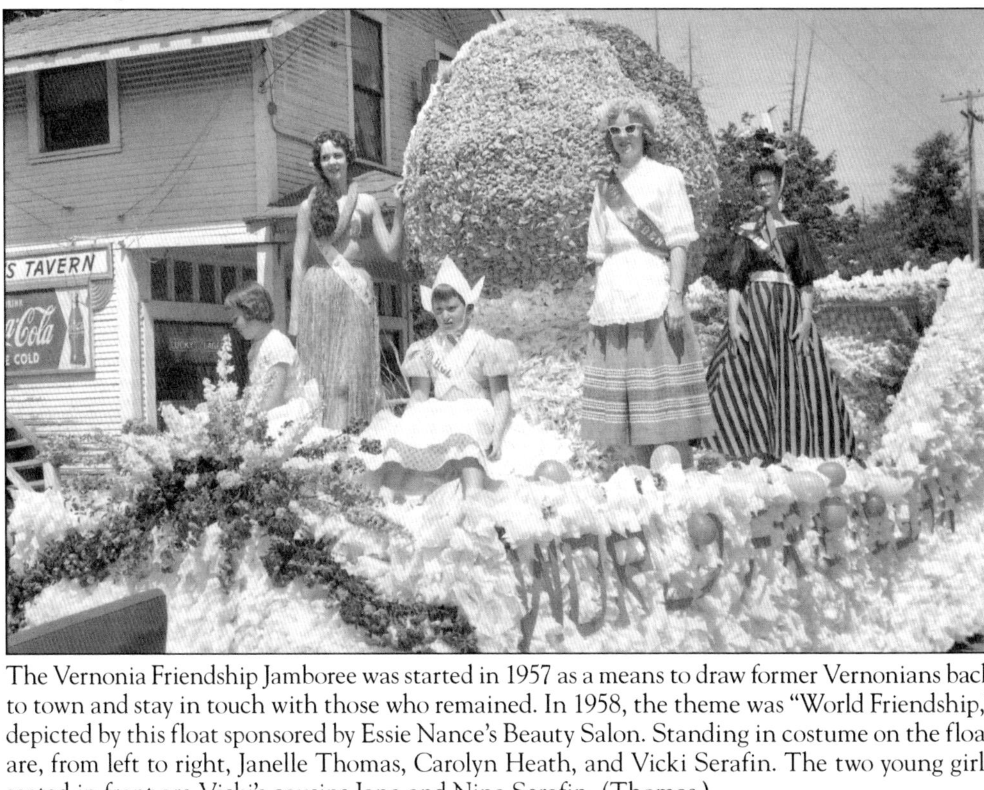

The Vernonia Friendship Jamboree was started in 1957 as a means to draw former Vernonians back to town and stay in touch with those who remained. In 1958, the theme was "World Friendship," depicted by this float sponsored by Essie Nance's Beauty Salon. Standing in costume on the float are, from left to right, Janelle Thomas, Carolyn Heath, and Vicki Serafin. The two young girls seated in front are Vicki's cousins Jana and Nina Serafin. (Thomas.)

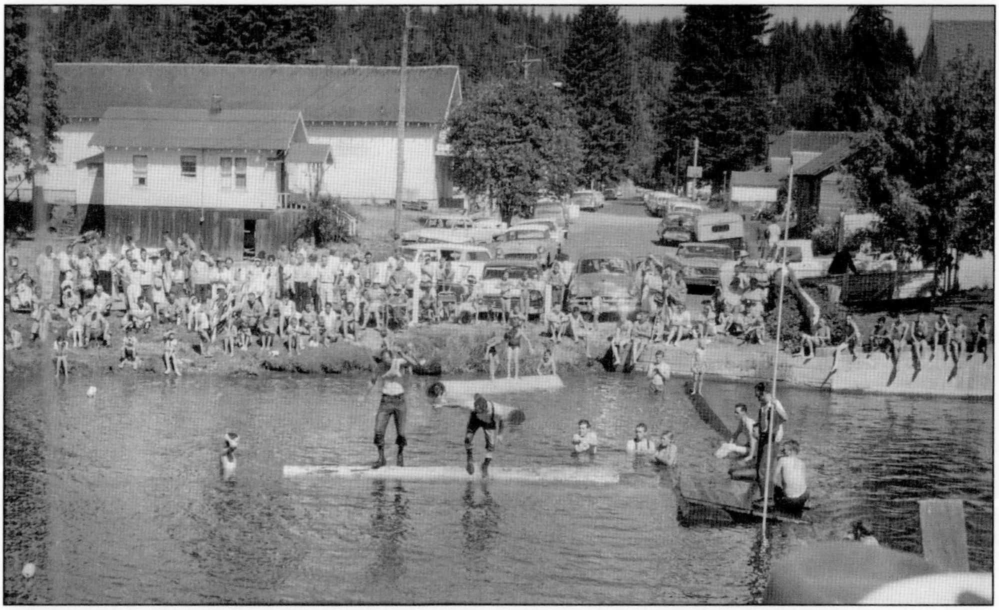

The Vernonia Friendship Jamboree includes a loggers's competition as part of its annual program. In one of the mid-1950s logging shows, Bill Pond and Gene Weller compete in log burling in Rock Creek. The photograph was taken from Hawkins Park, the site of the show. The object of the burling contest is to see which logger, wearing his calk boots, can roll the log but stay on the longest. Below, Bud Gibson saws down one of the upright logs that are brought in each year to the park to use for the falling contest. The object of the latter is to drop the cut log onto a stake and drive it into the ground. The most accurately hit stake determines the winner. Other contests include bucking (sawing), ax tossing, and choker setting. (Both, VPMA.)

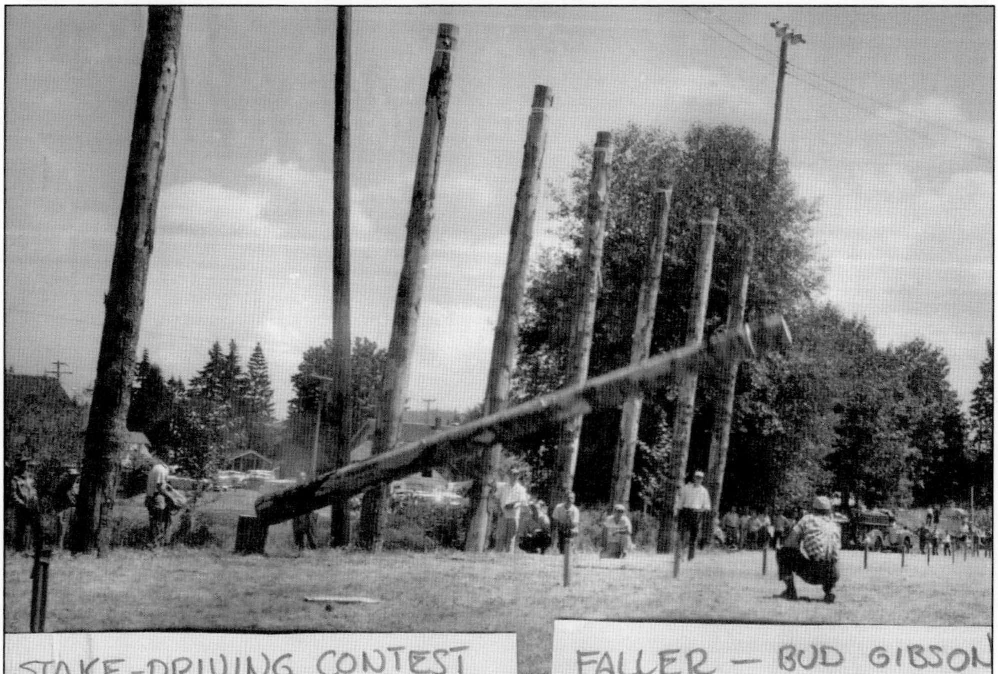

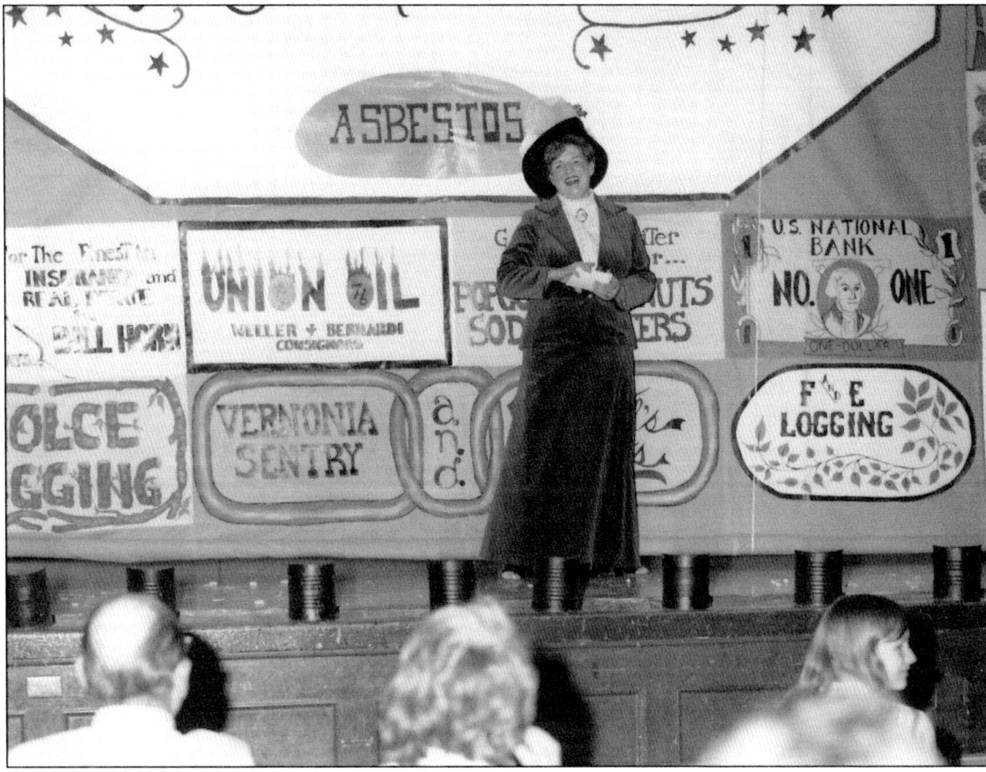

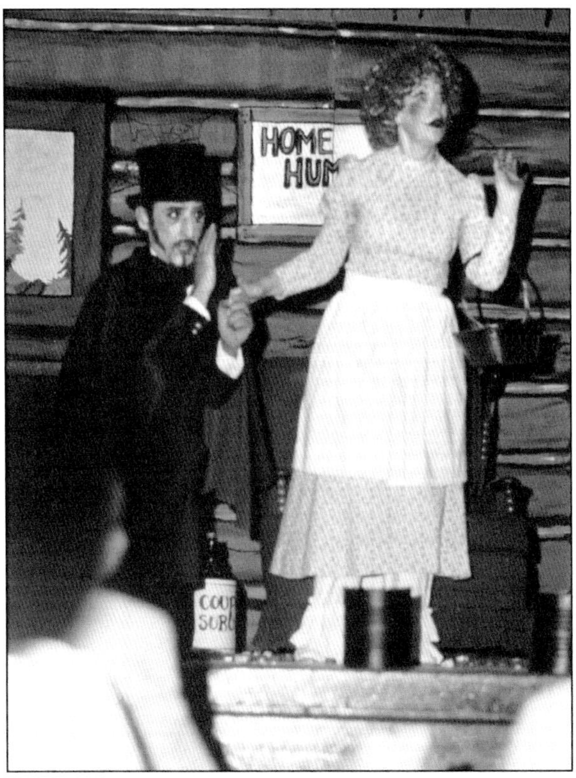

The Pauper's Playhouse melodrama was an annual event in the 1970s that raised funds for the American Cancer Society. The halls of Washington Grade School were turned into a Main Street with "shops" that sold flowers, sweets, and other fare. Following the melodrama tradition, musicians and singers gave short performances, known as "olios," between the acts of the play. The audience participated by shouting the appropriate boos and cheers and by throwing peanuts at the villain. Sally Biggs Harrison, currently Vernonia's mayor, directed and performed in most of the plays. She was frequently the mistress of ceremonies, as seen in the picture above. The stage curtain would have advertisements from local merchants that added to the revenue from the plays. In the photograph at left, the innocent heroine, played by Carolyn Keasey, looks away from the dastardly villain, played by Dee Stevens. (Both, VPMA.)

Filmed in 1958, the movie *Ring of Fire* starred David Janssen, Joyce Taylor, and Frank Gorshin. One of the former mill buildings was to be burned, and the producers of the film used it as a focal site in the movie's plot involving a big forest fire. David Janssen portrayed a small-town sheriff. Joyce Taylor and Frank Gorshin were delinquents who kidnaped the sheriff while the forest fire threatened the town. In the photograph at right, Bill Hanson (right) poses in front of the City Café with David Janssen. Below, David Janssen in his character's sheriff uniform signs autographs for local schoolchildren near the filming location. (Right, Meyer; below, VPMA.)

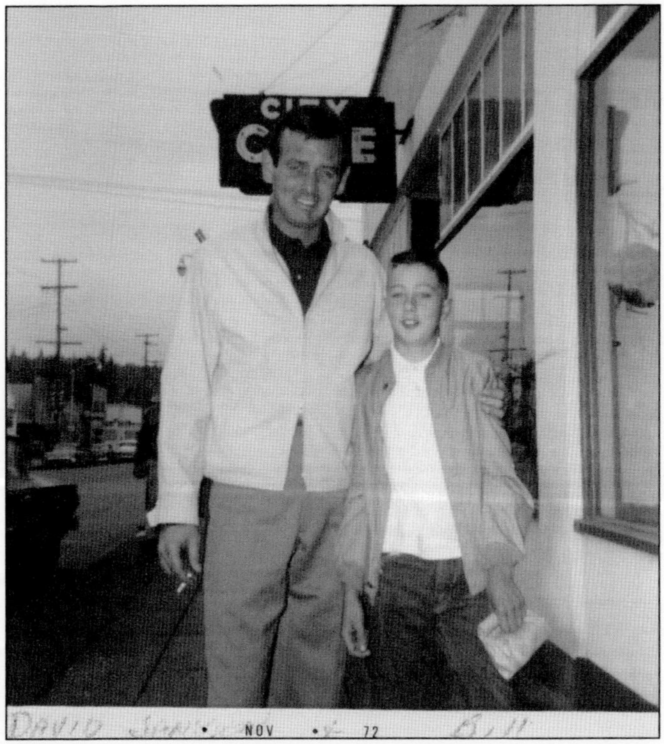

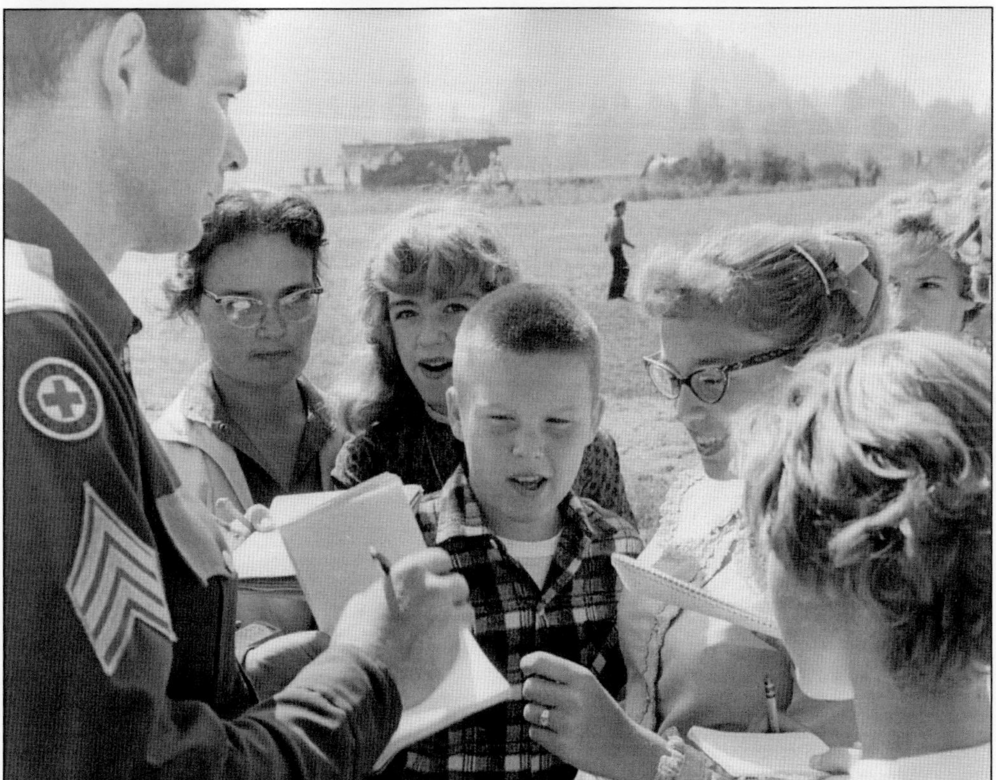

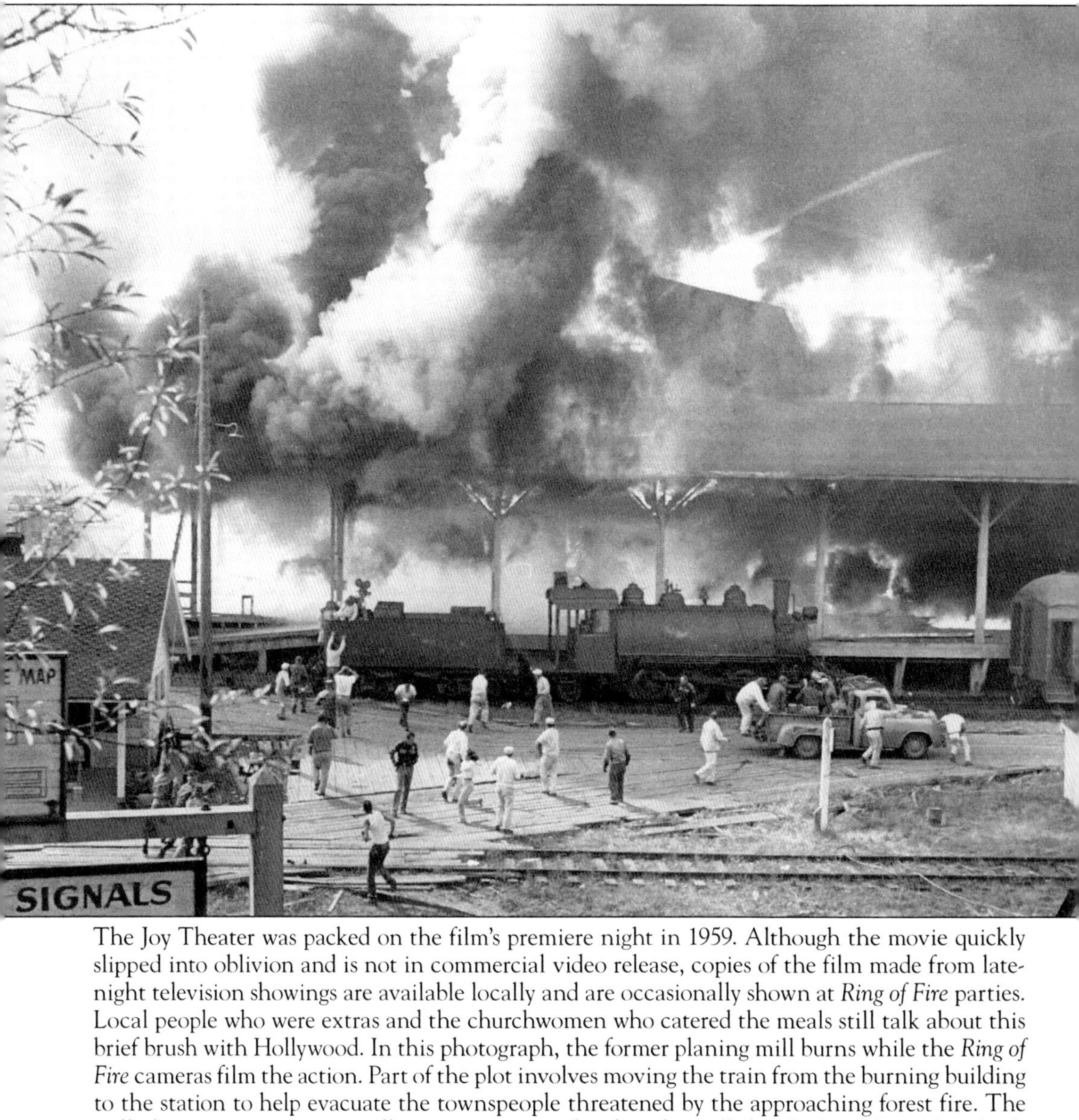

The Joy Theater was packed on the film's premiere night in 1959. Although the movie quickly slipped into oblivion and is not in commercial video release, copies of the film made from late-night television showings are available locally and are occasionally shown at *Ring of Fire* parties. Local people who were extras and the churchwomen who catered the meals still talk about this brief brush with Hollywood. In this photograph, the former planing mill burns while the *Ring of Fire* cameras film the action. Part of the plot involves moving the train from the burning building to the station to help evacuate the townspeople threatened by the approaching forest fire. The mill's burning was an especially poignant reminder that the mill that had employed hundreds and supported families and local businesses alike was really gone forever. (VPMA.)

Six

Logging Then and Now

Logging and the town of Vernonia have been intertwined since its founding. Located some 20 miles south of the earliest logging railroads in Columbia County, Vernonia eventually became a hub for a system of logging camps with railroads that supplied timber for the mill. As there were no roads into these areas, rail lines had to be constructed with numerous wooden trestles to cross the many ravines in the mountainous terrain. Lumber camp bunkhouses were built to be carried to the camps on the rail lines that brought in supplies and carried out logs.

The huge trees were felled by two men at either end of a crosscut saw, the "misery whip" that was the tool of the trade. Steam-powered donkey engines rigged to a spar tree hauled in the fallen logs and loaded them onto railcars.

Gasoline-powered chain saws eventually replaced the handheld saws, and modern road-building practices created roads for log trucks. It often took several of the earlier trucks to haul a single tree. Once the large old-growth trees were gone, logging became more mechanized and required fewer men to accomplish the same job. Specialized equipment can cut, limb, and load logs with amazing speed. Timberlands are replanted to create sustainable yields on both commercial and family-owned tree farms.

Despite the improvements in equipment and safety gear, logging remains one of the most dangerous jobs. The History Channel's reality series *Ax Men* was filmed in the area and featured two Vernonia logging companies in its first season. Although often edited for dramatic effect, the series depicts the risks and challenges faced by the people in this profession.

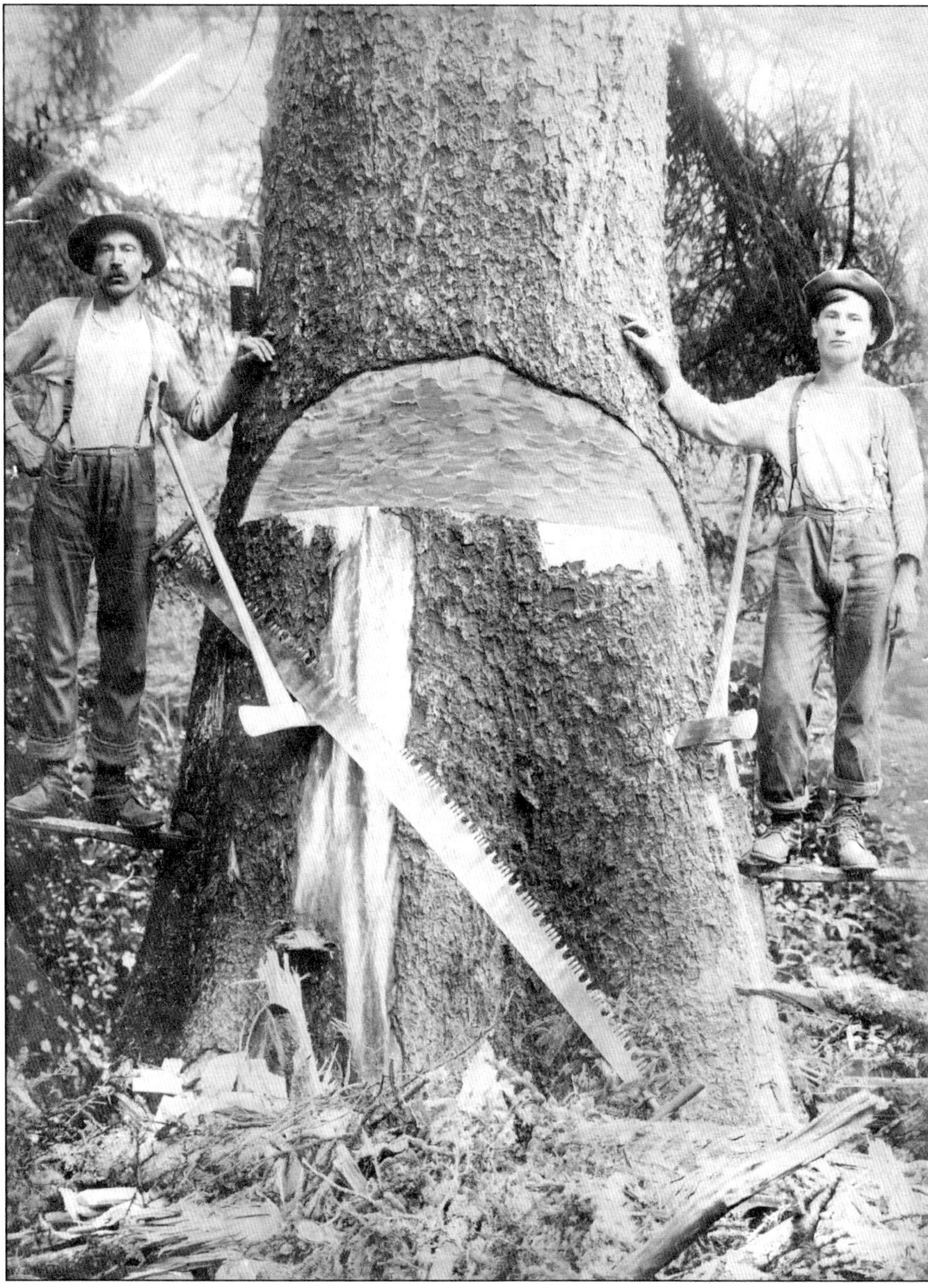

The northwestern corner of Oregon held one of the largest and best stands of old-growth Douglas fir—also known as yellow fir—in the world. The lands acquired by Oregon-American produced almost twice as many board feet per acre than an average good stand. The big trees had a slight flare at the base that had burly wood and was full of pitch. As a result, loggers used springboards driven into notches in the trees 4 to 6 feet aboveground as platforms for sawing. An undercut in the tree would first be hewn with axes before the saw work began. The wood above the springboard line was generally straight-grained and therefore yielded the best timber. In this photograph, two unidentified men stand beside a tree on springboards with the saw and axes of their trade displayed. (VPMA.)

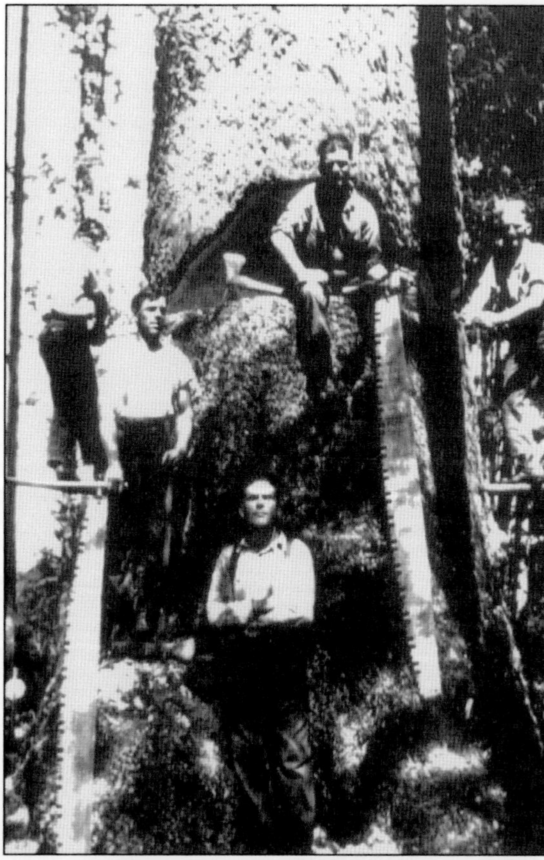

In the 1935 photograph at right, (from left to right) an unidentified man (possibly Eben Johns) stands on the springboard along with Vester Christensen, Chet Anderson, and Sam Anderson. Ted Anderson stands in front. Due to factors such as forest fires, disease, and windstorms, the trees in a given stand are not always uniform in size and age. Selective cutting of the prime timber can be done to leave the smaller trees to continue growing. In the 1928 photograph below, the woods crew of Lindsay Lumber uses horses to haul cut logs to the loading area. Vester Christensen is pictured third from the left. (Both, Queen.)

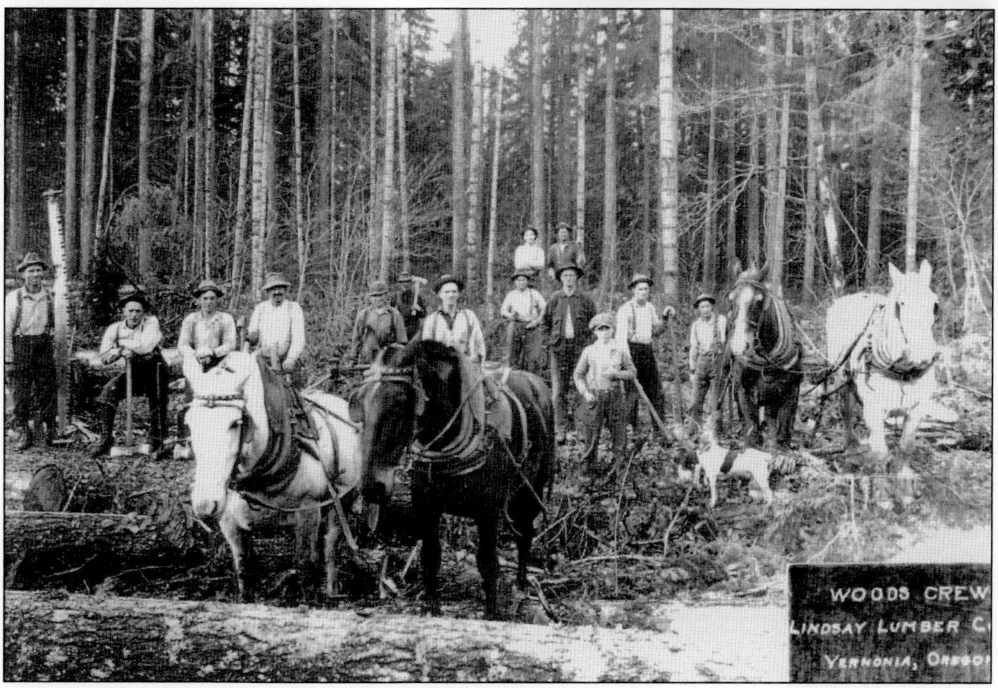

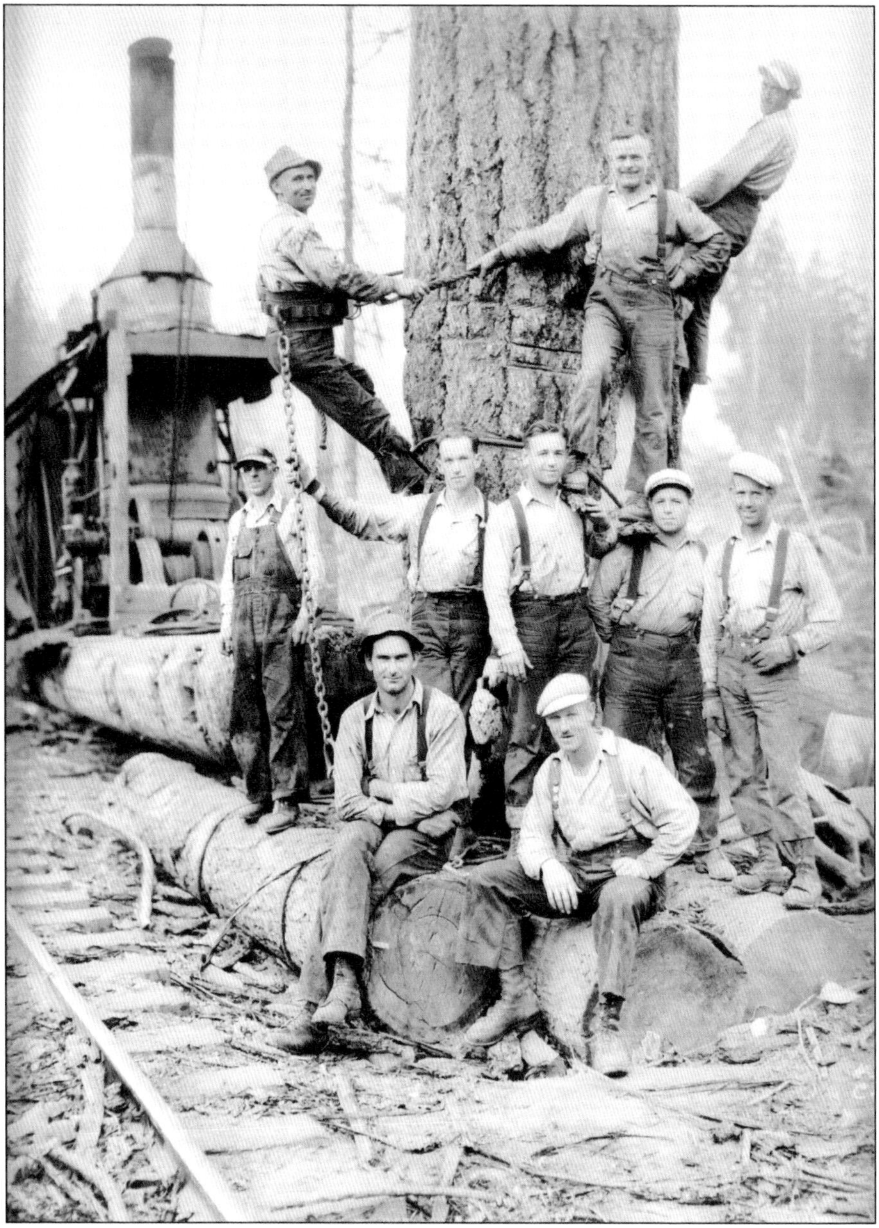

The tall timber in the Pacific Northwest was especially prized because it grew so densely that branching only occurred at the top; any lower limbs would die from lack of sunlight and fall off years before the tree was mature. Ike John Dass, a skilled high climber (topper), is seen in his safety belt and chain, posed along with other men in his crew at the base of the spar tree. Holly Holcomb (standing in the second row, third from left) later became the O-A planing mill foreman. The steam donkey in the background provided power to the hauling lines that were anchored on the spar tree. The high climber's job was to limb and top the spar tree for high-lead logging, rig it with blocks and cables, and later remove the rigging when the logging was done in that area. The men are dressed in the typical logger attire of heavy-duty work pants held up with galluses, heavy shirts, calk boots, and cloth or felt hats of all kinds. Those who ran the donkeys often wore bib overalls with pockets for tools. (Dass.)

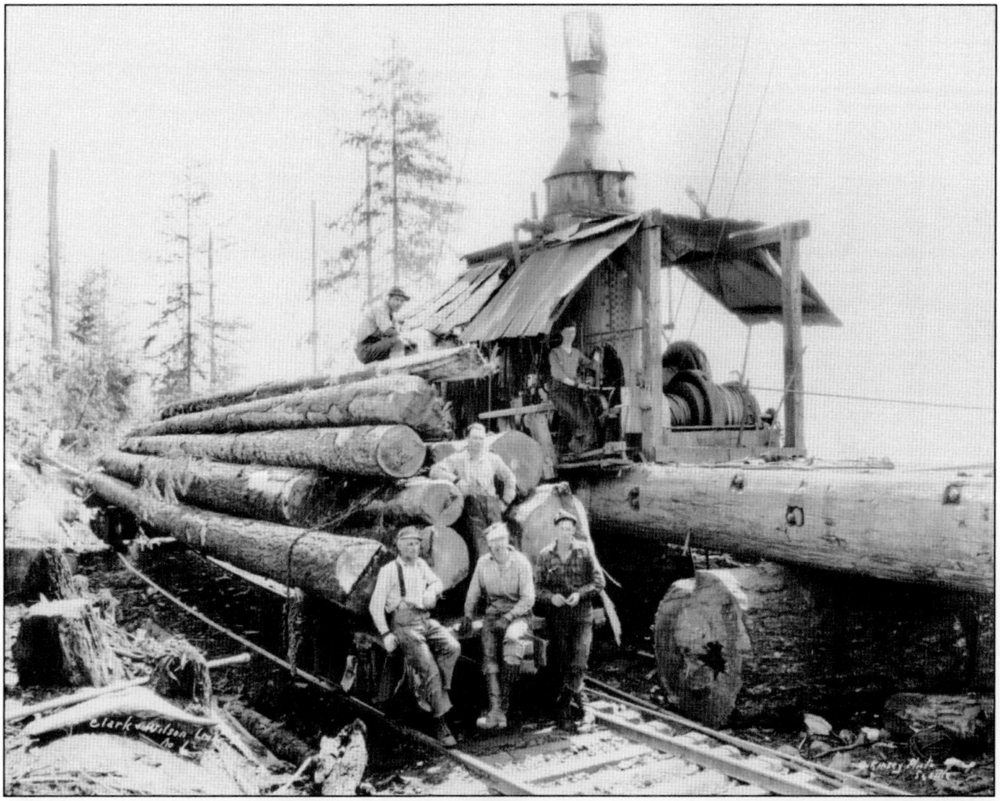

Above, an unidentified crew of men poses on and around the steam donkey after loading logs for rail shipment. Shown at right, the big logs were loaded onto railroad conveyances known as disconnected trucks (sets of railroad wheels on a heavy-duty framework). The length of the logs in a given load determined how far apart to space the empty trucks. The logs were set down on and chained to the trucks, which were then attached to a locomotive that hauled them to the mill. Andy Olson, the camp "push" (supervisor), directs loading operations. With rigging attached to the spar tree, the steam donkey in the left background powers the cables attached to the haystack boom, the flat log structure seen midair. This structure stabilized the movement of the log as it was lifted and swung for loading. (Both, VPMA.)

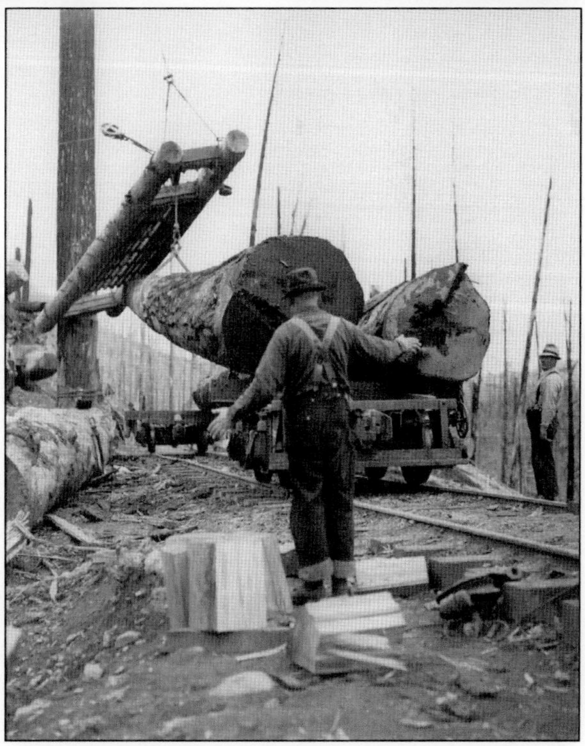

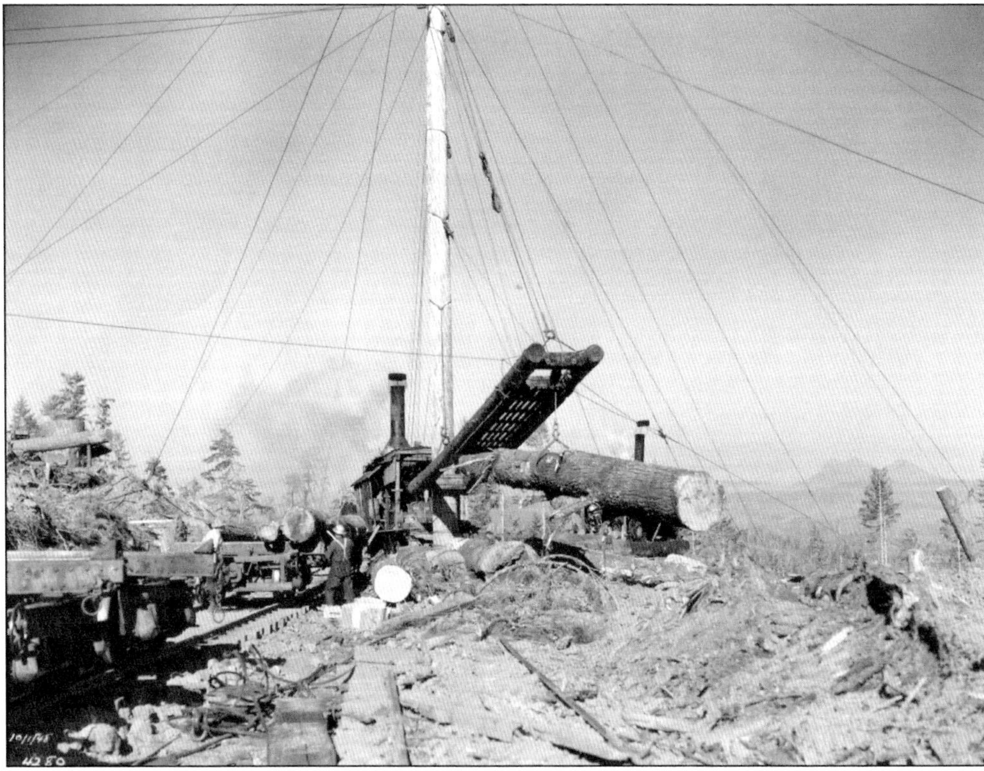

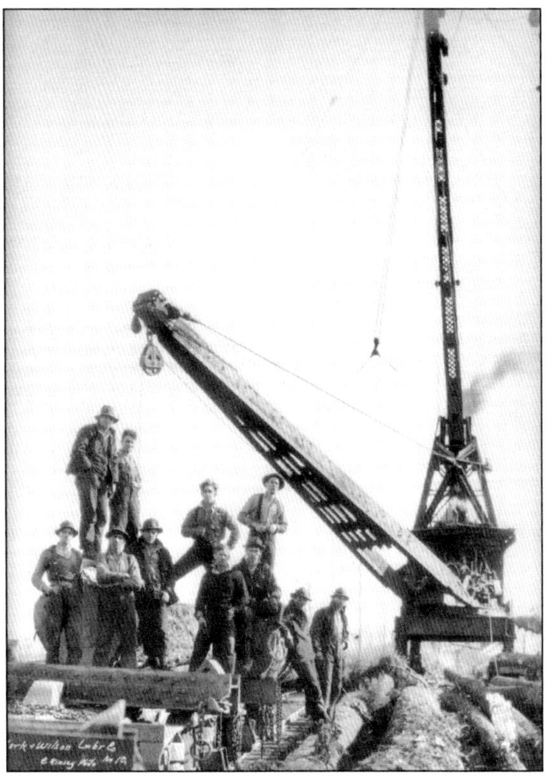

In the photograph above, more of the spar tree rigging is visible. This system of steam donkey, cable rigging, and spar tree was known as high-lead logging. Logs could be lifted and brought to the loading area above the obstructions on the ground. Donkeys were steam engines with vertical boilers patented by John Dolbeer in 1882. The tall boiler was fueled by the abundant scrap wood. The donkeys, also known as loaders or yarders, were mounted on log skids so they could be moved from site to site. To improve efficiency, new types of logging equipment were continually introduced. In the 1920s, the all-steel Lidgerwood tower skidder and heel boom began to replace the spar tree and wooden boom. Mounted on railcars, the tower skidder could be moved where needed without having to find an ideal spar tree. (Above, VPMA; left, Gwin.)

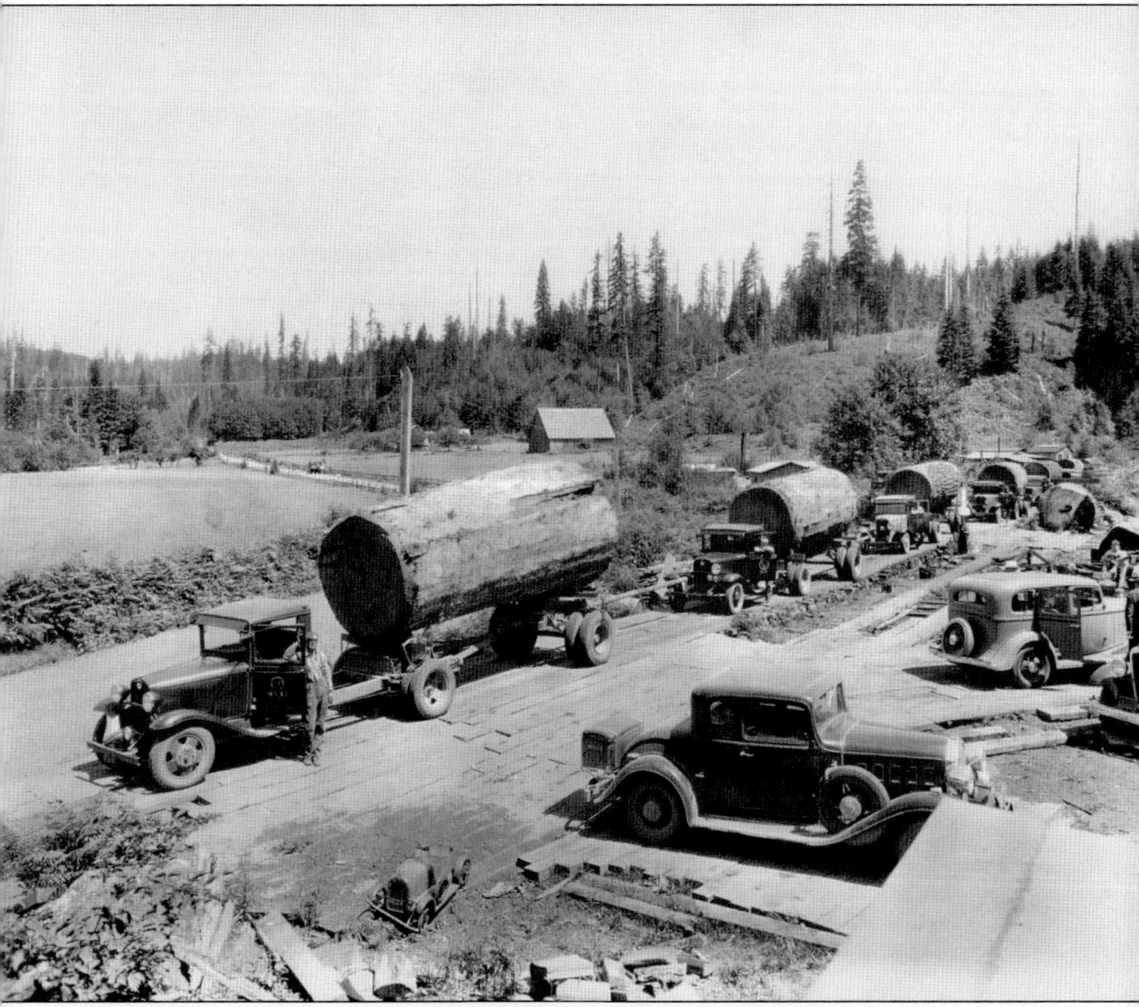

Log trucks began to replace the logging railroads in the 1930s as road-building equipment improved. It took seven trucks to haul this one big cedar out of the Jewell area; only five trucks are visible in this photograph. The George VanVleet Logging Company drivers were (from left to right) John Patrick, Vernonia High School graduate Bernard Dowling, Bud Larson, Eddie Ayers, John Hall, Joe Taber, and an unidentified seventh driver. (VPMA.)

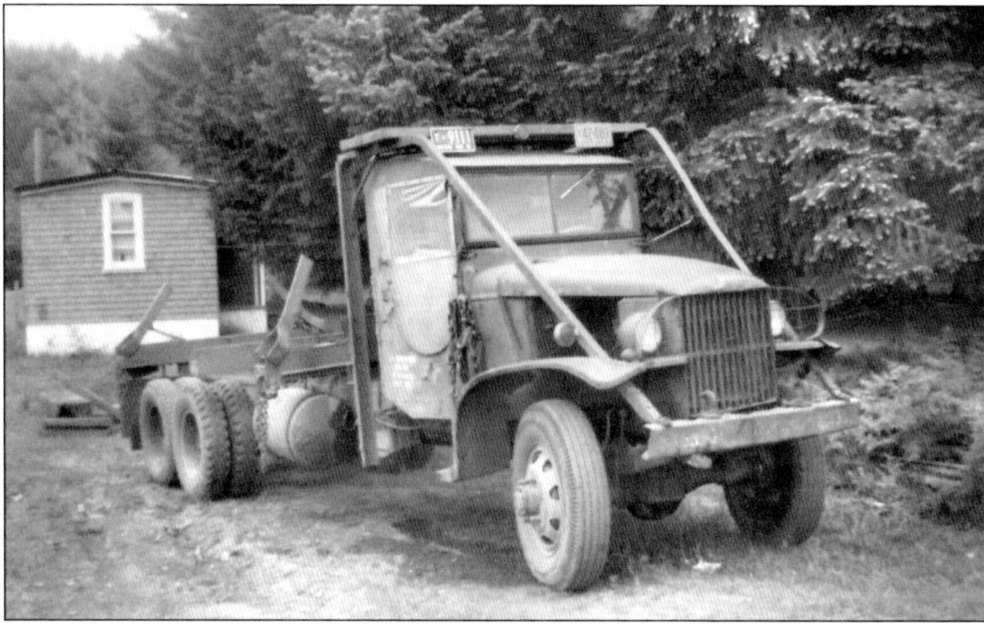

By the time these photographs were taken, logging roads and log trucks had replaced the small railroad lines and spurs needed when big timber was plentiful. Archie Dass worked for Wilfred Holce's logging operation in the 1950s. The 1942 GMC shown above in this 1957 photograph was Dass's first log truck. (Dass.)

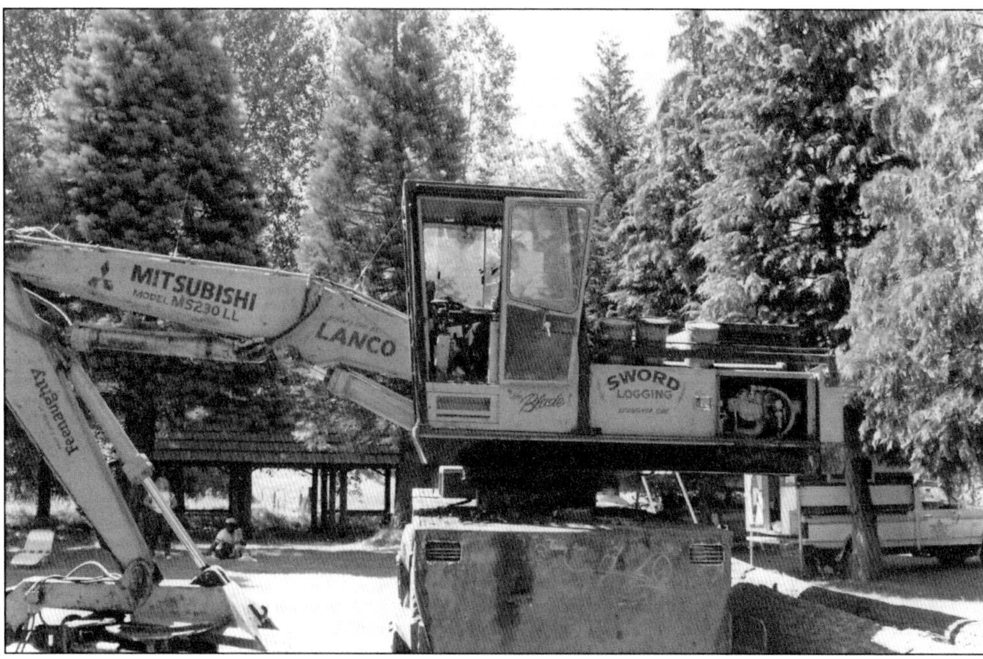

With the advent of gasoline and diesel engine power, the use of steam power came to an end and the methods of logging changed significantly. Beginning in the late 1940s, gasoline-powered chain saws began to replace the crosscut saw, and it took fewer men to accomplish the work overall. This 1985 loader, owned by Sword Logging, was used to load timber cut in thinning and second-growth operations onto log trucks. (Sword.)

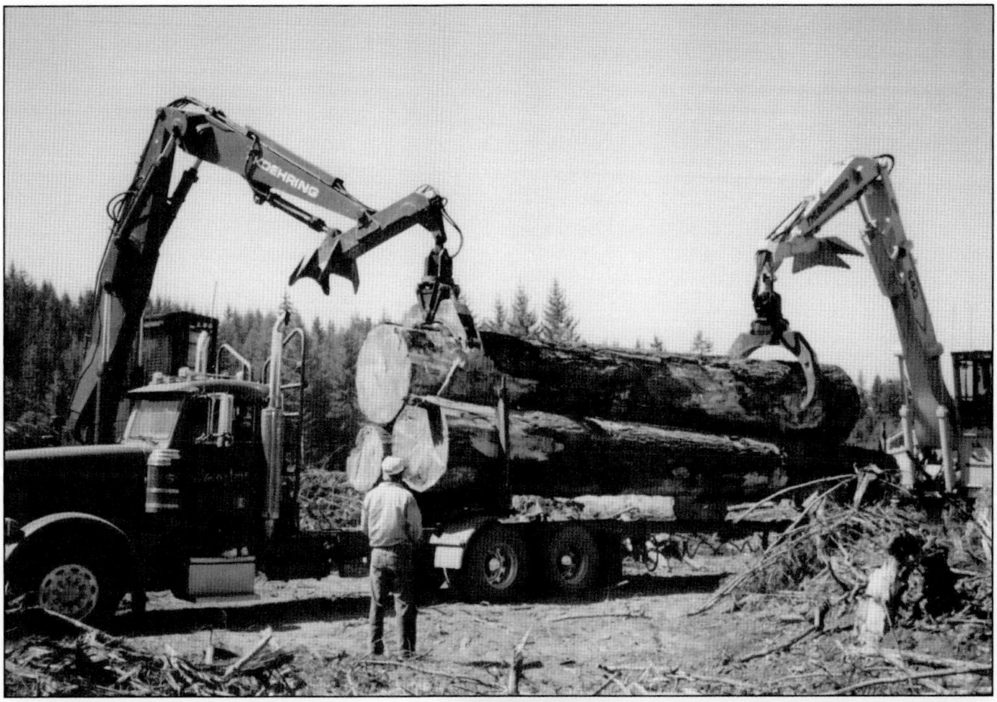

A mobile loader with a hydraulic-powered arm and tongs that grip, lift, and load logs is at work in the photograph above. While steel cables and chokers attached to the logs are still used as they were in the past, the Madill 70-inch, high-lead yarder is a more modern version of the steel tower skidders that replaced the donkey and spar tree to lift and haul in logs out of steep canyons and load them for transport to the mill. Taken about 20 miles south of Vernonia, the photograph at right shows the rigging and tower of a modern high-lead yarder in action. (Both, Gwin.)

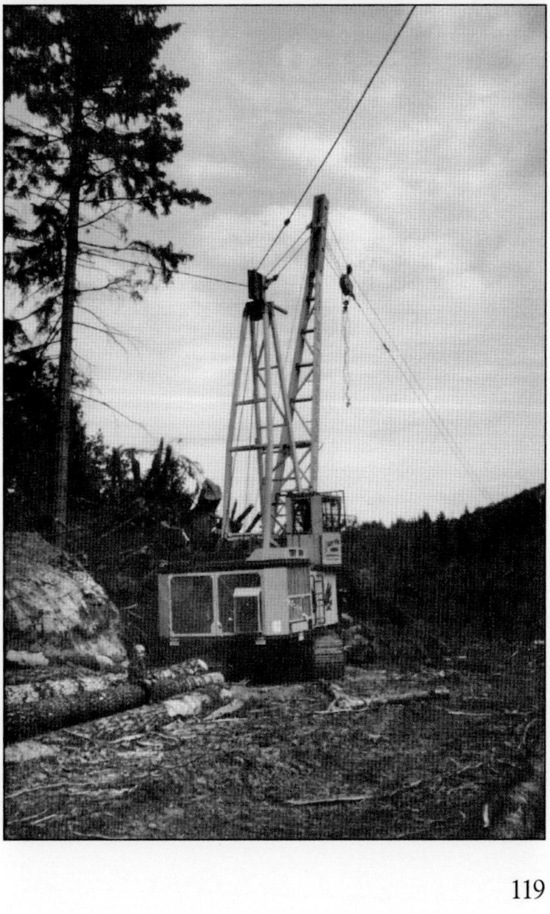

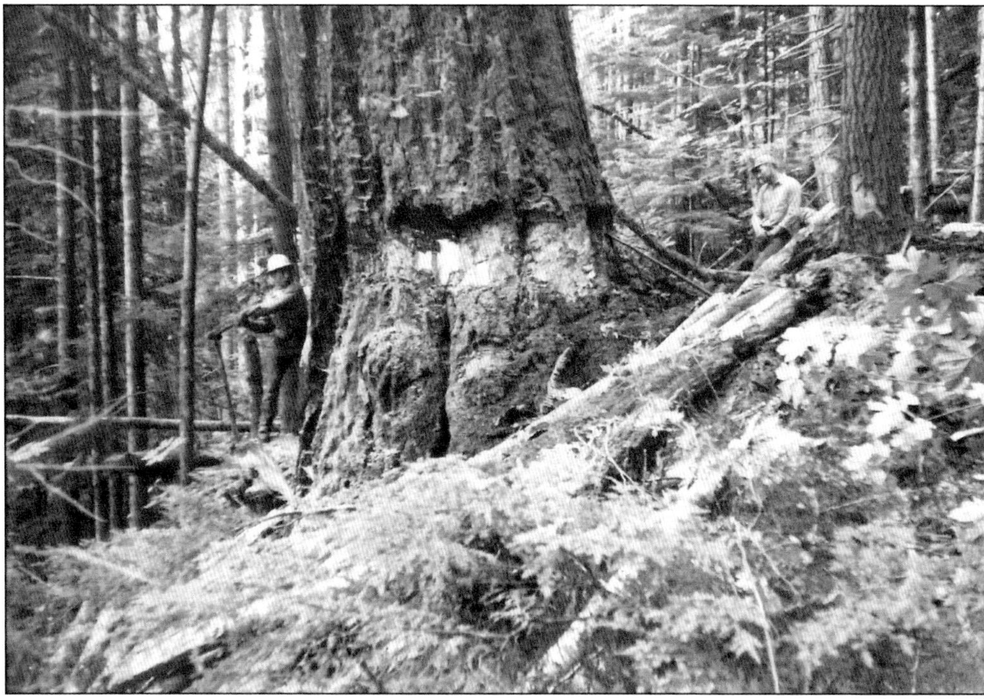

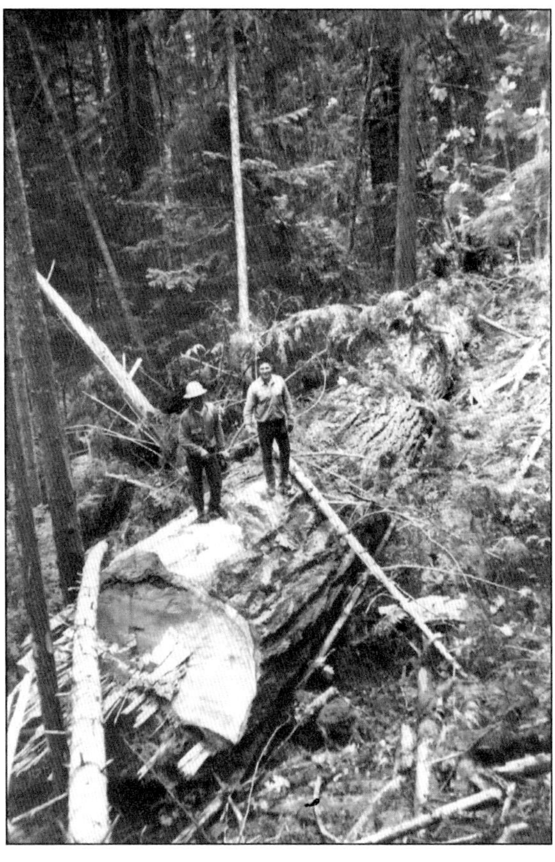

The bark of a Douglas fir could be 6 to 8 inches thick. In order to reduce the diameter of the tree before applying their chain saws, Archie Dass (left) and Wilfred Holce first chop away the bark in the 1961 photograph above. In the picture at left, Dass and Holce stand on the fallen tree. The angle of the undercut and other factors determine the direction a tree will fall. Expert loggers are skilled at evaluating a tree and its relation to other standing timber. They then can drop the tree exactly where they want it to land with minimal damage to the surrounding trees. (Both, Dass.)

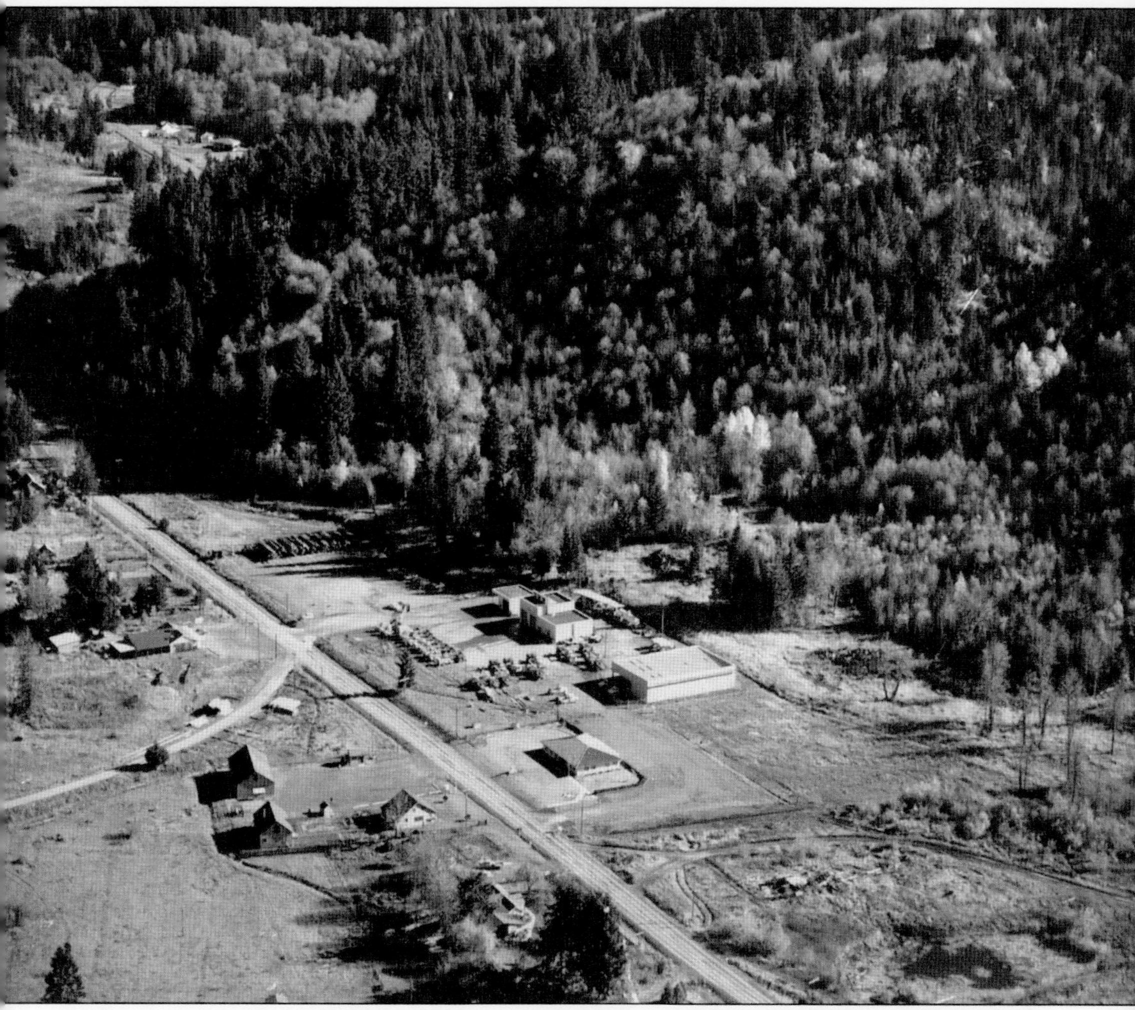

As the quantity of prime old-growth diminished with the intensive logging begun in the 1920s, timber companies started to look at the future. The concept of tree farming for sustainable forests was new, and with a minimum 60-year harvest cycle, it was not a source for short-term profits. Some companies, however, entered this new form of timber management. The Crown Zellerbach (CZ) Corporation acquired vast tracts of cutover forestland in the 1940s and 1950s from former timber companies such as Clark and Wilson. CZ developed extensive tree farms, including 47,000 acres near Pittsburg, as a source for second-growth and new trees for pulp and paper mills. This aerial photograph of the Pittsburg area was taken in the early 1950s and shows CZs shops and the Columbia (later named for Edward Stamm) Tree Farm headquarters that was located on State Highway 47, five miles north of Vernonia. CZs timber holdings have since been sold, and the building now stands vacant. (VPMA.)

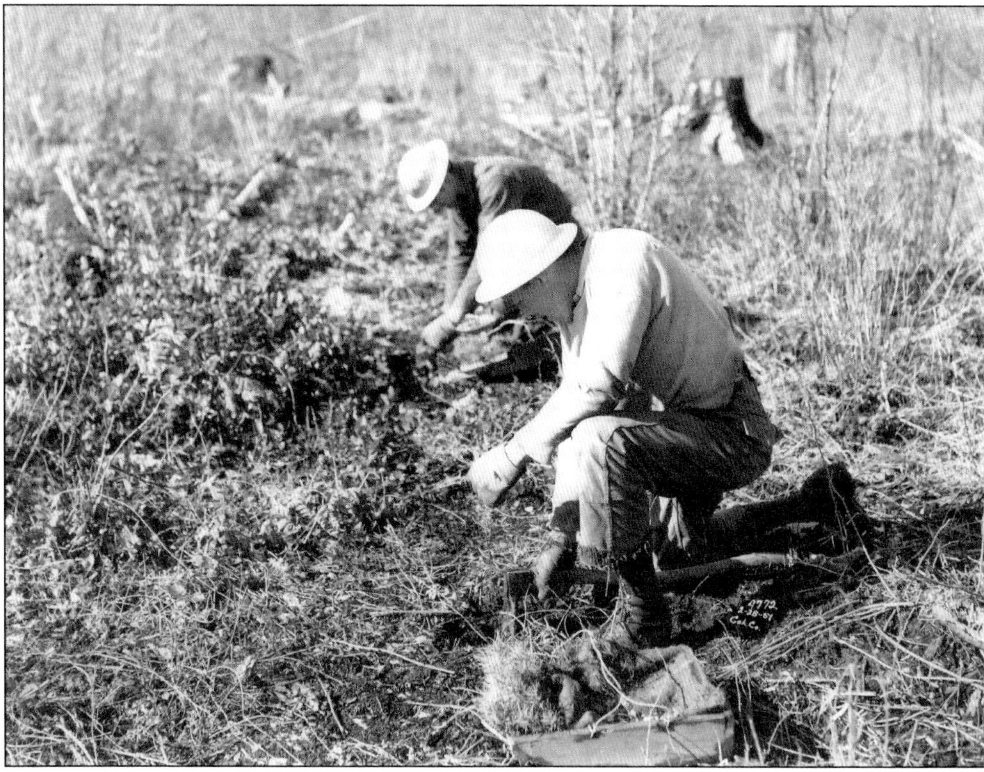

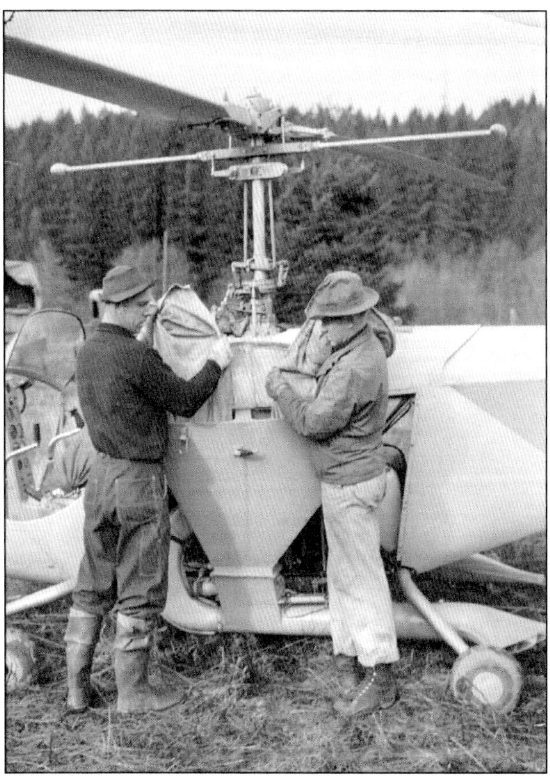

The series of fires from 1933 to 1951, collectively known as the Tillamook Burn, and the diminishing supply of old-growth brought the realization that harvested and burned trees needed to be replaced for future generations. Organized replanting of harvested or burned areas began in the late 1940s. In the 1950s and 1960s, school and civic groups participated as volunteers in the Tillamook Burn replanting project. The picture above shows Gordon Cline and other Longview Fibre employees planting two-year-old seedlings in a recently logged area near Vernonia in 1951. Tree farms also experimented with seeding forests by helicopter for a brief time. At first, fir seeds were broadcast from the air, much to the delight of resident rodents. Later seedlings were dropped in individual pointed plastic planters. The survival rate was not good, and the practice was abandoned in favor of hand-planted seedlings. (Both, VPMA.)

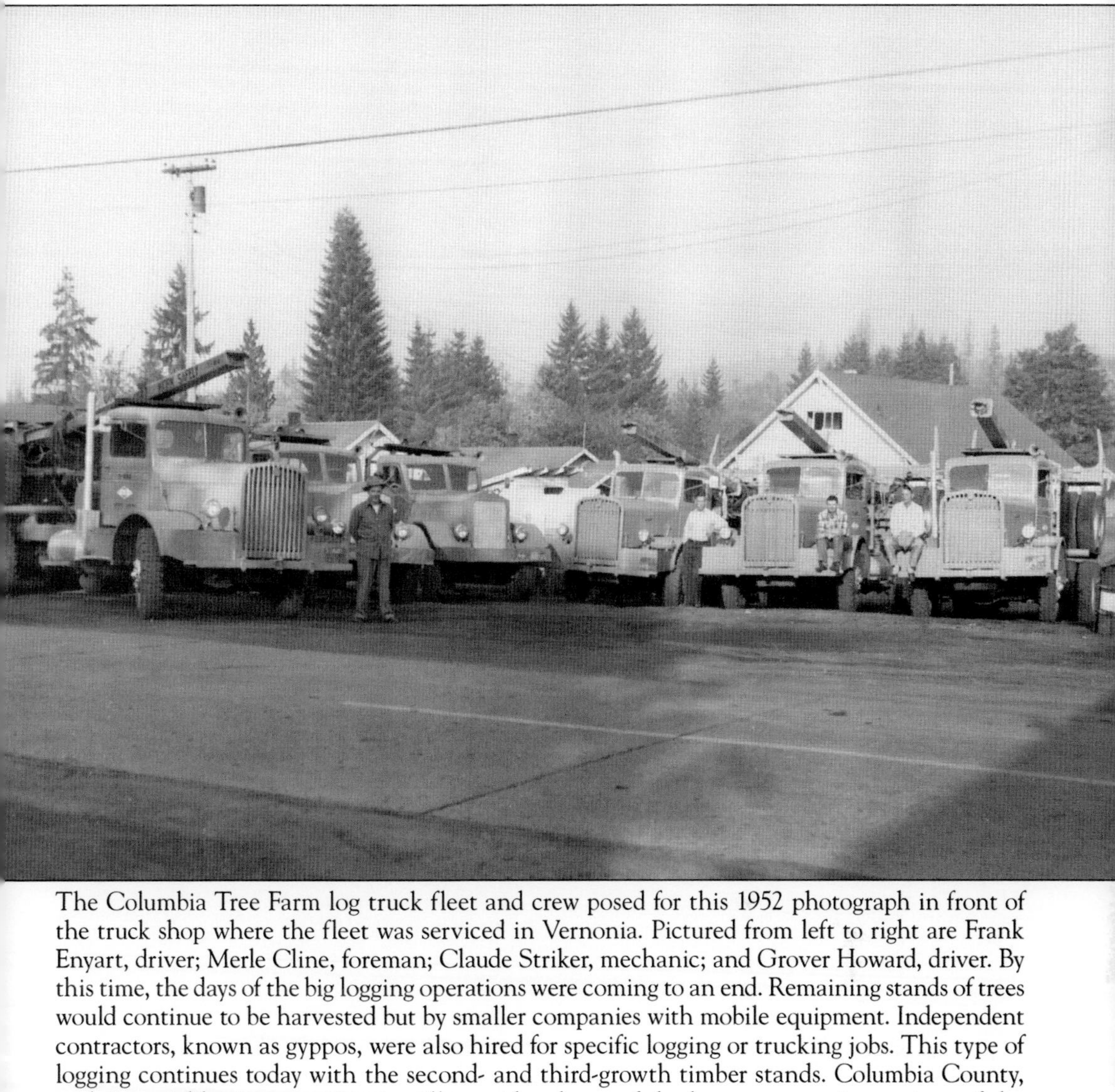

The Columbia Tree Farm log truck fleet and crew posed for this 1952 photograph in front of the truck shop where the fleet was serviced in Vernonia. Pictured from left to right are Frank Enyart, driver; Merle Cline, foreman; Claude Striker, mechanic; and Grover Howard, driver. By this time, the days of the big logging operations were coming to an end. Remaining stands of trees would continue to be harvested but by smaller companies with mobile equipment. Independent contractors, known as gyppos, were also hired for specific logging or trucking jobs. This type of logging continues today with the second- and third-growth timber stands. Columbia County, with its neighboring counties, is still considered one of the best tree-growing regions of the world. (VPMA.)

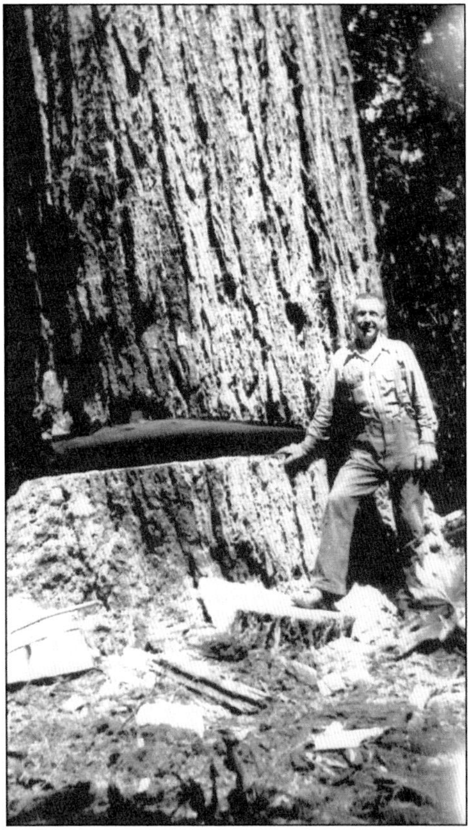

Harold Bergerson stands beside a big fir that has been undercut and is ready to fall in the 1959 photograph at left. Harold was the son of Charles Bergerson, one of the four Bergerson brothers who settled in the Nehalem Valley. While the other brothers eventually settled on Timber Route, Charles's homestead was on Rock Creek, 1 mile from Vernonia. Like so many others, Harold was both a farmer and a logger. Below, Patrick Sauer, an employee of Bergerson's logging company, stands in front of a log brought from the Keasey area to the Vernonia millpond. The O-A mill can be seen in the background. (Both, Gwin.)

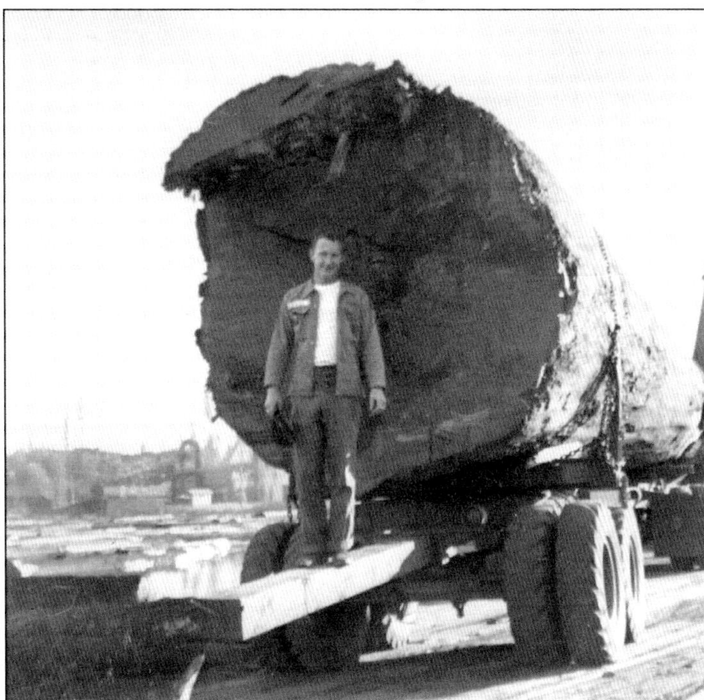

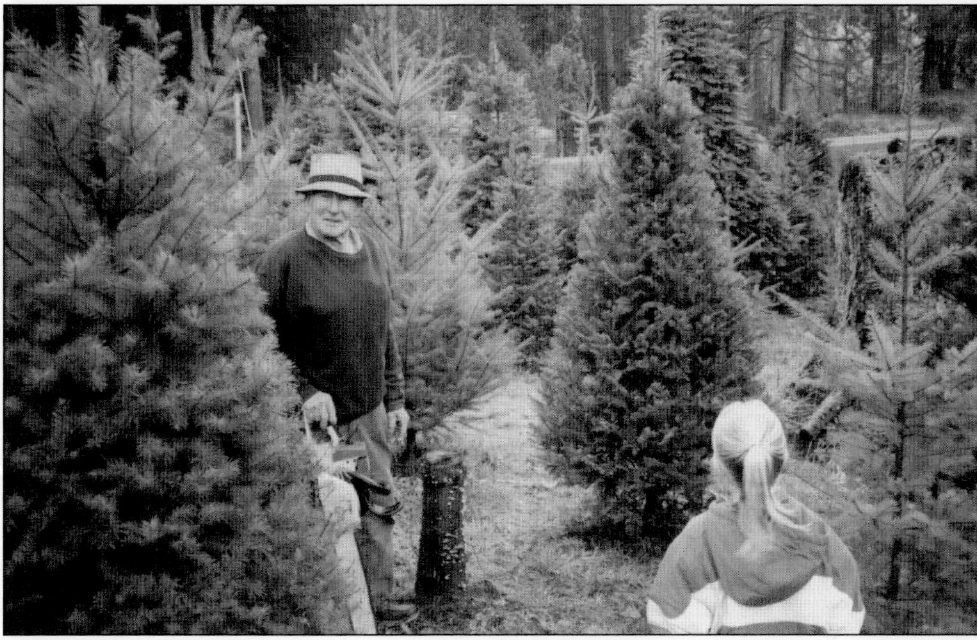

Marvin Meyer and Miranda Parsons are seen in December 1999 on the Meyer Christmas Tree Farm. Marvin and Ellen Meyer started the farm in 1962 for both retail and wholesale Christmas tree sales. Over the years, truckloads of trees have been shipped to other states, and many families have come to the Meyer farm as an annual Christmas season ritual. Oregon is the nation's largest producer of Christmas trees. In addition to its big timber-growing tracts, Columbia County has numerous Douglas and grand fir Christmas tree farms. In the picture below, Marvin Meyer saws the undercut in preparation for felling a big cedar on his property. (Both, Meyer.)

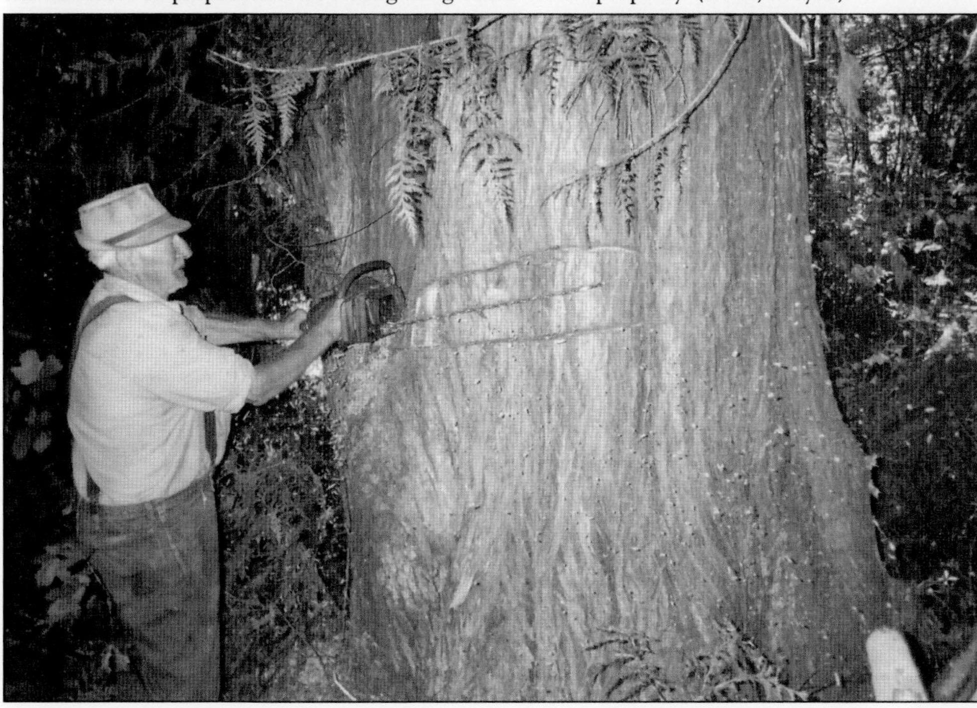

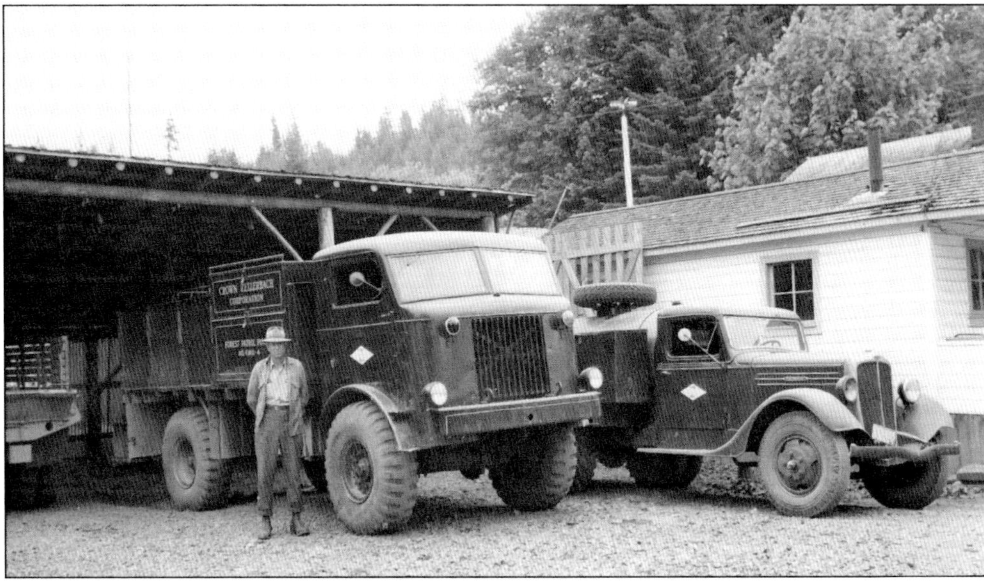

An unidentified man stands beside a fire truck that was used in the construction of the Alaska-Canada Highway during World War II. It was later shipped to Portland and purchased by Crown Zellerbach for use in its operations. It stands next to another tanker truck in the CZ fleet. (VPMA.)

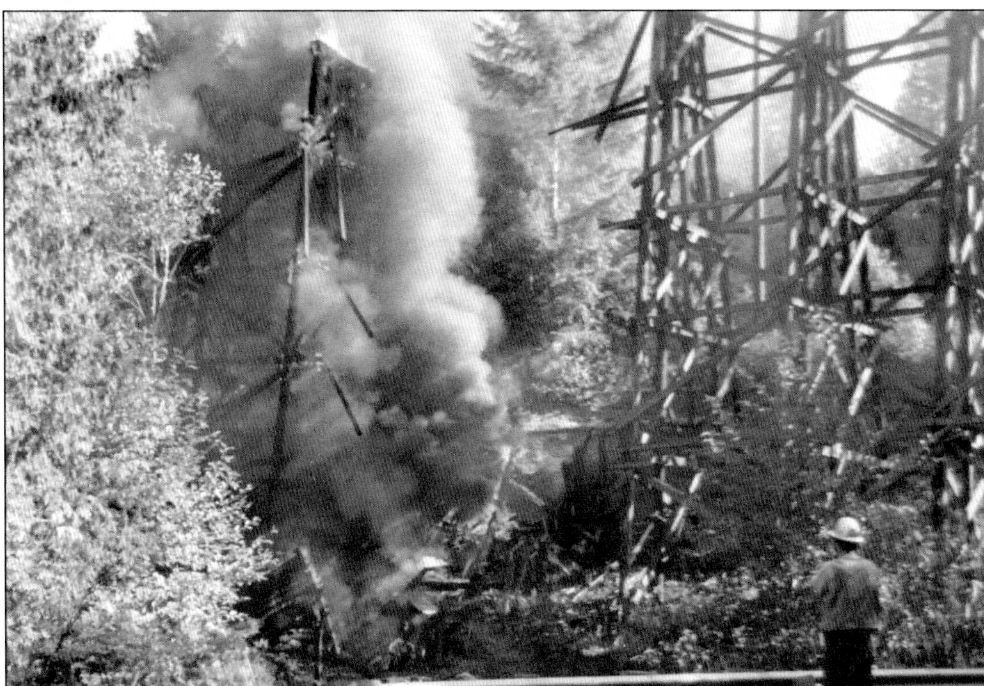

A forest fire takes its toll on the timber and any wooden structures in its path. In the 1987 photograph above, the high trestle that crosses Oregon Highway 47, the main route to the Upper Nehalem Valley, burns. After the fire was finally extinguished, half of the trestle was gone. The railroad had been abandoned for many years, so the trestle was not replaced. It stands today as a monument to Vernonia's railroad past. (Gwin.)

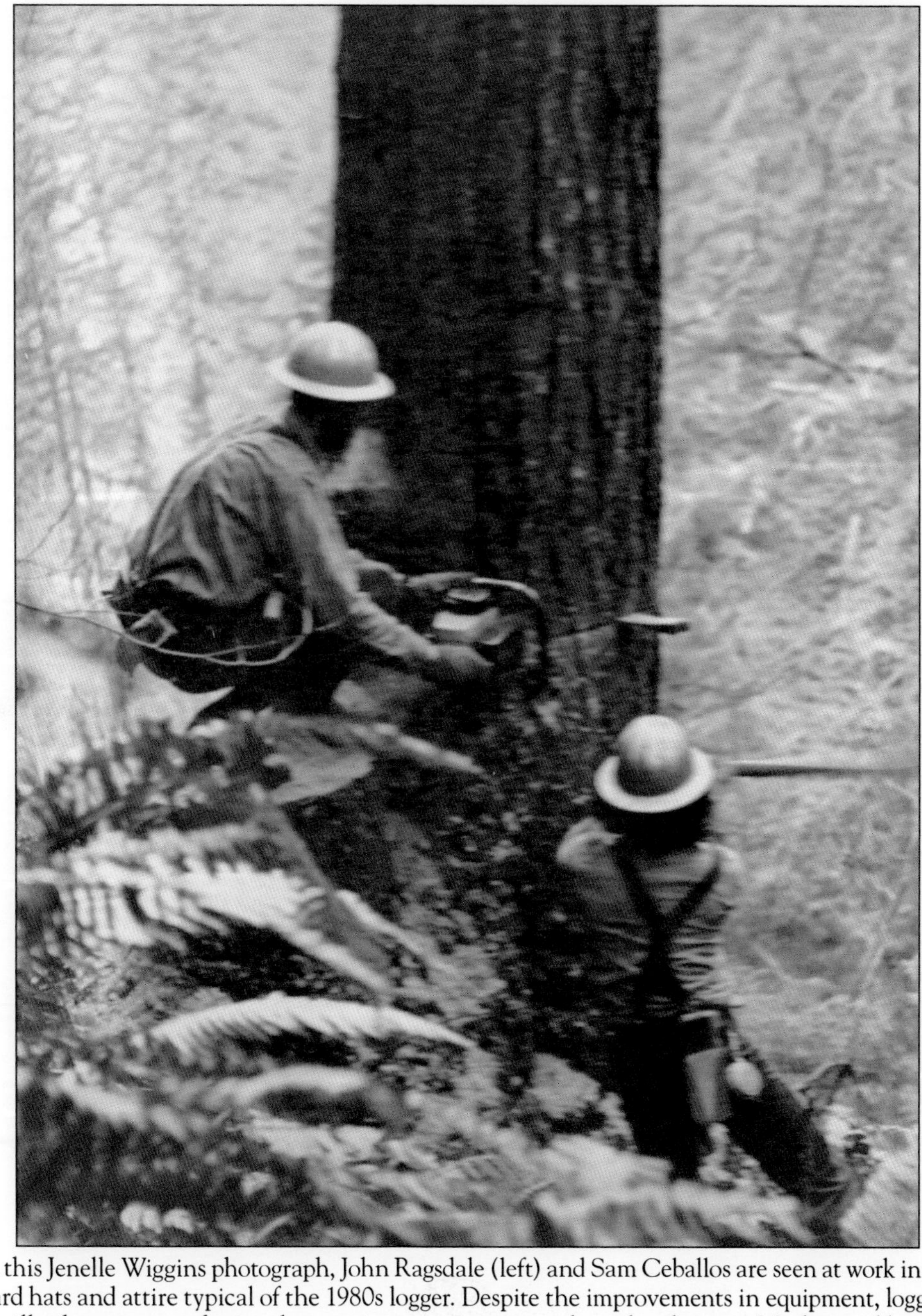

In this Jenelle Wiggins photograph, John Ragsdale (left) and Sam Ceballos are seen at work in the hard hats and attire typical of the 1980s logger. Despite the improvements in equipment, logging is still a dangerous profession that requires training, strength, and endurance. Mechanized logging equipment and the smaller second- and third-growth trees have reduced the large numbers of workers needed in earlier times. Fewer descendants of early logging families are able to continue in the business. To paraphrase the closing paragraph of Jim Blain and Ed and Greg Kamholz's excellent history of the O-A mill, *The Oregon-American Lumber Company—Ain't No More*, the future of Vernonia will depend on the pioneer spirit that characterizes those who live there to find new opportunities rather than wait the hundreds of years required to regenerate a "new" old-growth forest. (VPMA.)

Discover Thousands of Local History Books Featuring Millions of Vintage Images

Arcadia Publishing, the leading local history publisher in the United States, is committed to making history accessible and meaningful through publishing books that celebrate and preserve the heritage of America's people and places.

Find more books like this at
www.arcadiapublishing.com

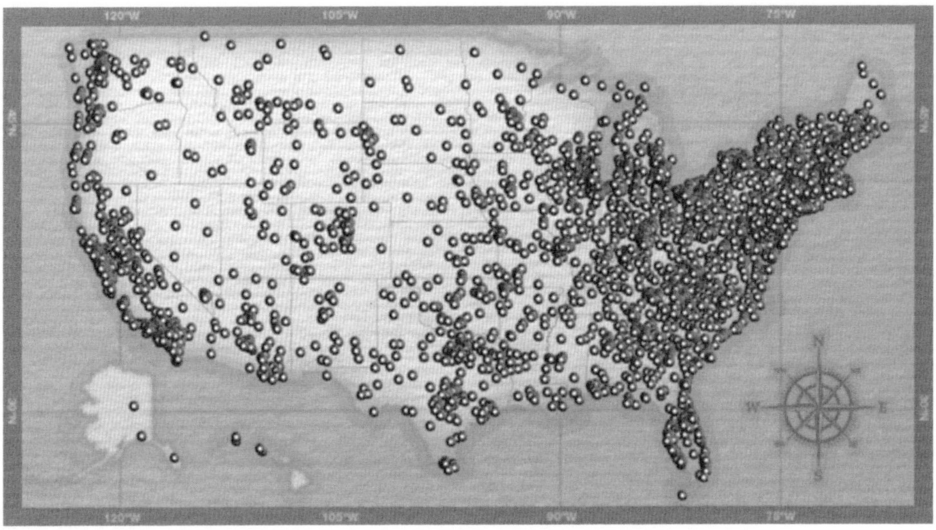

Search for your hometown history, your old stomping grounds, and even your favorite sports team.

Consistent with our mission to preserve history on a local level, this book was printed in South Carolina on American-made paper and manufactured entirely in the United States. Products carrying the accredited Forest Stewardship Council (FSC) label are printed on 100 percent FSC-certified paper.

MADE IN THE USA